Integrating Young Adult Literature through the Common Core Standards

Integrating Young Adult Literature through the Common Core Standards

Rachel L. Wadham and Jonathan W. Ostenson

 LIBRARIES UNLIMITED

AN IMPRINT OF ABC-CLIO, LLC

Santa Barbara, California • Denver, Colorado • Oxford, England

Library of Congress Cataloging-in-Publication Data

Wadham, Rachel L., 1973–
   Integrating young adult literature through the common core standards / Rachel L. Wadham and Jonathan W. Ostenson.
      pages cm
   Includes bibliographical references and indexes.
   ISBN 978–1–61069–118–5 (pbk.) — ISBN 978–1–61069–119–2 (ebook) 1. Reading (Secondary) 2. Young adult literature—Study and teaching (Secondary) 3. Language arts (Secondary)—Standards—United States. 4. Reading comprehension. 5. Teenagers—Books and reading—United States. I. Ostenson, Jonathan W. II. Title.
   LB1632.W25   2013
   418′.40712—dc23   2012036269

ISBN: 978–1–61069–118–5
EISBN: 978–1–61069–119–2

17 16 15 14 13   1 2 3 4 5

This book is also available on the World Wide Web as an eBook.
Visit www.abc-clio.com for details.

Libraries Unlimited
An Imprint of ABC-CLIO, LLC

ABC-CLIO, LLC
130 Cremona Drive, P.O. Box 1911
Santa Barbara, California 93116-1911

This book is printed on acid-free paper ∞

Manufactured in the United States of America

Contents

Introduction

The acts of teaching and learning are intricate endeavors. To succeed at them we must take a variety of elements and combine them into dynamic environments. The implementation of the new Common Core State Standards (CCSS) adds yet another element to that complex mix. However, we find that this dynamic time of change gives us just the recipe to make the engaging learning environments we seek. All we need to execute this recipe are the main ingredients: young adult literature, our classrooms, and the common core. In this book we are going to connect what we have, what we know, and what we are given in order to show you how these three powerful tools can create teaching and learning environments.

We begin by offering a statement of our own theoretical position: *Young adult literature should be an essential part of the classroom experience, and the new Common Core State Standards provide us with the framework to make it so.* The purpose of this book is to outline a practical approach to building independent readers who are college and workplace ready by applying the common core in inquiry-learning environments with young adult literature as our primary texts. As we outline both the philosophy of the common core and our own viewpoint, our purpose is to help you catch this vision that we hope will energize your teaching and your students' learning. We have filled these pages with straight talk, not only about the core but also about how young adult literature can be used with the new standards. Drawing from our own practical experience as educators and based in our passion for young adult literature, we hope to offer you the practical help and advice you will need to implement the Common Core English Language Arts Standards as effectively as possible.

To achieve our purpose, we have provided a broad research-based scope to our work. We have found that applying research-based practice is one of the important elements that supports good teaching and learning environments. Its application will also be more significant in the world of the common core as it also advocates for using research to inform our professional practice. To tie this broad research base together into one complete whole, we have organized our book into two parts.

Part one is devoted to an in-depth discussion of how we analyze texts to determine their complexity. As complexity is arguably the most important concept in the common core, if we wish to design learning environments based in the core, we must first focus our attention on applying this standard to the texts we use in our classrooms. In chapter one we provide an overview of young adult literature and its place in the classroom. Chapter two presents an overview of the CCSS and to the CCSS three-part model for determining text complexity that we hope will provide a balanced vision of the precise nature of the core. Chapters three though five build on this foundation to look at each of the three elements of the three-part model of text complexity, namely the quantitative, qualitative, and reader and text dimensions. The purpose of these chapters is not only to comment on and add depth to the explanations of the CCSS, but also to provide the structure for a model that can be put to practical use to evaluate all texts. Having created our model in chapter six we apply the model and provide a template that allows us to articulate our analysis. Lastly, we model our template with six young adult books.

Having judged complexity, the next step is to teach with those texts. Thus in part two, we turn to the practical classroom applications. In chapter seven we outline the pedagogy of inquiry learning, an approach that we feel is the best for building the environment that will ultimately create the types of independent readers the CCSS expects. Moving on to show how inquiry learning can be used successfully, we then outline in chapter eight a whole inquiry-learning unit. This chapter is unique in that it does not just present a bare-bones plan but instead walks though the planning process needed to achieve a full unit. In this chapter we hope to show you how we think as teachers as we plan units based on the common core standards that use young adult books.

We don't wish to leave you with just a foundation, so in the remaining chapters we provide you with the raw materials you will need to build the walls and roofs of your curriculum. In chapter nine we offer a variety of unit outlines, with essential questions, options for texts, and ideas for assessments that apply the core anchor standards. These outlines should provide you with the basic structure you need to create your own full units. In conclusion, chapter ten offers extensive book lists tied to the CCSS anchor standards. These lists will give you many more ideas for great young adult books that will meet the needs of the CCSS as well as engage your students in exploration of meaningful topics and ideas.

In total, then, this book provides a solid outline of how young adult literature, your classroom, and the CCSS can work together to create superior environments for teaching and learning. We hope that, like us, at the end of this book you will also have no doubt that the CCSS and young adult literature are fully compatible. As we connect great young adult books, our classrooms, and the common core, we have little doubt we can create a perfect recipe for building environments that create energized, independent readers. In the end this is what we believe every English language arts professional wants: a room full of creative, passionate, critical, and engaged lifelong readers.

Part I

Defining the Complexity of Young Adult Literature Using the Common Core Standards

Chapter 1

Young Adult Literature

We're sure if we asked you to name a book that changed your life as a reader and explain why, you would be able to immediately articulate the impact the book had on your life. For one of the authors that title was *The High King* by Lloyd Alexander, a vivid rendition of the triumph of good over evil, read during a time of great grief and pain for her as a young teen. For the other author, that book was Charles Dickens's classic *A Tale of Two Cities*, which he read on his own in eighth grade; our experiences with these books set us both on the path to becoming educators.

As classroom teachers, isn't this what we want, to show our students the power of literature? We want to show them that books provide us with valuable insights into the human condition in a way that other media cannot always match. We want our students to not only resonate with what they read but also to be changed by it. Sadly, despite our best efforts and our own love of literature, we often encounter not passion but blank stares and groans of frustration.

Taking our students from impassive to engaged is our great challenge, and while at times it feels that we should scrap the whole endeavor and turn to another profession, we are not naysayers but visionaries. If we use the construct of the Common Core State Standards (referred to hereafter as CCSS or as the common core) along with the powerful tool of young adult literature, we truly believe that our vision can come to life as we create passionate, critical, and engaged lifelong readers.

It doesn't matter whether you call it young adult literature, adolescent literature, or teen literature, the body of fictional works written for and read by young people ages 12–18 is vast and complex. Because of this we begin in this chapter by first offering our own definition of young adult literature and then moving to a brief history of young adult literature to contextualize the genre over time. Finding that lack of experience with the genre has created some myths about books for teens, we then share research and experience we hope will dispel those beliefs. We end with our theoretical perspective of the place of young adult literature in schools, discussing how these novels can become an essential part of any classroom reading. We advocate for a bold new approach that allows us to put young adult literature at the center of our practice.

What Is Young Adult Literature?

Articulating a brief yet comprehensive definition of young adult literature is a challenging task, in no small part because this definition has changed and evolved over the years. Scholars in the 1950s and 1960s defined young adult literature as anything read by those between the ages of 13 and 18 (approximately). This definition was very broad and included not only "young adult" books but also, significantly, books written for children and adults but read by teens (Cart, 2010).

Today, young adult literature has emerged as a distinct subset of works with unique qualities that differentiate it from adult and children's books. For a complete discussion of these qualities we suggest reading the fine work by authors such as Bucher and Hinton-Johnson (2009), Cart (2010), Cole (2008), and Donelson and Nilsen (2004). Rather than rehash lists of criteria or features of the genre, to articulate our own definition we will stick to a rather simple but helpful defining characteristic of young adult literature. We suggest this defining characteristic is that these books tell their story from a teenager's point of view; books that fall into the young adult category feature not only teen protagonists, but teenage perspectives on the world. So, by this definition, books such as Maya Angelou's *I Know Why the Caged Bird Sings* or Sandra Cisneros's *The House on Mango Street* would not be considered young adult. While these books do have teenage protagonists, they are not told from the point of view of a teenager; rather, they are retellings of memories and are rendered by an adult looking back on a life as a teenager. As a result, these books feature analysis or insight about events or characters that comes from an adult's reflections on the past. On the other hand, books that we would consider young adult, such as Elizabeth Scott's *Living Dead Girl* and Matt de la Pena's *Mexican White Boy*, not only have teenage characters but make use of the teenage point of view, embodying typical teenage feelings, language, and ideas.

For us, point of view is paramount in identifying a piece of young adult literature, and it makes up the main part of our definition. However, in today's market the publishers also play a very strong role in categorizing books, and we would be remiss not to consider that role. When a house publishes a book, it decides which audience that book is best marketed to, and their designation clearly holds a lot of power since publishers target certain librarians, readers, and booksellers to help them promote and market their works. These decisions influence whether or not books make it into teens' hands, and so we feel that how the book is marketed should also be considered when classifying books as young adult.

As we consider the role of publishers, however, we must note that it is not always clear how this decision is made and that sometimes decisions may change during the publication process. Markus Zusak's *The Book Thief*, for instance, was originally published in Australia as an adult book. When it was published in the United States, however, it was marketed as a young adult book—US publishers clearly saw a youth audience as more suitable for this title. In addition, the book's point of view is not that of a teenager, thus raising questions about whether it would meet our main criteria of young adult literature. It is also important to note that despite the fact the publishers try to dictate the market, in actuality the market does not always follow their instructions. This has been true for works such as Stephenie Meyer's Twilight series or J. K. Rowling's Harry Potter series, both of which have likely had as many adult readers as teen readers. Nevertheless, even with these challenges, marketing power plays a significant role in which books end up being read by teens, so we include its role as part of our definition.

So while others may add other characteristics or impacting issues, and you may add your own, we contend that at the very core young adult literature is: *A work that represents an entirely adolescent point of view that is mainly marketed to that same audience.*

A Brief History of Young Adult Literature

Scholars agree that the history of children's books began as early as 1600. However, books specifically for adolescents have had a much shorter history. This may be due in part to the fact that the adolescent years were not even considered a distinct part of one's life span until 1904, when G. Stanley Hall published his work, *Adolescence*. Even with this recognition, it was not until well into the 1940s that the world's economic and social conditions significantly changed to make it fully possible to have a period past childhood (Cart, 2010). Once the first group of postwar babies had reached their teenage years in the 1960s, society not only accepted the idea of adolescence but began to see this age group as one with distinct characteristics and needs. So it was, then, in the '60s and '70s, when new ideas about personal conduct and societal rules for teens became paramount, that we see the emergence of young adult literature as a separate genre.

Most critics agree that it was in 1967, with the publication of S. E. Hinton's *The Outsiders*, and in 1968, with Paul Zindel's *The Pigman*, that young adult literature was born. Hinton's and Zindel's groundbreaking works were the first to show the world through the eyes of a teenager. Following in their footsteps were Robert Lipsyte, M. E. Kerr, Robert Newton Peck, and, perhaps most famously, Robert Cormier's *The Chocolate War* (1974) and Judy Blume's *Are You There God? It's Me, Margaret* (1970). These early works were most often works of gritty realism, dealing with tough issues faced by complex characters that appealed to the teens facing the harsh realities of a time punctuated by rock and roll, war, and riots.

As the '70s came to a close, we saw changes in young adult literature. With media playing a much stronger role in the lives of teens, reading habits changed. The Baby Sitters Club, Sweet Valley High, and Fear Street, were favorites of many teens in this era (Bucher & Hinton, 2009). Groundbreaking books such as Cynthia Voigt's *Dicey's Song* (1983), Walter Dean Myers's *Fallen Angels* (1988), and Francesca Lia Block's *Weetzie Bat* (1989) also came on the scene during this period.

The 1990s saw another significant shift in the history of young adult literature. In a surge that many critics attribute to the "Harry Potter" phenomena (first published in the United States in 1998), reading became "cool" again. Publishers also began to see a strong market in teenagers who had lots of disposable income, and then began to create more books for this audience. By the turn of the century, young adult literature had become the fastest-growing market in the industry, with marketing intelligence companies such as Simba reporting approximately 2,000 new titles published each year. This impressive growth spans the gamut from realism to fantasy and is constantly embracing new formats from graphic novels to short stories. With the establishment in 2000 of the Michael L. Printz award, given by the American Library Association for a book that exemplifies excellence in young adult literature, we find that books for young adults have established a solid footing. As we move further into the 21st century, we are sure to see many advances in the genre that will bring exciting new adventures in this dynamically evolving body of literature.

Dispelling Some Myths

Today the field of young adult literature is exciting and vibrant; however, despite the call of vocal professionals (Crowe, 1999b; Gallo, 2001; Gallo, Hathaway, Wood & Fink, 2010; Hipple, 2000; Santoli & Wagner, 2004), negative ideas about young adult literature still pervade in many circles and greatly impact the overall acceptance of young adult literature as a tool for teaching. To dispel these myths, we address each one briefly in the hopes of revealing the true nature of young adult literature and its potential for teaching.

MYTH 1: Young Adult Literature Is Not Quality Literature

There are many who claim that the body of young adult literature lacks complexity and that titles published for this audience are shallow or poorly written. While this characterization surely holds true for some works of young adult literature, the sweeping statement that all works in this group are subpar is a gross generalization. Just as literature written for adults consists of titles ranging from poorly written to Nobel Prize worthy—so it is with the world of young adult literature. There are subpar works in any genre, and there are topics and styles that rise and fall in popularity in any group of work. Young adult literature, in the mature form it has taken today, contains as broad a spectrum of quality as works aimed at other audiences.

Young adult authors of today create works that rival the classics or the best modern works of adult literature. They use all of the literary elements in effective and innovative ways to convey exquisitely crafted, sophisticated, and challenging stories. Authors like John Green are among the writers working today who portray the world of teenagers in the quality literary form. His novel *Looking for Alaska* has been widely hailed as a work of significant quality. It tells of the coming-of-age of a young man in a prep school who must navigate a world of friendship, romantic entanglements, and issues of death and guilt; in its complexity and depth, it rivals other classic coming-of-age stories like *Catcher in the Rye* or *To Kill a Mockingbird*.

MYTH 2: Young Adult Literature Is Not Complex Enough for Deep Discussions and Intricate Analysis

We have encountered many who believe that young adult books are just for escapist or entertainment reading, and thus they have few classroom applications as they have nothing of real importance to say. Granted, young adult literature can be spare and straightforward, eschewing the complex syntax and long descriptive passages of adult novels or the classical canon. Part of this is due to the audience: teens have lots of competition for their attention, and authors writing for teens must construct their works to stand up to this. Everything in a quality young adult novel has a purpose; much of the superfluous is stripped away in these works. But to assume that this simplicity means a lack of complexity is, once again, far from true.

While some literature written for teens features shallow themes and follows pop culture trends, there are also many books that explore complicated themes and feature authentic characters in meaningful settings that can be used to engender classroom discussion and analysis. Young adult books offer us an expression of the complexities of the human condition, both the good and the bad. For example, Ruta Sepetys's novel *Between Shades of Gray* is the story of a 15-year-old Lithuanian girl in 1941 who is forced into a hard-labor camp in the Arctic where her life is turned upside down, and her primary concerns are finding food and caring for her ailing mother and brother. This book can undoubtedly inspire deep discussion of man's inhumanity to man, the power of family, the indomitable human spirit, and the futility of war. This and any number of other young adult books provide abundant material for the intricate analysis that professionals are looking for.

MYTH 3: Young Adult Literature Is Not Challenging Enough for Good Readers and Is Better Suited to Remedial or Reluctant Readers

Because of its relatable characters, recognizable settings and conflicts, and approachable modern syntax, young adult literature has often been advocated for struggling or reluctant readers. While the genre certainly has potential to help these readers, we should not view this as the only application for these books. Less able readers can benefit from young adult novels; however, we should not let this prevent us from seeing that there are young adult books out there that meet the needs of good readers as well. There are high-quality, deep books that meet rigorous standards for complexity that will meet the needs of almost any teen reader. We must take care in conflating accessibility with simplicity. The fact that a book features familiar characters, settings, and conflicts does not mean it does not also present those elements in complex and authentic ways that provide challenges to all levels of readers.

While this brief discussion only scratches the surface, we hope that it allows you to view young adult literature in a new light. Young adult literature is rich and interesting. It is complex and represents high quality. Reading even a few of the top titles in young adult literature today, it becomes very apparent that these novels are full of just the right stuff for teaching and learning. As such, we believe that young adult literature should be the foundation for all students in the middle and high school classrooms.

Young Adult Literature in the Classroom

The publication of the CCSS and its widespread adoption offer a perfect context to use young adult literature for instructional purposes. We understand, though, that this idea might seem incredible, especially for those who have held to some of the myths we explored in the previous section. The tradition of the classical canon is strong in our educational system, and we need to make a strong case for enhancing or replacing those books with young adult titles. Let's consider some ways we could make this case.

We first contend that we ought to determine if young adult literature can fit with the general outcomes we expect in a classroom. Stotsky, Traffas, and Woodworth (2010) note that there are two major functions of the literature curriculum: to make students familiar with the heritage of English language literature and to help them develop the language skills necessary to attend college. These two outcomes also seem inherent in the CCSS, with the standards clearly articulating in more specific terms these same goals. For example, a standard like Grade 8, Reading Standard 9 asks students to show how modern fiction draws on forms from the past such as myth (National Governors Association & Council of Chief State School Officers, 2011; Note that due to the nature of this book we will no longer give the full citation when we discuss the CCSS. All references to it come from the documentation given at this source; when necessary we will cite locations and pages numbers, but we will not give the full citation). This standard seems to address Stotsky's outcome of connecting to our literary heritage. The CCSS also fully articulates the second function as it was designed to prepare students for college, even going as far as to title the reading standards, "College and Career Readiness" standards (p. 35).

In addition to what Stotsky and the CCSS articulate, we would like to add one additional outcome: to give our students a love of reading and books. A vocal advocate for young adult literature, Don Gallo (2001) also indicates that he would love to see the love of reading as the first goal of every English language arts curriculum. Kelly Gallagher (2009) feels so impassioned about instilling a love for reading that he dedicates his entire book *Readicide* to exploring the reasons why students leave school uninterested in reading. We believe the goal of the CCSS to have students read complex texts at a proficient level independently is only realized when they understand the power of reading and willingly engage in it on their own, without intervention from a teacher. Creating passionate, engaged, lifelong readers ought to be one of our primary goals—after all, what benefit is reading ability if we aren't interested in reading at all?

Having determined what outcomes we expect, we should next consider the texts that are most likely to help us reach these goals. We contend that young adult literature will not only help us meet the outcomes we have outlined, but it can do so more efficiently and with greater success. Let's consider how young adult literature can meet some of the main objectives required to meet our stated outcomes.

First, the heritage of English language literature is vast, and no list or canon can adequately encompass it all—in fact, we can hardly agree on what this list should be.

For example, Donelson (1978) recounts an experience he had in a class for English teachers during a debate about books that were so significant that no high school student should graduate with reading them. After 15 of the students made lists of what books they thought would fall into the above category, the class found that there were no common titles on the list. Some have also questioned the makeup of our idea of the traditional canon, questioning the exclusion of many minority and alternative viewpoints; these researchers call for more works by women and people of color to be part of our literary heritage (Guillory, 1993; Landt, 2006; Pike, 2003; Whaley, 1993). If our objective is to connect students to their literary heritage, we contend that the viewpoint of young adults is one that should be included as part of our literary heritage, especially when the individuals reading these books are young adults themselves.

Second, as we consider the need to develop skills required for college- and workplace-level work, some would argue that only the classical canon is suitable for this task. Many scholars with wide experience in the field of young adult literature suggest, on the contrary, that this mature field now contains numerous examples of complex, sophisticated texts that can provide a meaningful context for students' development of critical language and reading skills (Gallo, 2001; Hipple, 2000; Moore, 1997; Santoli & Wagner, 2004).

Lastly, we agree with Santoli and Wagner (2004) that young adult literature is the most significant way to increase students' satisfaction with the literature they are reading. The characters, settings, conflicts, point of view, and themes of these books are more familiar and more relevant to teen readers. If teens find that these books meet their interests and needs, they are more likely to read and read more, thus becoming the lifelong readers we hope to create.

No matter the design of our course or the curriculum, young adult literature can provide us with the essential building blocks for our curriculum. Scholars and advocates clearly show that works of young adult literature:

- Can serve to answer essential questions in a thematic unit because these books address themes worthy of study, the same universal themes explored by the classics (Hipple, 2000; Santoli & Wagner, 2004; Scherff & Groenke, 2009)
- Can be used to teach any and all forms of literary theory and criticism (Moore, 1997; Scherff, 2007; Scherff & Groenke, 2009)
- Can be used to teach literary elements and devices (Salvner, 2000; Scherff & Groenke, 2009)
- Can be used as tools for reflection and self-development, to show adolescents how literature can broaden self-perceptions and world experiences (Bean & Harper, 2006; Glasgow, 2001; Landt, 2006; Scherff & Groenke, 2009)
- Can engage readers in deep conversation and application of literature to personal and community experiences in a way that other texts that do not represent a teen point of view cannot (Santoli & Wagner, 2004).

Young adult literature can do all of these things, and in many scholars' opinions it can do them better than the accepted canon because the works of this genre find personal appeal and connections for the readers who are reading them. We often encounter students who clamor to read something like *The Hunger Games* yet will only read the CliffsNotes for their assigned English text. So if even our best readers are not reading the canon (Broz, 2011), we believe that it is high time to embrace young adult books. There may be those who think embracing young adult literature is a kind of surrender: we just accept that readers are going to read young adult books, so we must accept into our classrooms this inferior form of literature. However, this is far from true: we are not embracing a trend because it is inevitable; we are accepting an extremely useful tool. For us, reading the classics is like using a hammer when a screwdriver is what is called for. Let's start using the right tool to develop engaged and critical readers; for us that tool is young adult literature.

There are all types of ways to use young adult literature in any classroom: It can be used as part of a personal independent reading program; it can be used for whole class assigned reading; it can be used as a bridge to the canon; it can be used independently for reading by groups or individuals as part of a curriculum unit. The opportunities are endless, and if we include young adult literature, we open up a whole toolbox of options. No matter how, who, or where you teach, we know that you can use young adult literature. We hope this book will help you to see that young adult literature is an outstanding option for the classroom and that it will arm you with all you need to advocate for its use in meeting the demands of the CCSS.

Embracing Young Adult Literature

Since young adult books are a good fit for the outcomes in our classes, we wonder why there is still such great resistance to their use in classrooms. Why don't more professionals embrace young adult literature? Why do biases against it exist in spite of the voices of scholars and advocates who show what a great tool young adult literature can be? There may be no clear answer to these questions and no single answer that satisfies, but we would like to take a moment to discuss some of the reasons we think professionals may use to exclude young adult books. Doing so will help us understand the barriers we face and how we might overcome them.

One of the first reasons many may not embrace young adult books is a general lack of understanding of the genre, along with the proper training to use it. Many professionals come out of their training programs with no significant experience with young adult novels. Others who have had some exposure may still not feel comfortable teaching it (Christenbury, 2000; Herz, 2005; Santoli & Wagner, 2004). Unsure about where young adult books fit into the curriculum, we rely on this training and end up continuing the traditions of the canon.

In this training we were learning to read and respond to the literature that our college professors found important; we were not learning to read and respond to the literature that our current middle and high school students will find significant. In addition, the critical theories, learning outcomes, and teaching situations that our professors used to structure their own teaching are not the same ones that should be used to structure our own teaching. Relying on our training alone, sadly, can give us a very biased and limited basis for our own teaching. If you feel your own training has not prepared you to engage in the world of young adult literature, we encourage you to expand upon it. Reading the professional literature written by experts who know how to teach young adult books is one way to expand your experience. The bibliography at the end of this chapter provides a good basic start to this literature. Talking to other professionals and checking out libraries will lead to many other significant articles and books as well. In addition, attending professional conferences and workshops such as the one offered by the Assembly on Literature for Adolescents (ALAN) every November is also a great resource.

Another barrier may be our own attitudes, beliefs, concerns, and fears. Some have real concerns about the quality of young adult literature and its potential in the classroom. Others may hold the belief that if we don't read the classics, we will help to create an unlearned society. Some might fear going against the traditional wisdom that other professionals espouse. Others may fear how students, other teachers, administration, and parents will respond, concerned about controversy or the potential of offending someone. These concerns, born out of a sincere desire to give our students the best education, can prevent us from seeking out alternatives. We hope that this book will help you to reconstruct any ideas you hold that may lead to misunderstandings about the literature. We, too, have faced similar concerns in our own careers, but have found that while many of them are challenging, it is certainly possible to overcome them.

If we ground ourselves in the belief that we want to find the best curriculum and texts to create outstanding learning experiences for our students, any concerns we have will be easier to confront. We recommend national professional associations such as the American Library Association (ALA), the International Reading Association (IRA), and the National Council of Teachers of English (NCTE) as great resources for those who need support—especially those facing administration concerns or censorship attempts. The professional support that these organizations provide, at both conferences and online, will be extremely helpful.

Yet another barrier we must confront is the weight of the load teaching puts on us. Teaching is hard, no doubt about it. Creating engaging and interesting lessons and activities on a daily basis only adds to the challenge. For many, to add something further just seems out of the question. However, adding in young adult literature need not take us down an entirely new path. We can use much of what we've done before with young adult literature. The reality is that we're teaching the same skills and content, just with different texts. While we realize that it may not be simple to transfer, the process is much less demanding than it might seem at the outset.

While the initial work may be daunting, the reality is that this work is only at the beginning. There may be a lot of work initially and a steep learning curve in the initial steps, but it will get easier as you go along. With every day of experience there is less learning and work. In addition, you don't have to do all the work yourself. Along with what we provide in this book, many teachers have already created lesson plans and activities for a variety of young adult books. A good web search for "lesson plans for young adult novels" will bring up many interesting ideas for you to use. We often tell our pre-service teachers that the most creative teachers are those who take what others have done and adapt it for their own use. These resources can provide you with all the raw material you need to create lessons, units, and activities, with much less work than if you created them from scratch. In addition, the articles, books, and professional association resources we have mentioned before can also provide so many great ideas to help reduce the workload of planning.

Lastly, we believe that one of the biggest barriers to the use of young adult books is the pressure on curriculum that comes from outside forces. We recognize that not everyone gets to choose the books that are used in their classrooms, but many teachers do. In fact, in her study, Samuels (1983) found that things like censorship, funding, or district and department requirements were not a major factor in teachers' decisions to include or not include young adult novels as part of their curriculum. Also Stotsky, Traffas, and Woodworth (2010) note that fully 70 to 80 percent of teachers choose their own texts. For the majority of teachers who have autonomy in choosing texts, the advent of the common core provides us with a unique chance to rethink some of our decisions in the past and consider a larger role for young adult literature. For the minority who really have no control, with mandates preventing them from including young adult books, we find that there is certainly room for change. The adoption of the common core offers us the perfect opportunity to open the dialogue with committees and administrators about the great potential that young adult books have for our classrooms. The common core also gives us a great deal of ammunition to successfully argue for the inclusion of young adult texts at the heart of our curriculum.

The common core offers no predetermined pedagogy, placing much of the responsibility to meet the standards on the individual teacher. In the CCSS, teachers are free to use whatever tools and knowledge their professional judgments and experience identify as most helpful for meeting the standards. We contend that one of these tools is young adult literature. As noted above, many have clearly shown though their professional judgment and experience that young adult literature is a helpful tool in the classroom to engage readers. With this background and experience we have no reason not to believe that young adult books should play a significant role in the freedom teachers have to apply the CCSS. So no matter what outside forces impact your teaching, let's start the conversation and campaign for change. If you need to, start small by talking to your fellow teachers and librarians to get them on board, then expanding out and talking to your principals and administrators. The more we articulately advocate for what we know can work with our students, the better able we will be to serve them in all their learning endeavors.

Our Bold Approach to Young Adult Literature

At a recent conference of the National Council of Teachers of English, a colleague of ours gave a presentation discussing articles about young adult literature that had been published in the last 100 years of a journal for that association. One comment he made struck us: He noted that an overarching theme in many articles was the perceived need to justify or apologize for young adult literature. While these authors advocated strongly for the genre's use, at the same time they also downplayed it since they did not wish to disregard traditional teaching practices. With all due respect to these writers, we choose not to apologize for or downplay the role young adult literature should play in the classroom.

We are going to take a bold approach. We are passionate about our contention that young adult literature should be at the forefront of today's middle and high school classrooms. We also believe that there is no need to bow to tradition in the hopes that it makes our position stronger, for if it is not strong enough on its own merits, it is not worth believing in the first place. As professionals, we know what works for us and for our students. Research has proven and our experience has shown which pedagogies and materials are the most effective. However, as the modern landscape of education is filled with potholes, we often let ourselves be distracted by them to the detriment of what we know is right and best. We believe that the time is ripe for us to eliminate those distractions and embrace the best tools we have.

The CCSS provides us with a solid basis. With an emphasis in these standards on teacher choice and expertise in applying the standards, we finally have the wind at our backs, pushing us forward toward creating the very best curriculum with the very best materials. We believe that young adult literature should form the basis for all integrated instruction in all content areas for all students ages 12–19. Young adult literature has often played no role or only one supplementary to other works; however, it need not be the black sheep any longer. We are not going to make any apologies for our view nor try to soften it by taking time to pay homage to the canon and its usefulness in the curriculum.

We know that this radical approach may be troublesome to some. However, we believe in its value, as we have seen it at work in our own classrooms. We also feel that we need to take creative and innovative steps in order to see what the future could look like. We encourage you to experiment and find what works best for you and your situation. And while we realize that not everyone is going to implement what we advocate, as the CCSS emphasizes empowering professionals to do what is the very best for their students, we also believe that in the end, this is what this book is about as well. We hope to help you take the elements of the CCSS and empower yourself to find the right tools to apply to your situation. We hope that as you read, you will look for ideas and elements that will work for you. We have purposely been broad and all-encompassing in our recommendations of books and in our outline of lessons and activities. We want you to read on and empower yourself to create dynamic and interesting curricula that are the very best for your students.

Bibliography

Bean, T., & Harper, H. (2006). Exploring notions of freedom in and through young adult literature. *Journal of Adolescent and Adult Literacy, 50*(2), 96–104

Broz, W. J. (2011). Not reading: The 800-pound mockingbird in the classroom. *English Journal, 100*(5), 15–20.

Bucher, K. T., & Hinton-Johnson, K. M. (2009). *Young adult literature: exploration, evaluation, and appreciation.* (2nd ed.). Upper Saddle River, NJ: Prentice Hall.

Cart, M. (2010). *Young adult literature: From romance to realism.* Chicago, IL: American Library Association.

Christenbury, L. (2000). Natural, necessary, and workable: The connection of young adult novels to the classics. In V. R. Monseau & G. M. Salvner (Eds.), *Reading their world: The young adult novel in the classroom.* (2nd ed.). Portsmouth, NH: Heinemann.

Cole, P. (2008). *Young adult literature in the 21st century.* Columbus, OH: McGraw-Hill.

Crowe, C. (1999a). Dear teachers: Please help my kids become readers. *English Journal, 89*(1), 139–142.

Crowe, C. (1999b). English teachers are from Mars, students are from Venus (but YA books can help interplanetary understanding). *English Journal, 88*(4), 120–122.

Crowe, C. (1999c). Rescuing reluctant readers. *English Journal, 88*(5), 113–116.

Crowe, C. (2000). Dear knucklehead: Wise up. *English Journal, 90*(1), 149–152.

Crowe, C. (2001). AP and YA? *English Journal, 91*(1), 123–128.

Donelson, K. (1978). The classics are never enough. *Curriculum Review, 17*(5), 371–381.

Donelson, K. L., & Nilsen, A. P. (2004). *Literature for today's young adults.* (7th ed.). Boston, MA: Allyn & Bacon.

Gallagher, K. (2009). *Readicide: How schools are killing reading and what you can do about it.* Portland, ME: Stenhouse Publishers.

Gallo, D. R. (2001). How classics create an aliterate society. *English Journal, 90*(3), 33–39.

Gallo, D., Hathaway, J., Wood, K., & Fink, L. (2010). Ice cream/I scream for YA books. *Voices from the Middle, 17*(4), 8–14.

Glasgow, J. (2001). Teaching social justice through young adult literature. *English Journal, 90*(6), 54–61.

Guillory, J. (1993). *Cultural capital: The problem of literary canon formation.* Chicago, IL: University of Chicago Press.

Hall, G. S. (1904). *Adolescence: Its psychology and its relations to physiology, anthropology, sociology, sex, crime, religion and education.* New York, NY: D. Appleton and Company.

Herz, S. K. (2005). *From Hinton to Hamlet: Building bridges between young adult literature and the classics.* Westport, CT: Greenwood Press.

Hipple, T. (2000). With themes for all: The universality of the young adult novel. In V. R. Monseau & G. M. Salvner (Eds.), *Reading their world: The young adult novel in the classroom.* (2nd ed.). Portsmouth, NH: Heinemann.

Landt, S. M. (2006). Multicultural literature and young adolescents: A kaleidoscope of opportunity. *Journal of Adolescent and Adult Literacy, 49*(8), 690–697.

Mitchell, D. (2001). Young adult literature and the English teacher. *English Journal, 90*(3), 23–25.

Moore, J. N. (1997). *Interpreting young adult literature: Literary theory in the secondary classroom.* Portsmouth, NH: Heinemann.

National Governors Association & Council of Chief State School Officers. (2011). *Common core state standards initiative.* Retrieved 2011 from http://www.corestandards.org.

Pike, M. A. (2003). The canon in the classroom: Students' experiences of texts from other times. *Journal of Curriculum Studies, 35*(3), 355–370.

Salvner, G. M. (2000). Time and tradition. Transforming the secondary English class with young adult novels. In V. R. Monseau & G. M. Salvner (Eds.), *Reading their world: The young adult novel in the classroom.* (2nd ed.). Portsmouth, NH: Heinemann.

Samuels, B. G. (1983). Young adult novels in the classroom? *English Journal, 72*(4), 86–88.

Santoli, S. P., & Wagner, M. E. (2004). Promoting young adult literature: The other "real" literature. *American Secondary Education, 33*(1), 65.

Scherff, L. (2007). Getting beyond the cuss words: Using Marxism and binary opposition to teach *Ironman* and *The Catcher in the Rye. ALAN Review, 35*(1), 51–61.

Scherff, L., & Groenke, S. (2009). Young adult literature in today's classroom. *English Leadership Quarterly, 31*(4), 1–3.

Seney, B. (2008). Bridging to the classics. *Understanding Our Gifted, 20*(3), 3–5.

Stallworth, B. J. (1998). The young adult literature course: Facilitating the integration of young adult literature into the high school English classroom. *ALAN Review, 26*(1), 25–30.

Stotsky, S., Traffas, J., & Woodworth, J. (2010). Literary study in grades 9, 10, and 11: A national survey. *Forum: A Publication of the ALSCW,* (4), Retrieved January 10, 2012 from http://www.alscw.org/Forum4.pdf.

Whaley, L. (1993). *Weaving in the women: Transforming the high school English curriculum.* Portsmouth, NH: Boynton/Cook.

Wold, L., & Elish-Piper, L. (2009). Scaffolding the English canon with linked text sets. *English Journal, 98*(6), 88–91.

Chapter 2

The Common Core State Standards

The Common Core State Standards were initiated through a joint effort of the National Governors Association Center for Best Practices and the Council of Chief State School Offices. These two groups also worked with Achieve Inc., an education reform group based in Washington, D.C. These groups' shared purpose was to create a common set of standards that were research-based and that states could voluntarily adopt. The impetus for this work was grounded in the long-term movement toward accountability and standards-based reform that began in the early '90s. So while this type of reform is not really new, the creation of standards philosophically grounded in research that can then be applied across state lines represents a significant attempt to reexamine educational benchmarks.

The standards for the English language arts (ELA) and mathematics were released in June 2010; as of March 2012, 46 states and the District of Columbia have formally adopted the standards, committing that the common core will replace at least 85 percent of state standards by 2015. The hope of the groups involved in developing the CCSS is that these standards will be better aligned with current workplace expectations and that they will encourage rigorous skill development in students. Whether these standards will achieve that goal, of course, remains to be seen. But with so many states adopting the standards and with vigorous efforts underway to develop assessments to match the standards, it behooves all educators to begin closely examining the CCSS documents and consider the implications of these standards for our classrooms and teachers.

The English language arts standards of the common core are divided into four basic strands: reading, writing, speaking, and listening. For each strand, the CCSS articulates overarching anchor standards that are then subdivided into grade-specific standards. These anchor and grade-specific standards articulate the specific skills that the authors of the common core believe are essential for students at each grade. In addition to the standards, three supportive appendices are provided; the first two outline a methodology designed to help teachers effectively evaluate texts used for reading instruction. We will discuss these appendices later in this chapter. The remaining appendix, designed to help teachers assess student writing, will not be of primary concern to us in this book. Additional documentation includes information about applying the standards to students with disabilities, English language learners, and non-ELA content areas.

All of these documents are important reading if we want a clear understanding of the CCSS, and we encourage professionals to take the time to read and study them. To help support this reading we will now explore what the CCSS is and is not as well as some of the basic assumptions and problems with the CCSS that are particularly germane for us to understand if we intend to use them to support the inclusion of young adult literature into the classroom.

The Precise Nature of the Common Core Standards

The CCSS is a set of educational standards. A standard is a statement or rule that helps us to ensure quality, the implication being that if we apply the standard, a certain level of quality will be met. The same holds for the CCSS, which were designed to provide a clear statement of what students are expected to learn. These standards are performance based rather than prescriptive, meaning that they describe what students ought to be able to do (determine the theme of a text, for instance) rather than what teachers ought to do (have students compare poetry from different cultures). We should consider the standards as the building blocks to everything else that goes on in a classroom, including assessments, curriculum design, and student interventions.

We feel it is critical to note that the CCSS does not seek to standardize anything but the measurable outcomes of student learning. Individual teachers and school districts decide how to design instruction that meets those standards. The CCSS does not mandate specific texts or curricular approaches, nor does it dictate how teachers should teach. For example, a closer reading of the documents clearly reveals that the exemplar text lists are only examples of the kinds of texts and levels of complexity that students ought to be exposed to during their schooling rather than a mandate that specific books be taught in classrooms. Instead, the three-tiered model of text complexity offered by the CCSS provides teachers with a template and methodology to use in judging any text, thus opening up a wider range of possibilities for teachers.

There is significant potential in this approach, as the common core opens exciting possibilities for every professional. The implementation of the common core can help us to celebrate innovation and change as we strive to develop and improve curriculum and instruction. The focus on research-based outcomes can help us renew our understanding of pedagogy that has proven to be more effective than techniques that we may currently be using. Here we see great opportunities to use effective active and inquiry-based learning strategies. In the common core documents, we also see a stronger focus on our students as individuals, a focus that allows us unprecedented ability to think of our students' learning needs and develop effective ways to meet those needs.

In this spirit we offer the primary argument of this book: *Young adult literature, when coupled with inquiry-based learning designs, can meet students' needs and help them develop skills that will meet the demands of the common core.* The changes the CCSS advocates make this an exciting time to speak up about some of the best pedagogy and tools out there to enhance student learning.

We acknowledge that the CCSS has its detractors (Beach, 2011; Kendall, 2011, Tienken, 2011), and will leave it to others to make their case. We find that the widespread adoption of these standards and the fast-approaching publication of large-scale assessments matching the CCSS demand that we accommodate these standards. Fortunately, we believe that under the direction of passionate, creative, and engaged professionals, the application of the common core can provide us with the right set of conditions to create the quality learning environments we have always tried to achieve.

Assumptions and Implications of the CCSS

The fundamental need for public education to prepare students for college and the workplace is almost universally accepted. In recent years our focus has been sharply tuned to this fact as scholars and theorists have argued that our schools are failing in this regard.

For example, Tony Wagner (2008) argues that the current system does not prepare students to meet the demands of a modernized global workplace. Other studies have also shown that students are not prepared for the rigors of reading and writing in both college and work contexts (Casner-Lotto & Barrington, 2006; Wilkins, Hartman, et al., 2010; Williamson, 2008). These studies, among others, informed the standards of the CCSS and their attempt to reverse this trend. This basic tenet, that standards need to be aligned with current college and workplace expectations, pervades the CCSS; however, there are the three other important beliefs inherent in the CCSS we need to consider: the increased emphasis on informational texts, the need for texts to be more complex, and the need for readers to develop independence.

Increased Emphasis on Informational Texts

To prepare students for college and work, the CCSS encourages teaching the skills of reading, writing, and speaking in an interdisciplinary context. Research (Fang & Wei, 2010; Kane & Rule, 2004; Ruiz, Thornton, & Cuero, 2010; Stevens, 2006) and practical experience have shown that the integration of basic skills across the curriculum enhances overall student achievement. In light of this, the common core standards also place strong emphasis on informational texts. The CCSS does not suggest that ELA teachers are solely responsible for incorporating greater informational texts, but that these texts should be included in all other curricular areas as well. This call for more informational texts does not require that we stop reading novels or other forms—the standards do not expect us to do one or the other but both.

This provides an exciting opportunity and a challenge. One of our great opportunities is to expand the repertoire of texts used in our ELA classrooms. Making connections between topics and characters in fictional texts to informational nonfiction and biographies is an exciting way to enhance the teaching of any text. But with this opportunity also comes the challenge of expanding our knowledge of available texts both for our use and to help support their content area colleagues in the identification and use of a wide variety of texts. This will require ELA teachers to be more conversant in a wider range of texts. Building knowledge and experience with so many different forms will certainly be a constant endeavor in our future professional development. This challenge, however, also allows us to partner with our colleagues in new and exciting ways as we work to help each other find the very best texts. We encourage you to collaborate by looking to fellow teachers as well as other important sources such as your school librarian to help you expand your knowledge of the wide variety of texts that are available. Young adult literature—both fiction and nonfiction—provides a good foundation for this partnership since young adult books will be appropriate for all content areas in the same way that they fit ELA classrooms.

Text Complexity

One of the fundamental underpinnings of the CCSS is that in order for students to be ready for college and the workplace, they need to be engaging with texts of greater complexity. The CCSS documentation outlines research that shows that texts used in schools have been declining in complexity while demands of out-of-school reading have remained the same or increased. While we could debate at length this research and its conclusions, we will leave that to others now speaking up (Allington, 2012; Tienken, 2011) and to future research. That the fundamental progression of all educational pursuits should be upward, however, seems to be a basic principle accepted by most of us. We grow and learn by moving from simple ideas and tasks to more complex ones; this trajectory should be the same for our students' reading.

Much space and attention in the common core documentation is devoted to conveying the CCSS vision and purpose for calling for greater text complexity, making this one of the most critical beliefs inherent in the CCSS. The assumption that in-school reading is not complex enough drove the creation of the three-tiered model for judging text complexity. This model gives us a means for making choices about texts and a pattern for increasing rigor throughout the grades. We will fully discuss the issues related to text complexity in our next three chapters, but for now we note that this increase is one that works well in theory, but in practice will no doubt provide us with challenges. With readers of different skills and abilities in every classroom, we may find it difficult to create environments that take all readers to higher levels of complexity. The use of young adult literature, however, can help mediate some of these challenges: it can meet the stated demands of text complexity outlined by the CCSS and provide us with a wide variety of texts to help us meet individual readers' needs.

Reader Independence

The last and, we feel, most important assumption of the CCSS is that to be ready for college and the workplace, students must be able to read and write at a high level of independence. Moving toward independence is a complex process involving the intricate interplay between the tools and pedagogy that are used in the classroom every day. While this certainly involves teaching students helpful skills and strategies, we also know that it entails helping students develop a positive disposition toward reading—reading skills and a positive attitude are intertwined, in fact, in independent, competent readers. This goes beyond earning a grade or some kind of external reward—it is an inner motivation and understanding about the power that the act of reading has. Unfortunately, the research and commentary (Gallo, 2001; Herz, 2005; Pike, 2003) on current classroom practices indicates that they can turn kids off to reading, discouraging a lifelong passion for it. We believe that young adult literature in the classroom is not only a good tool to help our students build the critical and analytic skills they need, but that it is the body of literature with the greatest likelihood to build positive attitudes toward reading for the maximum number of readers.

Filling the Holes in the CCSS

We admire the way that considerations of informational texts, complexity, and independence cause us to revisit our assumptions about the texts we use in the classroom. However, based on our professional experience and knowledge of research of what creates the best conditions for readers, we believe that two important points are left out of the CCSS. The lack of discussion about amount of reading and reading for pleasure are critical elements to consider if we hope to build students who can read a variety of complex texts independently so they can ultimately comprehend texts in college and the workplace.

Amount of Reading

The CCSS makes a brief note that for students to achieve the standards, they need to read a great deal; however, this small mention is not explored further and is then eclipsed by the focus on complexity. Studies have shown that the amount of reading a student does is directly linked to achieving the type of higher-order independent reading the CCSS asks for, and that increased volume has been positively linked to increased reading comprehension, vocabulary, and writing skills (Allington, 2012; Brozo, Shiel, & Topping, 2007; Cipielewski & Stanovich, 1992; Krashen, 1993).

While the intent of the CCSS is to expose readers to more complex texts over time, reading one or two texts over the years—even if they increase in complexity—is unlikely to make independent readers. A high volume of reading is one of the significant additions we believe is critical if we are going to make the types of readers the CCSS envisions. If we look closely at our classrooms, we can see that as the complexity of texts may have declined over the years, so has the amount of reading students engage in. Far too few schools have built large amounts of reading into the curriculum, instead focusing on skill development in the hopes that students will pass standardized tests. The amount of reading also declines as we move up though grades: Look at a kindergarten or first-grade classroom and you will mostly see numerous books and opportunities for children to engage in them. On the other hand, Gallo (1968) found that the eleventh-graders he studied read only 11 books per year. A recent conversation one author had with a high school teacher confirms Gallo's finding; this teacher indicated that including both in-class and out-of-class reading, her students read the equivalent of 12 books a year. This limited volume of reading is never going to be sufficient for students to obtain the high levels the CCSS requires. And this is just reading assigned for school—what about reading that teens do on their own, outside the demands of teachers? Research has shown that adolescents are doing much less voluntary reading (Bauerlein, 2010; National Endowment for the Arts, 2007; OECD, 2011; Ratcliffe, 2009), which complicates this problem even more. While the intent of the CCSS is to expose readers to more complex texts over time, reading few texts—even if they increase in complexity—is unlikely to make independent readers. A high volume of reading is one of the significant additions we believe is critical if we are going to make the types of readers the CCSS envisions.

The increasing role that digital technologies play may bring some potential changes to this problem. With a recent survey showing that nearly two-thirds of teens use the Internet daily (Lenhart, Purcell, Smith, & Zickuhr, 2010), it's likely that these students are encountering increasing amounts of text online. While not full-length novels, the Facebook pages, search result listings, or comment boards that teens peruse certainly count as reading in the sense of decoding and comprehending text. There are also suggestions that the rise of popularity of e-books may have an impact on the amount of reading teens do. Industry reports claim that sales of young adult e-book titles are significantly outpacing paper sales or sales of other genres (Springen, 2012). However, there's no clear data yet as to whether these figures mean that teens are reading more. Whatever the digital future may hold, we contend that of equal importance to students being exposed to a higher level of complexity in the text they read, they also need to increase the sheer amount of their reading.

Reading for Pleasure

To create independent readers, the environment we create in our classrooms should not only portray how to read at a critical level but also how to engage with reading on a personally pleasurable level as well. Our students should experience the thrill of staying up all night to finish a book or the eager anticipation for the next book in a series. Some of our students find relevance in reading car repair manuals or video game hint guides—as Smith and Wilhelm (2002) found in their study. But these reading experiences are often denied them in schools. Helping students appreciate reading is vital to creating the type of independent readers we want, so a focus on reading for fun and pleasure is essential to any implementation of the CCSS.

The only real mention made of this in the CCSS is a note that students need all kinds of opportunities with reading to not only stretch themselves in complexity but also to have the pleasure of easy, fluent reading. Our concern is that the emphasis on complexity may overshadow concerns about building a love (or at least an appreciation) of reading. This has been very clearly shown in the research from those like Bauerlein (2010) and Gallo (2001) who note that difficult classics used in the classroom often have the effect of turning students off reading entirely. Gallagher (2009) talks about students who, exposed to reading as merely a way of preparing for tests or completing school tasks, become *aliterate*—able to read but choosing not to because they find it irrelevant and tedious. This results in the type of student that one author encountered in a literature class for pre-service teachers who admitted to her, with much pride, that she had not read a book for pleasure since the seventh grade. This type of student who can read but chooses not to seems to us to be the antithesis of the type of independent engaged reader that the CCSS is asking us to create.

As professionals, there are many things we can do to create the types of environments that will produce not only critical readers but passionate ones as well. Techniques like letting students pick their own books, having silent reading time, and using inquiry learning to engage students in literature in authentic ways can go a long way to helping students understand the joy and value of reading. Once again, we contend that young adult literature can play a valuable role here in that it provides accessible and relevant texts to teen readers. The exploding numbers of young adult titles testifies, we suggest, that teens are hungry for books that speak to them and eager to read when they find the literature personally compelling. Sadly, we have encountered professionals who talk about young adult books in disparaging ways, an attitude we find disrespectful to teens and their interests. A respect for young adult books helps teens to know that their perspective and ideas are valid, thus also creating the kind of learning environment that allows teens to see the joys and pleasures of reading more easily. Using literature that is developmentally appropriate, that discusses issues of importance to the audience we are addressing, and engages their interest goes a long way to helping students see reading as pleasurable.

Applying the CCSS

The CCSS provides us with the theoretical underpinnings and the basic tools necessary to apply the standards to achieve excellence in ELA. However, the common core does not provide us with the practical, day-to-day application of its ideas; this is left entirely up to professional judgment. It is our job to translate what the documentation has to offer into concrete activities, lessons, and structures that will allow us to create effective learning experiences. No matter what structures you use to apply the CCSS in your classrooms (just as we will use the structure of inquiry learning later on), the first step in the process will always be to judge texts to determine if their construction meets the expectations of the CCSS for text complexity. The CCSS outlines a three-tiered model that is used for this analysis.

The Three-Tiered Model of Text Complexity

One of the most important assumptions of the CCSS is that students need to read works of increasing complexity. To help professionals apply the notion of complexity to texts, the standards' authors offer a model to be used as a template to judge texts. This model contains three components to measure text complexity and to guide teachers' decisions about selection of texts for study in the classroom: quantitative dimensions, qualitative dimensions, and reader and task considerations.

Quantitative dimensions cover the application of mathematical formulas to a text to discover a numerical score that indicates the relative ease or difficulty of reading of the text. Qualitative dimensions address elements of a text that are not as easy to measure quantitatively, including the complexity of its structure, language, and format. Reader and task dimensions cover the role the reader plays in making and determining meaning from a text as well as how the text will be applied in teaching situations. The common core notes that each of these three elements is of equal importance in judging a text's complexity level. This will not be a

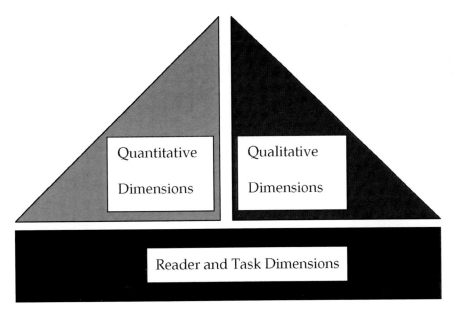

Figure 2.1   The CCSS Three-Tiered Model of Text Complexity

surprise to ELA professionals who know from experience that each of these dimensions plays a significant role in text complexity and text selection. Because of this balanced approach, we find that the three-tiered model provides us with a good basis to not only evaluate texts but to articulate an individual text's role in our classroom instruction.

This model is conceptualized in the standards documents as a pyramid, with reader and task providing the base, and then qualitative and quantitative methods providing the two sides of a triangle (see Figure 2.1). The location of reader and task dimensions at the foundational part of the pyramid may be happenstance, but we believe that its location as foundation communicates a lot. Our professional experience has shown that considerations of readers' needs and tasks often do make up the basis of many of our text choices. We strive to match students' interests to specific texts, knowing that they'll be more likely to read about settings, characters, or themes that they find familiar or relevant. In addition, skilled teachers know that certain texts are well suited to specific tasks—to teach students about making inferences, for instance, a good teacher will carefully select a text that requires such skills and that allows for an authentic context in which to develop them. In our view, these two considerations really do provide the foundation for judging all texts and, coupled with the other two dimensions, offer a robust vision of how texts should be analyzed and selected. Nevertheless, there are three significant problems with the CCSS view of text complexity as presented that should be considered as we use this model.

The CCSS Portrays Certain Biases

As with any work of this sort, the CCSS displays a bias toward certain theoretical perspectives, and as with most ELA instruction over the decades, the bias here seems to be toward new critical or formalist applications for literature study and analysis. As Tyson (1999) explains, these approaches, while no longer practiced in the mainstream of literary criticism, have colored the way we read, write, and teach literature. These theories, with their focus on the use of textual evidence to support claims and on a close reading of iconic texts, have pervaded much of classroom instruction for decades (Beach, 2011). The application of formalist traditions is evident in the standards as they also ask students to identify and compare a variety of texts using textual evidence.

Box 2.1 Publication Date Ranges of CCSS Exemplar Texts

Date Ranges	K–1	Grade 2–3	Grade 4–5	Grade 6–8	Grade 9–10	Grades 11 and up
pre-1800					3	2
1800s			1	2	2	8
1900–1930			1		3	4
1940–1949		1	2			1
1950–1959	1				2	1
1960–1969	3	1	1	2	2	
1970–1979	3	2	2	2	1	1
1980–1989		4		1	1	
1990–1999		1	2	3	1	1
2000–2005		4			1	1
2005–2010	1		1			
	8	13	10	10	16	19
% of texts pre-1930			2%	2%	50%	73%

This tradition is also evident in the selection of the core's exemplar texts. For example, we find it telling that in the lists of exemplar texts for K–3, no text listed as an exemplar was published before 1930, and on the lists for grades 4–5 and 6–8, only 2 percent of the texts were published before 1930. However, when we move to the grade 9–10 list, fully 50 percent of the texts were published before 1930, and on the 11-and-up list, fully 73 percent of the texts were published before 1930. In addition, the only lists that give texts published in the last five years are the K–1 and the 4–5 lists. (See box 2.1). This overabundance of older texts might imply that few texts appropriate for grades 9–12 have been published since the 1930s. However, this is far from true. While classic texts meet the complexity standards of these grade levels, there are also thousands of modern texts that meet the standards for rigor, and the standards' authors have failed to acknowledge these.

Another issue we find is that, while the K–8 text exemplars are filled with examples of children's books, the 9–12 texts list only adult texts. Of the 35 texts given in appendix B on the 9–10 and 11+ reading lists, only one could be considered a young adult book, and even that designation is debatable. This title, *The Book Thief* by Markus Zusak, since it was first published in Australia as an adult book and does not truly reflect an adolescent point of view, is a questionable fit for the description of true young adult literature. The standards gloss over a whole body of literature that can match the developmental needs of the teen readers it is targeted to. Such does not seem to be the case when we examine the lists for younger readers, leading us to ask: If it is appropriate to teach children's books to children, then why not young adult books to young adults?

Without a doubt the exemplar texts offered by the standards for grades 6–12 are significantly biased toward classic works. While these exemplar lists are intended to serve only as examples of how the standards for text complexity can be applied, not as a finite list of required texts, our concern is that the CCSS bias may only reaffirm old habits instead of opening up possibilities. Today we have a whole wealth of literature that could meet the complexity standards, and if we look past this bias toward using this model to analyze all texts, we will find this bounty open to us.

We recognize that the power of tradition and of our own training can be powerful forces. In spite of the apparent bias in the common core documents, we feel the standards rely on professional expertise, and the suggestions to apply the standards locally actually encourage us to revisit our current practice to find significant possibilities for revising instruction in progressive ways.

The CCSS Lacks Proper Sequencing

The stated purpose of the CCSS is to create environments where students will achieve independent facility with increasingly complex texts over time. The model provides the foundation for this purpose as it is the tool by which we will judge and communicate how texts fall into this progression. This idea that students should be provided texts in a logical sequence throughout their studies that gives them stepping-stones to greater complexity is not new. In fact, the pattern used to sequence texts in this way was articulated by Dr. Teri Lesesne (2010) in her book *Reading Ladders: Leading Students from Where They Are to Where We'd Like Them to Be*. The model articulated by Lesesne supports a concrete view of how a steady increase can be achieved.

However, despite its intent to increase complexity over time, a close look at how the CCSS presents the application of the model reveals a significant lack of proper sequencing between grade levels and texts. For example, in the 6–8 grade exemplar list we encounter *The Tale of the Mandarin Ducks* by Katherine Paterson a 20-page retelling of a Japanese folktale illustrated by Leo and Diane Dillon. Then moving up to the 9–10 grade examples, we find Franz Kafka's *The Metamorphosis*, an intriguingly bizarre work originally written in German and first published in 1915. We find it hard to believe that just the few months of movement between grades 8 and 9 would prepare students to move from Paterson's work to the significantly more complex work of Kafka with ease. These huge leaps from more obviously simple texts to what we consider overly challenging texts just do not make much practical sense. They also do not display the type of gradual progression of texts that the CCSS states we should have.

In addition, we find that many of the texts the CCSS applies the model to in the higher-grade bands demand large amounts of background knowledge from their readers, thus in our opinion making them far too complex for the age groups they are recommended for—at least if students are expected to read them independently. With the diversity of ability and experience we encounter in classrooms, to ensure that all students in a class will be able to comprehend overly demanding texts may require far too much intervention on the part of the teaching professional to really be practical. Choosing texts that are just as rigorous in their complexity but that do not make inordinate demands allows us to focus more on other tasks such as showing readers how to analyze structure. We find then that there is a great deal of intervening complexity that the CCSS does not acknowledge. Filling in these significant gaps with books that are appropriately leveled by our own application of the model will be the job of professionals as they apply the CCSS to the classroom. Young adult literature can help provide titles that fill in these gaps.

The CCSS Outline of Complexity Measures Is Unbalanced

While the CCSS outlines its case for the three-tiered model very well, it remains just that, an outline. The common core lacks depth by sometimes only offering a few vague descriptions of several elements of the model. Despite the suggested importance of all the dimensions, the CCSS documentation fails to fully address important issues. In fact, a careful reading of the CCSS documents shows a bias in favor of the qualitative and quantitative measures. For instance, in some of the in-depth discussion about text selection, the common core recommends that professionals use several quantitative measures and that a qualitative analysis of the text can easily override these measures. This clearly puts the emphasis on qualitative measures, a good recommendation since quantitative measures tell us very little, but here the core fails to state what role reader and text considerations play. Do these override both the qualitative and quantitative measures? Or should they be considered equal to the other measures? Without more clarity on how the three factors are to work together, we worry that teachers will impute more importance to quantitative and qualitative measures, thus ignoring their student readers or slighting them in some way.

We can also see the discounting of the reader in other ways. For example, in the discussion of text complexity, nearly four full pages of appendix A are dedicated to how to determine the complexity of a text from a quantitative and qualitative perspective, but only about one paragraph and half a page of commentary are dedicated to explaining how to consider readers and tasks. Furthermore, these brief explications provide a narrow focus on reader characteristics, noting, for example, the nonlinear development of reading ability and the need for classroom support for texts that are beyond grade or ability level. While important, these statements fail to fully capture the complexity of the concept of text and reader characteristics. We see very little mention of the important aspects of how texts should be matched to readers' interests, of the value of building on readers' previous experiences, or of the role that motivation plays in readers' development.

Not only does the common core gloss over reader and text characteristics in the explanation, it also does so when providing examples of how to apply the standards to texts. In the model-in-action exemplar samples, four paragraphs discuss the application of qualitative measures, one paragraph the quantitative measures, and a single sentence covers the reader and task considerations (by essentially delegating the job to a local professional). This approach offers little guidance as to how to consider this measure; glossing over these elements suggests to us that the authors of the common core may not be as serious about considerations of readers and the task as they claim to be. Granted, the standards authors do place their confidence in teachers who best know their students and the tasks best suited to their classrooms; however, without providing more in-depth exploration of how teachers are to make these decisions, it seems possible that teachers may rely more on quantitative and qualitative measures at the expense of students' needs. We, of course, hope that our exploration of these issues in this book can equip teachers with what they'll need to make sound decisions about texts based on all three considerations.

Conclusion

There is no doubt that the CCSS has its problems, and as we implement it we will have to face many challenges as it is interpreted by states, districts, and individuals. We have seen in many schools the applications of good ideas gone very wrong, a phenomenon that we are in danger of repeating as we apply the CCSS. Because the CCSS is not always clear and gives most of the power to individuals to make interpretations, we must ensure that we create environments that foster open and honest dialogues about the CCSS and its application. The CCSS does not call for extreme measures, nor should we let it reaffirm old habits that are outdated and fail to work. We need to embrace the opportunity the CCSS offers us to be engaged and critical about our practice so we can avoid any potential misinterpretations of the core that will lead us down the wrong path.

We are optimistic that the common core gives us an opportunity to incorporate new and interesting ideas into our practice. For us this means we now have the opportunity to heed the urgings of practitioners and researchers to incorporate young adult literature into the classroom. If we recognize the biases and problems the CCSS contains and do not let them influence our implementations inappropriately, we have the opportunity to build new traditions that can not only fulfill the requirements of the CSS but will also engage students in their own genre of literature. By so doing, we can develop students who will be prepared to be passionate, critical, and engaged readers throughout their lives.

The basic vision we have offered of the CCSS and its three-tiered model of text complexity prepares you to start applying the model on your own. We now turn to a full description of that model. In our next three chapters we will look at each of the three dimensions of the model in turn. Then in chapter six we will use this discussion to show how the model is actually applied to real books.

Bibliography

Allington, R. L. (2012). *What really matters for struggling readers: Designing research-based programs.* (3rd ed.). Boston, MA: Pearson.

Bauerlein, M. (2010). The new bibliophobes. *Educational Horizons, 88*(2), 84–91.

Beach, R. (2011, December). *Analyzing how formalist, cognitive-processing, and literacy practices learning paradigms are shaping the implementation of the Common Core State Standards.* Paper Presented at the Annual Meeting of the Literacy Research Association. Retrieved April 2, 2012, from EBSCOHost ERIC database. (ED527334)

Brozo, W. G., Shiel, G., & Topping, K. (2007). Engagement in reading: Lessons learned from three PISA countries. *Journal of Adolescent & Adult Literacy, 51*(4), 304–315.

Casner-Lotto, J., & Barrington, Linda. (2006). *Are they really ready to work? Employers' perspectives on the basic knowledge and applied skills of new entrants to the 21st century U.S. workforce.* Washington, D.C: Partnership for 21st Century Skills. Retrieved Feb. 29, 2012, from EBSCOHost ERIC database. (ERIC Document Reproduction Service No. ED 519465).

Cipielewski, J., & Stanovich, K. E. (1992). Predicting growth in reading ability from children's exposure to print. *Journal of Experimental Child Psychology, 54*(1), 74–89.

Fang, Z., & Wei, Y. (2010). Improving middle school students' science literacy through reading infusion. *Journal of Educational Research, 103*(4), 262–273.

Gallagher, K. (2009). *Readicide: How schools are killing reading and what you can do about it.* Portland, ME: Stenhouse Publishers.

Gallo, D. R. (1968). Free reading and book reports: An informal survey of grade eleven. *Journal of Reading, 11*(7), 532–538.

Gallo, D. R. (2001). How classics create an aliterate society. *English Journal, 90*(3), 33–39.

Herz, S. K. (2005). *From Hinton to Hamlet: Building bridges between young adult literature and the classics.* Westport, CT: Greenwood Press.

Hiebert, E. H., & Sailors, M. (Eds.). (2009). *Finding the right texts: What works for beginning and struggling readers.* New York, NY: Guilford Press.

Kane, S., & Rule, A. C. (2004). Poetry connections can enhance content area learning. *Journal of Adolescent & Adult Literacy, 47*(8), 658–669.

Kendall, J. S. (2011). *Understanding Common Core State Standards.* Alexandria, VA: ASCD.

Krashen, S. D. (1993). *The power of reading: Insights from the research.* Englewood CO: Libraries Unlimited.

Lenhart, A., Purcell, K., Smith, A., & Zickuhr, K. (2010). Pew Internet & American life project: Social media & mobile internet use among teens and young adults, from http://pewinternet.org/Reports/2010/Social-Media-and-Young-Adults.aspx.

Lesesne, T. (2010). *Reading ladders: Leading students from where they are to where we'd like them to be.* Portsmouth, NH: Heinemann.

Marlowe, B. A., & Page, M. L. (2005). *Creating and sustaining the constructivist classroom.* Thousand Oaks, CA: Sage Publications.

McEwan, E. K. (2007). *40 ways to support struggling readers in content classrooms, grades 6–12.* Reston, VA: National Association of Secondary School Principals; Thousand Oaks, CA: Corwin Press.

National Endowment for the Arts. (2007). *To read or not to read: A question of national consequence.* (Research Report No. 47) Washington, D.C.: National Endowment for the Arts. (ERIC Document Reproduction Service No. ED 499045).Retrieved Feb. 29, 2012, from EBSCOHost ERIC database.

National Governors Association & Council of Chief State School Officers. (2011). *Common core state standards initiative,* 2011, from http://www.corestandards.org/.

Organisation for Economic Cooperation and Development. (2011). *Do students today read for pleasure? PISA in focus. no. 8.* Paris, France: OECD Publishing. (ERIC Document Reproduction Service No. ED 526809). Retrieved Feb. 29, 2012, from EBSCOHost ERIC database.

Pike, M. A. (2003). The canon in the classroom: Students' experiences of texts from other times. *Journal of Curriculum Studies, 35*(3), 355–370.

Ratcliffe, A. (2009). Reading for pleasure? What a concept! *Education Digest: Essential Readings Condensed for Quick Review, 74*(6), 23–24.

Ruiz, E. C., Thornton, J. S., & Cuero, K. K. (2010). Integrating literature in mathematics: A teaching technique for mathematics teachers. *School Science and Mathematics, 110*(5), 235–237.

Springen, K. (2012). Are teens embracing e-books?: The digital divide. *Publishers Weekly,* from: http://www.publishersweekly.com/pw/by-topic/childrens/childrens-industry-news/article/50707-are-teens-embracing-e-books-.html.

Stevens, R. J. (2006). Integrated reading and language arts instruction. *RMLE Online: Research in Middle Level Education, 30*(3), 1–12.

Smith, M. W., & Wilhelm, J. D. (2002). *Reading don't fix no Chevys: Literacy in the lives of young men.* Portsmouth, NH: Heinemann.

Tienken, C. H. (2011). Common core state standards: An example of data-less decision making. *AASA Journal of Scholarship & Practice, 7*(4), 3–18.

Tyson, L. (1999). *Critical theory today: A user-friendly guide.* New York: Garland Publishing.

Wagner, T. (2008). *The global achievement gap: Why even our best schools don't teach the new survival skills our children need—and what we can do about it.* New York, NY: Basic Books.

Wilkins, C., Hartman, J., Howland, N., & Sharma, N. (2010). *How prepared are students for college level reading? Applying a Lexile[R]-based approach. Issues & answers.* (Report No. REL 2010-no. 094) Washington, D.C.: Regional Educational Laboratory Southwest. (ERIC Document Reproduction Service No. ED 513585). Retrieved Feb. 29, 2012, from EBSCOHost ERIC database.

Williamson, G. L. (2008). A text readability continuum for postsecondary readiness. *Journal of Advanced Academics, 19*(4), 602–632.

Chapter 3

Quantitative Dimensions of Text Complexity

Take a look at the following list of six books and their brief annotations. As you consider this list, try to determine how you would rank these books if you were determining their complexity. Which would you rate as the least complex? Which as the most?

1. *The Little House* by Virginia Lee Burton. A Caldecott Award–winning picture book with color illustrations on every page originally published in 1942; it illustrates the story of a small country house that is swallowed up by the big city.
2. *Fahrenheit 451* by Ray Bradbury. A dystopian adult novel published in 1953 that addresses themes of censorship, imagination, and power. It is set in a future America where firemen burn certain kinds of books.
3. *Paddington Helps Out* by Michael Bond. An early chapter book, originally published in 1960, with scattered line-drawn illustrations about a lovable bear who came from darkest Peru to live in London.
4. *The Flunking of Joshua T. Bates* by Susan Shreve, illustrated by Diane DeGroat. A children's book with selected full-page illustrations published in 1984 in which Joshua learns that he must repeat third grade.
5. *Before We Were Free* by Julia Alvarez. A young adult novel published in 2002 that tells the story of 12-year-old Anita de la Torre as she lives under a dictatorship in the Dominican Republic.
6. *An Abundance of Katherines* by John Green. A young adult novel published in 2006 that tells the story of child prodigy Colin and his friend on a road trip where they meet new friends and Colin is finally able to work out his romantic problems.

Given this limited information, how would you rate these books on complexity? Our own rankings from least to most complex would come out something like this:

1. *The Little House*
2. *Paddington Helps Out*
3. *The Flunking of Joshua T. Bates*
4. *Before We Were Free*
5. *An Abundance of Katherines*
6. *Fahrenheit 451*

These ranking are based on numerous criteria such as the audience of the book, the format of the book, the thematic presentation, and other variables. While others' rankings may vary slightly, few would disagree that these books constitute a definite range of complexity levels.

This ranking only remains true, however, until you rank them using a readability formula. Every one of these six books, when processed though the Lexile Framework for Reading, receives a score of 890. As far as the Lexile measures are concerned, all of these books are on the same reading level and represent the same level of complexity, a level that translates out to about a fourth or fifth grade. However, we know of very few educators who would find *An Abundance of Katherines* or *Fahrenheit 451* a good fit for an average fourth-grader.

This simple example brings to light some of the complex problems related to text measurement tools. While these formulas have their benefits, they also are rife with problems. In this chapter we will take a close look at readability formulas, their history, their types, and the strengths and weaknesses of these tools. Understanding readability formulas from this broad scope can help us to appropriately apply them as part of the CCSS three-tiered model for determining text complexity.

History

While the idea of using mathematical applications to determine a text's readability has been around for a long time, the intensive study of concrete formulas began in earnest in the 1920s. This study came as a reaction by teachers and researchers as they faced the need to assess the complexity of texts in conjunction with rising numbers of children attending school. Laws that outlawed child labor and compulsory schooling laws meant that thousands of children from diverse backgrounds were coming out of the labor force and into the classroom, and researchers were concerned about how they would be able to read the textbooks that were used in schools. Finding that many were too difficult for most of these readers, they set out to create methods to determine how complex a textbook was. The intent in creating these formulas was to find out how to make textbooks easier to read so that schools could offer more efficient learning for a more diverse population.

Importantly, during this time, sight approaches to learning to read were the dominant pedagogy, not phonics instruction. Since students were not being taught phonetically how to decode but to recognize words as a whole, texts had to be easier for students to read. This pedagogical approach also encouraged researchers to find ways to make reading reflect those most simple words that could be sight read with ease (Zakaluk & Samuels, 1988).

In these efforts to determine ease of reading, researchers looked at a variety of variables that they knew comprised text complexity; however, the majority of research at this time focused on two particular variables, semantic and syntactic difficulty. In their seminal work, Gray and Leary (1935), for example, came up with a list of 24 variables that contributed to a book's readability. Ultimately they focused on two of these, vocabulary and sentence length. The remaining 22 were qualitative in nature and were considered too challenging to reduce to numbers; like most readability theorists in the '20s and '30s, Gray and Leary abandoned other possible measures and focused on vocabulary and sentence length. Because of their ease of measurement, most researchers, like Gray and Leary, found that these variables alone could provide interesting information about a work's readability. This became a tradition, and all subsequent formulas ultimately included only semantic and syntactic difficulty in their calculations.

We see the fruits of these early theorists at work not only in the formulas we use today but also in the core's emphasis on easier texts. The CCSS writers show that while demands on readers have held steady or increased in recent years, the difficulty of textbooks has declined.

As we consider the CCSS, we understand that their logic is sound and the principles they espouse are solid, but at the same time we must realize the ideas of these early pioneers who were trying to create education open to a broader citizenry have trickled down to today. Professionals must understand more fully the complexity of these formulas and their history if we are to apply them appropriately in the CCSS model.

Types of Formulas

There are a variety of quantitative readability formulas. At a very basic level these formulas take a text, or oftentimes a selected part of the text, and then, using certain variables contained in a mathematical formula, a number is computed that purports to represent the relative reading difficulty level of the text. All base their calculations on two general variables: semantic difficulty (measured in various ways including word length, word familiarity, or word frequency) and syntactic difficulty (measured by sentence length or the average number of words per sentence).

Each formula represents different assumptions about the purpose of measuring readability. Some were developed by theorists trying to help people learn to read better; others were developed by companies to support a specific product. The frequent use of these two variables makes the formulas appear similar, but because of the different application of variables and mathematical operations, different formulas will produce different results. For example, some formulas result in a raw number, while others result in a number representing a grade-level equivalent.

Since each formula has its own unique perspective to offer, we have chosen to briefly outline eight different formulas. There certainly are other formulas, programs, and approaches out there. In fact, the CCSS documentation mentions one, the Coh-Metrix, that we have chosen not to include in our discussion. This measure attempts to go beyond the standard formulas to measure how the text conveys information. Like the writers of the CCSS, we find this measure to be very complex and recognize that it lacks widespread validation. While this measure has and may yet yield some interesting information, it lacks usefulness at the current time.

Of all the approaches, we find the ones we have outlined to be the most direct, cost effective, and most easily applied formulas available; however, we encourage readers to find the formulas that work best for them and their students. No matter the formula used, they all have similar constructions and biases, and we also encourage professionals to fully research any formula that they are called upon to use. Understanding how a formula measures texts, what biases may be inherent in the formula and its application, and how it matches a reader and a text are important steps to correctly applying quantitative measures to texts not only for the CCSS but for all instructional situations.

Flesch-Kincaid Formula

Developed in 1975 by J. Peter Kincaid and Rudolf Flesch as part of a contract with the United States Navy, this formula soon became the standard used by the Department of Defense to assess the reading difficulty of their technical manuals. Today this formula is one of the most widely used; in fact, it is the formula that word processing programs, including Microsoft Word, use to determine reading levels. The formulas use sentence length and the average number of syllables per word as the basis for their calculations and predict about a 91 percent comprehension rate. The Flesch-Kincaid Formula is easily calculated using word processing programs or other online tools. The only caveat is that the score must be calculated on a digital version of the text, so a sample either must exist digitally first or must be created. It is recommended that three samples of 100 consecutive words be used to calculate the score, so entering these by hand—if no digital version exists—is not likely to be too demanding (Burke & Greenberg, 2010; Trollinger & Kaestle, 1986).

SMOG

G. Harry McLaughlin developed the SMOG formula in 1969; it has been widely used successfully since that time to assess the complexity of health education materials in particular. This formula is unique in that it tries to predict 100 percent comprehension. This means that the resulting score usually represents one to two grade levels higher than other formulas. The formula is calculated using a sample of 30 sentences from the text, scorers counting the number of words with three or more syllables; using this number, they figure the square root and then add three. The resulting number will represent the grade level at which the text is readable. There are online calculators that will generate this number when sample text is entered (Burke & Greenberg, 2010; McLaughlin, 1969).

Coleman-Liau

Created by linguists Meri Coleman and T. L. Liau in 1975 to evaluate the readability of textbooks used in the United States, this formula uses a sample of 100–300 words and then computes a grade-level result by counting the number of letters per word and the number of sentences in the sample. Coleman and Liau focused on the variable of letters per word instead of number of syllables in the word like other formulas for two reasons: they believe that longer words are harder to read, and it is easier for a computer to count characters than syllables. This application of computer ease makes this formula straightforward to apply because scans and optical character recognition (OCR) programs that recognize character and sentence boundaries can be used. It is not required to create a digital copy of the text as is required by many of the other formulas. However, while there are online calculators that will generate this number, these will not use scans or OCR, so if these are used, a sample text must be entered by hand (Coleman & Liau, 1975).

Automated Readability Index

Like the Coleman-Liau formula, the Automated Readability Index uses as its variables the numbers of characters per word, but unlike the former, it then uses the number of words per sentence to calculate a grade-level indicator. Again, this makes this formula easier to calculate since computers can much more easily recognize characters than syllables. Using a sample of 100–300 words, this number can be easily calculated using online calculators (Thomas, et al., 1975).

Gunning Fog Index

In 1952, Robert Gunning found that many newspapers, magazines, and other business documents were being written at a very complex level. In order to help writers learn to express themselves clearly, Gunning developed the Fog Index. The Gunning Fog Index uses a sample of 100 words for its calculations of the average sentence length and the number of words with three or more syllables. This index is unique in that in identifying these words it excludes any words that are proper nouns, compound words, jargon, or words with -es, -ed, or -ing suffixes. This formula then generates a grade-level indicator. Online calculators can easily generate this number (Gunning, 1952).

Dale-Chall

Used widely in scientific research and considered to be the most reliable and validated of all the readability formulas, the Dale-Chall Formula was developed by Edgar Dale and Jeanne Chall. In addition to sentence length, the formula compares the text to a predetermined list of

3,000 words that are familiar to most fourth-graders. Dale developed this list in response to the creation of vocabulary-frequency lists popular in the 1940s that had been designed to help teachers and publishers introduce children to words they would encounter frequ-

Box 3.1 Free Online Readability Formula Calculators

Free Text Readability Consensus Calculator: Gives numbers from seven popular formulas including Flesch-Kincaid, SMOG, Gunning Fog, Coleman-Liau, and Automated Readability
      http://www.readabilityformulas.com/free-readability-formula-tests.php
OKAPI!: Calculates the Dale-Chall Formula
      http://www.lefthandlogic.com/htmdocs/tools/okapi/okapi.php
Readability Calculator: Flesch-Kincaid Grade Level, SMOG, Coleman-Liau, Automated Readability
      http://www.online-utility.org/english/readability_test_and_improve.jsp
Text Readability Scores: Flesch-Kincaid, SMOG, Coleman-Liau, Gunning Fog, and Automated Readability
      http://www.addedbytes.com/lab/readability-score/
Words Count: Readability: Flesch-Kincaid, SMOG, Gunning Fog
      http://www.wordscount.info/wc/jsp/clear/analyze_readability.jsp

ently. The logic behind this comparison is that readers will find it easier to comprehend words they are familiar with than those words they are not. The inclusion of these frequent words makes the Dale-Chall Formula unique, but it is also harder to apply since texts must be compared to this list. The formula provides three scores for comparison: a raw score, a grade-level range, and a number/percentage of "hard" words in the text. These numbers predict about a 93 percent comprehension rate. There are online calculators that will generate results when sample text is typed in (see box 3.1), so the application of this formula faces the challenge of converting a text to a digital format (School Renaissance Institute, 2000).

All of the previous formulas we have discussed were developed by theorists whose main motivation was to help people learn to read better. While these formulas are very useful, the most common ones used in schools and in the CCSS document were developed by companies to help support a product. Let's take a look at each of these formulas.

ATOS/Accelerated Reader

Developed by Judi and Terry Paul beginning in 1984, the Accelerated Reader Program was designed to match readers to texts, to help readers move from guided to independent reading, and to give teachers a tool to measure both readers and texts. Now distributed by Renaissance Learning, the Accelerated Reader Program is widely used in the United States. The foundation of this program is a series of computer-mediated assessment tests that can be purchased from the company. These multiple-choice tests are designed to help teachers monitor students' reading and then apply needed interventions to assist readers in their progress. To match students with the right books, individual titles and their associated quizzes are analyzed with the ATOS readability formula to assign them a grade level. One of the unique things about this formula is that instead of using small samples as all the others have, the text of the entire book is analyzed; this gives a more accurate picture of the difficulty of the entire text. In addition, scores are reviewed by a panel of experts for reasonableness and adjustments are made, especially when it is obvious that the formula is not accounting for certain elements of the text.

The ATOS formula uses three variables: words per sentence, average grade level of words, and characters per word. The formula is reported as a grade level that indicates grade year and month where this book would be readable; a score of 7.2 indicates the book to be appropriate for a seventh-grader in their second month of schooling. These scores provide a granularity of application that other formulas do not have, although many argue these grade/month indicators are misleading because it is impossible to say that every child within a certain month of schooling will be reading at a certain level. In addition to the grade-level score, the Accelerated Reader Program also gives an interest-level indication. This designation does not indicate the readability of the text but intends to give a general idea of a grade range where students will find the text interesting. The intent of this level is to give an indication of a book's content, which is not measured by the ATOS formula, and to account for books that have low readability scores but contain challenging content that does not match that score.

Renaissance Learning provides a free database that lists reading and interest level for many books at AR Book Finder (http://www.arbookfind.com/UserType.aspx). The biggest challenge with this resource is that only those books that have been processed through the program will have a score in this database. If a book is not listed in this database, there is no way to calculate this score independently, so professionals are very reliant on the titles that the company has decided to include as part of their offerings (School Renaissance Institute, 2000; What Works Clearinghouse, 2010).

Lexile

The Lexile Framework for Reading was developed in the mid-1980s by A. Jackson Stenner and Malbert Smith, the founders of MetaMetrics. The Lexile formula is calculated based on average word frequency and average number of words per sentence. The Lexile measure for both student and book is communicated by a number with an L at the end of it; higher numbers represent more difficult texts, and Lexile scores predict about a 75 percent comprehension rate. It is important to note that all the number gives is a raw score; scores can be converted to grade-level equivalents or ranges that show where texts might match grade levels or abilities. So a reader measured at an 860L reading level will be expected to comprehend about 75 percent of a book also rated as an 860L. In addition to the raw score, Lexile also provides additional information in Lexile Codes. These codes indicate material that is difficult to measure, such as graphic novels or non-prose texts; they also address items that rate outside of the expected range such as books that are nonconforming (e.g., a nonfiction book aimed at first-graders that gets a Lexile measure much higher than that audience suggests) or books that would need adult direction (e.g., picture books that are meant to be read aloud).

MetaMetrics' goal is to develop scientifically based assessments for learning, so many of their resources are available for free; this includes a free database of books with their assigned Lexile scores. Like the ATOS database, the biggest challenge with this resource is that only those books that have been processed though the program will have a score. However, if a book is not listed in this database, the company offers a free Lexile analyzer to registered users that will analyze 1,000 words and return a score. As with other calculators, the sample text will have to be digital to use this tool. Educators can also request to have longer samples analyzed or recommend books for inclusion. Among other things, the availability of the free tools to apply the Lexile Framework for Reading makes this formula not only the one cited most frequently by the CCSS, but also the most accessible and easy to use for most educators (Smith, 2000; Stenner, 1999).

Strengths of Readability Formulas

The quick, objective score from readability formulas such as the ones outlined above provides us with a basic foundation when determining how readable and/or complex a text is. While they do not give us comprehensive information, they certainly can help us match readers and texts, promote independent choices, and help us evaluate students' progression.

Studies have shown that in order to have successful reading experiences, children should read books that are not too challenging but not too easy. Books that frustrate readers do not lead to successful experiences, so matching a reader's level and the book's complexity is an important issue (Allington, 2012). The use of quantitative formulas is a good starting point to help us make that match. Through testing we can determine a range of reading ability for almost any child; using that range, we can match their ability to a text using the formulas that measure the text's complexity. Matching book readability to students' reading level ensures that the books they read are challenging enough to provide useful practice but not so hard as to be frustrating.

These formulas can also promote student independence by encouraging self-selection of books. If students know their reading level, online tools or other information can guide them to books on that same level. While we would hope that children would be able to self-monitor their reading selections, as adult readers do, sometimes these behaviors have not been taught or learned, so simple readability measures can help guide them to new and interesting books.

In addition, these formulas can also help us to see that students are reading increasingly complex works. In order to know if students are moving from less complex to more complex texts, we need to know where the books they read fall along that continuum. A simple numerical representation of a text's readability provides us with a solid foundation to determine how complex a text is. And these scores can then help us to clearly see if the students are progressing in their reading skills.

Potential Problems with Readability Formulas

While quantitative measures of a text's readability do provide us with a basic foundation, there are many potential weaknesses with these formulas. Let us take a closer look at some of the issues that may arise with the use of readability formulas.

The things they measure don't necessarily make something harder or easier to read, because language is contextual   In order to quantitatively measure a text's readability, it is essential to reduce that text to readily measurable qualities. However, this is inherently problematic since no semantic or syntactic measure can capture the complexity of language. Words only have meaning in context, and words that are not easy to understand in isolation often may be easier to understand in context. When you condense a text to its semantic and syntactic variables, you strip out all context. While this kind of study of language in isolation can give us a useful tool to predict suitability, it will never be able to fully capture the complexity of a text. Quantitative formulas will never measure the difficulty of concepts or the grammatical coherency of text, two important factors that contribute to complexity. This problem is clearly shown in a simple example: If we take a simple sentence that reads a very low level and scramble the order of words, the resulting sentence would still score the same but, to a reader, would be incomprehensible (Trollinger & Kaestle, 1986; Zakaluk & Samuels, 1988). For example, using one of our sentences above: "When you condense a text to its semantic and syntactic variables, you strip out all context," when muddled "Condense context you semantic when a you variables text strip syntactic to its and you out all" would get the same score by a quantitative formulas, but it is easy to see how incomprehensible it is without the coherence provided by proper syntax.

Stripping down a text to its semantic and syntactic variables does not give us a complete picture as to how complex a text will be for an individual child. This is true because as Zakaluk and Samuels (1988) note, readability is the interaction between text characteristics and reader resources. Since readability formulas don't analyze the context of the book, this can make for a large mismatch between book and reader, such as a book with adult-level content being graded for a second- or third-grade reader. Without the context, we will never be able to have a full picture of a text, nor will we be able to accurately match a text with a reader and task.

Looking at only a portion of text can give us an inaccurate picture   To facilitate ease of use, many of these formulas rely on a sample of the text to determine readability. As statisticians will tell you, this can lead to many problems with sampling error. When you rely on only a portion of the text, you run the risk of not getting the whole picture of the work. For example, if the 300 words for a sample are chosen from a very simple portion of the text—a selection of dialogue, for instance—then the text may rate very low, but an analysis of the entire text would rate the text much higher. In a 2009 study, Hiebert found that when analyzing only selections of a book, Lexile scores within one title could vary as much as 10 grade levels, with one section scoring at a third-grade level while another section scored at a college level. This sampling error is less of a problem with formulas that do full text scans of the book; however, if companies that do this have chosen not to rate a text that a teacher wishes to use, their only recourse will be to turn to sampling formulas, which are prone to this type of error.

Different measures give different results   Even when they apply the same or similar variables, no two readability measures will come up with the same score for two texts. This is due to a variety of factors such as text sampling and the structure of the formula itself. For example, the book *Sword Song* by Rosemary Sutcliff, a piece of historical fiction about a young Viking swordsman, scores on the Lexile scale at 1240L. Under the CCSS guidelines, this book would be considered for grades 9 to 12. However, on the ATOS scale, the book comes out at 6.8, which puts it toward the last part of the sixth grade. At best, this represents a discrepancy of two grade levels, at worst, six grade levels. Given this wide disparity, it could be difficult to use just these measures to find the best grade level for this text. In addition, these formulas do not correlate perfectly: Some generate grade levels, others a numerical score. While we can make conversion charts, these different formulations will never describe the exact same idea of a level. We suggest that the way to avoid the pitfalls and bias that are inherent in how each formula measures and gives results is to consult a variety of formulas. Just as scatter plots show us better correlation when we have a greater number of data points to see where correlates lie, so does having a number of formulas give us a better picture.

Some scores are easier to come by and to calculate   Each of these formulas has varying availability, and some are easier to calculate than others; those that are proprietary are perhaps the least accessible. In addition, some require digital text, which teachers may not have access to nor time to create. In a busy school day, finding time to analyze texts using multiple formulas may be difficult, and professionals may turn instead to the most accessible and easily calculated formulas. As it is best to not base decisions on one formula alone, this can make decisions more complicated for teachers. Nevertheless, if time or other factors force us to rely on a single measure, we must be aware of what we are giving up and the biases that may be inherent in only using one measure to judge a text.

Producers have a vested interest in their formulas Whether for financial or intellectual motives, formula creators have a vested interest in their creation. While those who only have an intellectual interest may have less invested than those who are creating products for profit, there are always going to be some biases. Like any salesman, those who promote these formulas may try to present their ideas and products in the best possible light, playing down the negatives in order to make a good impression. This, of course, means consumers may not get the whole picture. While we do not contend that any of these formulas or companies try to pull the wool over teachers' eyes or sell inferior products, we must admit that because of their vested interest there will be bias present. As professionals, we need to look critically at these biases, deciding after looking at all the options what works best for us and our students.

Texts vary When you boil a text down to its semantic and syntactic variables, all texts begin to look the same as they are all made up of these basic elements. But clearly not every text is the same: A novel is going to have a much different purpose than an informational text, and a novel written in the 1880s is going to require a different approach than one written in 2010. Hiebert (2009) shows how this works by comparing a novel that receives a Lexile score of 1100 and a science textbook that earns a score of 1130. As far as Lexile is concerned, these two books are on the same reading level, suggesting that they do not vary significantly. But a closer look shows us that an average biology textbook includes more new words than one would be exposed to in one semester of learning a foreign language. Obviously, the vocabulary demand of the biology book is higher than the novel, but the Lexile score fails to take this into account. Not taking into account this variance of text creates one of the greatest challenges with using readability measures.

Readers vary Not only do texts vary, but readers do as well. Most teachers know this from firsthand experience. Readers' interests, characteristics, motivation, and a host of other factors come into play here. Many of you may have encountered a student like one of ours who tested at a second-grade reading level but found a complex bike repair manual—one that was completely incomprehensible to us despite our graduate degrees—to be a fairly simple read. These formulas only measure characteristics to predict the grade at which an average reader could comprehend the text; but the reality is that not all of our readers are going to fully match these expectations.

Many texts require previous experience or intervention to understand, and readers without that knowledge or support may struggle. Trying to pin down a reader's ability to a grade level is inaccurate at best because, again, we are only describing a hypothetical, average person. They also assume that there is a point when the text is too hard and a reader will not persist. However, this is far from true: Readers will persist with texts they are interested in, even if they find them challenging, a fact we will discuss in more depth later. The metrics used to measure both reader and text, while helpful, may not deliver a precise or comprehensive picture. They may not fully match readers on their ability scales, and rarely attempt to match readers to their own interests.

One important thing to remember is that no experimental studies have established standards that are optimal for learning, comprehension, interest, and efficient reading. These vary so widely for students that no one has been able to find a magic formula that allows us to predict the best zone for all readers. In addition, a reader may be at different levels depending upon the task they are asked to complete. If we read a text independently, we will require a different reading level than if we have instructional assistance to navigate the text. Many educators and researchers, the authors among them, believe that these types of formulas are best used for fourth grade and below. This makes them relatively inaccurate when it comes to judging reading materials for teenagers and adults. Once a student becomes fairly adept at the skills of decoding texts, which most often happens around third grade, other skills and elements take precedence. Formulas, however, are concerned with decoding skills alone; since they don't measure the more complex areas, they soon become irrelevant for skilled readers. Also, readers and texts don't naturally progress upward in a linear fashion. You would suspect that as readers move up a trajectory, there would be harder and harder texts until you could find the most difficult. However, when we get to the college level, there is no more progression, the levels top out, and formulas really give no further meaning to interpreting the text. This makes the highest levels inaccurate at best since, once again, it is the text construction, vocabulary meaning, and other elements that make the text more difficult (Zakaluk & Samuels, 1988).

Requiring students to read on a certain quantitative level biases them against a wide selection of quality literature   A major concern we have with the implementation of the CCSS is that as we try to move students toward more complex texts, some may feel they need to force students into a particular reading "box" that does not allow for natural selection of books that are either above or below a certain level. Consider these two questions: Do you read works above your reading level that you consider too hard for you? Do you read books that you would consider below your reading level or that are too easy for you? We're sure the answer to both of these questions is probably yes. For most readers this is true; we often read both above and below our reading level. If we prevent children from exercising the same freedom, we run the risk of not only giving them a limited viewpoint of what books are, but also preventing them from finding books they enjoy.

While the CCSS espouses increasingly complex texts, it does not espouse that every text has to be at a certain level of complexity. This suggest to us that texts of both high and low complexity should be included as part of our students' reading while the overall movement should be upward. We cannot let an interpretation of the CCSS limit us to certain types of texts, first and foremost because not all of the readers in our classes will be at the same level. It is disheartening to see an eighth-grader who tests at a second-grade reading level disinclined to read because all the books at his level are considered "baby books" and he feels self-conscious when reading in front of his peers who are reading higher-level novels. When it comes to books, there should be no judgment; works should not be judged by a readability formula in a way that would bias students toward or against them. Older readers should feel equally able to read a complex picture book or a classical work. Reading above as well as below one's level is a natural thing to do, and a strict application of readability levels does not allow readers to explore the great breadth and depth of quality literature.

English has changed and will continue to change   Researchers have shown that English language usage has simplified over time. In the modern world, the way we express ideas is less complex than it was 100 years ago. This leads us to ask is if it really valid to compare something written in the 1800s to something written today. It is not that language in the 1800s was better, it was just different; admittedly it was often more complex, but this is not always a good thing. Much of the language used in older texts includes flowery excesses that most English teachers would consider too wordy if it appeared in their students' writing. In addition, older texts use different conventions of grammar and sentence structure than those we use today, even using complex forms of words that have gone out of current usage. The reality is that we just don't have a level playing field for comparison. For example, the works of Jane Austen range in Lexile score from 1110L to 1180L, but one of the popular adult authors of today, Jodi Picoult, writes works that range from 760L to 900L. Both authors explore complex themes and address settings and characters relevant to their own lives, but because of their era they write at different Lexile levels, indicative of their time and contemporary linguistic style. While many may consider this simplification of language to be a bad thing, the reality is that it exists and we need to be careful when considering the complexity of texts and take into account what age they were written in to help us have a more level ground on which to judge (Danielson & Lasorsa, 1989).

Possibilities for the Future

In its implementation, the CCSS shows us that readability formulas, while a good tool, do have their problems. The writers of the common core even note that the quantitative formulas need to be updated and call upon researchers to develop more accurate formulas. We question whether it will ever be possible to fully quantify something as complex as texts. When the task itself is so complex, especially when you take into account readers' knowledge and other variables that can vary so much between two people, we believe that it may never be possible to reduce a text to a numerical score.

However, we do believe that these formulas can be made better. Some researchers have tried to develop new formulas, such as those that use syntax as part of the measure. There are others who have worked out how density (the number of concepts a text represents) affects a text's complexity. Others have been looking at the presence of cues and other textual signals that allow readers to find their places in a text. Yet others are exploring how we could measure coherence of story flow. Even formulas that take into account the age of a text and changes of language over time would be a fine addition to our current formulas (Danielson & Lasorsa, 1989; Trollinger & Kaestle, 1986). Sadly, many of these formulas have proved and will continue to prove expensive and difficult to implement, so it is questionable whether they will become readily useful for practical application. In the future, we may see many new options that will add to our arsenal; however, even with these innovations, without measures that look at the whole text as well as the reader and his or her knowledge, even these innovative formulas will never give us a full picture of a book's readability.

Bibliography

Allington, R. L. (2012). *What really matters for struggling readers: Designing research-based programs.* (3rd ed.). Boston, MA: Pearson.

Burke, V., & Greenberg, D. (2010). Determining readability: How to select and apply easy-to-use readability formulas to assess the difficulty of adult literacy materials. *Adult Basic Education and Literacy Journal, 4*(1), 34–42.

Coleman, M., & Liau, T. L. (1975). A computer readability formula designed for machine scoring. *Journal of Applied Psychology, 60*(2), 283–284.

Dale, E., & Chall, J. S. (1948). *A formula for predicting readability.* Columbus, OH: Bureau of Educational Research, Ohio State University.

Danielson, W. A., & Lasorsa, D. L. (1989). A new readability formula based on the stylistic age of novels. *Journal of Reading, 33*(3), 194–197.

Gray, W. S., & Leary, B. E. (1935). *What makes a book readable: With special reference to adults of limited reading ability, an initial study.* Chicago, IL: University of Chicago Press.

Gunning, R. (1952). *The technique of clear writing.* New York, NY: McGraw-Hill.

Hiebert, E. H. (2009). *Interpreting Lexiles in online contexts and with informational texts.* Retrieved Feb. 29, 2012 from: http://www.apexlearning.com/documents/Research_InterpretingLexiles_2009-02%281%29.pdf.

McLaughlin, G. H. (1969). SMOG grading: A new readability formula. *Journal of Reading, 12*(8), 639–646.

School Renaissance Institute. (2000). *The ATOS[TM] Readability Formula for books and how it compares to other formulas. Report.* Madison, WI: Wisconsin School Renaissance Institute. (ERIC Document Reproduction Service No. ED449468). Retrieved May 6, 2011, from EBSCOHost ERIC database.

Smith, R. R. (2000). How the Lexile framework operates. *Popular Measurement, 3*(1), 18–19.

Stenner, A. J. (1999). *Instructional uses of the Lexile Framework.* (ERIC Document Reproduction Service No. ED435976). Retrieved May 6, 2011, from EBSCOHost ERIC database.

Thomas, G., et al. (1975). Test-retest and inter-analyst reliability of the automated readability index, Flesch reading ease score, and the fog count. *Journal of Reading Behavior, 7*(2), 149–154.

Trollinger, W. V., & Kaestle, C. F. (1986). *Difficulty of text as a factor in the history of reading. Program report 86-13.* Madison, WI: Wisconsin Center for Education Research. (ERIC Document Reproduction Service No. ED312652). Retrieved May 6, 2011, from EBSCOHost ERIC database.

What Works Clearinghouse. (2010). *Accelerated Reader [TM]: What Works Clearinghouse intervention report.* Washington, D.C.: Institute of Education Sciences. (ERIC Document Reproduction Service No. ED511267). Retrieved May 6, 2011, from EBSCOHost ERIC database.

Zakaluk B. L., & Samuels S. J. (Eds.). (1988). *Readability: Its past, present, and future.* Newark, DE: International Reading Association.

Chapter 4

Qualitative Dimensions of Text Complexity

Quantitative measures provide us with the first guide to determine the relative complexity of a text, but these numbers do not give us a full or oftentimes accurate picture of the text. To gain a complete picture we must apply other measures, some of which are qualitative. In this chapter we will focus on these measures and how they create complexity within a text.

When focusing on qualitative factors, there are three main issues we must confront. First, these elements cannot be easily reduced to a number, so it is difficult to numerically quantify them. Second, since quantifying these elements is challenging, judgments about them are often open to charges of subjectivity since two readers may not judge the relative quality or complexity of these elements in the same way. Lastly, these factors require skill and time to apply. Despite these challenges, the expertise that teachers have built though experience and training suggests that these issues are problems that can be overcome.

To make the process of qualitatively analyzing a work easier, in this chapter we will look at a variety of factors individually. However, this does not mean these factors should be considered separately when evaluating a whole work; all of these elements will play off one another. One element may appear to make a book less complex, but when we consider it in conjunction with other elements, we may see that the book actually becomes more complex than a single element might suggest. Consideration of the interplay of all the elements and features of a work is essential when analyzing each of its elements.

We propose six categories that should go into a qualitative assessment: format, audience, level of meaning, structure, language conventions, and knowledge demands. These categories both reflect and add to the elements outlined in the CCSS. As we look at each element we will first present essential questions to consider. These questions will provide the foundation for your own analysis as you apply these principles.

Format

The style, makeup, and format of a book all play into its readability, as found in the extensive study by Gray and Leary (1935). How a book is presented can make it easier or harder to read, thus making it more or less complex. There are six elements of format to consider: size, font, layout, construction, organization, and illustrations.

Size of the Book

What is the physical size of the book? How many pages does it have?

Statistics from the National Reading Practice database indicate that longer books are generally more difficult to read, and thus more complex, than shorter books (School Renaissance Institute, 2000). When we consider size, we must take into account not only the physical size and shape of a book but also the number of pages it contains. On one end of the spectrum, we have children's books, which are usually quite large with very few pages, and on the other end, we have more complex adult novels, smaller in dimension with many more pages. It's important to note that today standards are not always applied uniformly. Graphic novels are quite complex when you consider visual literacy needs and thematic representation, and they are often closer to picture books in physical size. Also, some young adult books are very long, such as *Harry Potter and the Deathly Hallows* by J. K. Rowling at 759 pages and *Inheritance* by Christopher Paolini at 860 pages; in spite of their length, many would consider them to be less complex thematically or conceptually.

Font

What kinds of fonts are used in the text? Is the font represented in a nonstandard way (indented or margined differently, presented in different colors, etc.)? Is the font consistent throughout the book or does it vary? If it varies, why does the font change and how is the author using that change?

When considering the complexity of a work, looking at the types and fonts used is important since certain fonts are easier to read than others. While most books will use one font style throughout, some authors change fonts or style for effect or to make certain things stand out in a text.

If the font used in a book is consistent throughout, a judgment on how its size and readability affects the text is all that is necessary to judge complexity in this area. However, if nonstandard fonts are used or fonts vary, we must consider how these effects impact the work's complexity. In general, a work that uses nonstandard fonts will be more difficult to read, especially when these fonts are extremely elegant or represent some other nonstandard focus. A recent trend, for instance, has been to use fonts printed in color, as in Maggie Stiefvater's *Wolves of Mercy Falls* series. These can make a text more complex since colored fonts can be harder to read than black text on a white background. Authors can also use changes in font to indicate structural changes. Sometimes these changes represent forays into memory or the thoughts and actions of a different character. For example, in Marie Lu's *Legend*, two different fonts and colors represent two characters' different points of view. The convention of switching a character's point of view makes this work more complex, and the number of fonts used is the indicator of that complexity.

Layout

How is the text laid out? How long are the lines? How wide are the page margins? How dense is the text block? Is the layout expected or is it unconventional?

How a text is laid out can also affect how readable it is. Books with more white space around the text block are often less complex to read since the layout affects how densely the text is packed onto a page and more text on one page will make the work more complex.

In addition to white space and density, sometimes how the text is laid out will be more unconventional than with a text block divided into sections. When text is portioned in different areas of the page or is divided by illustrations or other elements that intervene, it can be more complex. For example, in Jeff Kinney's popular *Diary of a Wimpy Kid* series, the text blocks are broken up by line drawings. This division is often in the middle of a paragraph, making the layout unconventional; the reader has to read both text and picture to gain meaning. Authors of children's and young adult literature seem to be very willing to play around with varied layouts, so this element is significant when analyzing the complexity of these works.

Formatting that does not maintain standard margins can also add complexity. Sometimes different margins are used to set off a section, such as layout that is used to represent a poem or song lyric. For example, in most novels in verse, such as in Karen Hesse's *Out of the Dust* or Virginia Euwer Wolff's *Make Lemonade*, the layout is that of a poetic work, so the margins vary greatly. The unconventional indentations of these margins indicate that this work is representing a more complex form and makes different demands of a reader.

Construction

What is the quality of the construction of the work? Is the paper of good quality? How is the work bound?

How much work is put into the construction of a book can be an important indicator of its intended or perceived complexity. Publishers make judgments daily about the purpose and audience of a book, and these decisions then impact its construction. Very few publishers are going to use top-quality paper and leather binding for a work of subliterature intended for a less sophisticated audience: While you can find leather-bound copies of the works of Shakespeare, we are unlikely to see the *Gossip Girl* series sold this way. The overall implication is that more sophisticated construction on the outside can be indicative of a more complex text.

Organization

What organizational structures does the author use to divide or arrange the work? Are these atypical? Does the organizational structure seem logical or consistent with the rest of the text?

While elements of organization are most often considered when looking at the complexity of informational texts, they are important to literary texts as well. Fundamentally, literary texts are organized into sentences, paragraphs, and chapters. Looking at the length and size of each of these elements can help us determine complexity. In general, longer sentences or chapters indicate greater complexity, while shorter elements indicate less complexity. However, this rule should not be applied without considering other elements of the text. Novels in verse, for instance, often have shortened organizational structures, but, given their poetic nature, they are typically more complex than the short sentences might lead us to believe.

Many authors use larger divisions to separate the work into sections that are greater than chapters. In *Blood Red Road* by Moira Young, chapters are grouped into larger sections with a bolded heading centered on an empty page that groups the chapters into sections indicating the changes in the characters' location over time. Other elements, such as headings at the beginning of chapters, can contextualize the upcoming narrative or give the reader time and location indicators. In *Strings Attached* by Judy Blundell, for example, the beginning of each chapter gives a statement of the time and location of the events to come, the only indicator of the many changes in setting in this work. Readers must attend carefully to these indicators in order to make sense of the book, and this can make a text like this more complex.

Authors of young adult literature today use unique organizational forms that can increase the complexity of the text. With books written like a movie script or in the form of a series of e-mail exchanges, for example, unique demands are made on a reader to make sense of the text. Since authors use these structures to give information and to contextualize the work, these often subtle indicators require more of the reader's attention. Thus, anything that is outside of one's normal experience with fictional text structures will make the text more demanding and more complex for the reader.

Illustrations

What role do the illustrations play? Are they merely illustrative or are they integral to the story? What visual literacy skills are necessary for the reader to interpret both the text and the pictures?

The presence of illustrations in a work can indicate either simplicity or complexity. For instance, let us first consider the picture book format. This format is usually targeted at a younger reading audience, and the pictures support the words and help the reader to interpret them. We might judge a book like this as less complex given the supportive relationship between words and images. On the other hand, innovative works such as *The Invention of Hugo Cabret* by Brian Selznick and *Countdown* by Deborah Wiles show how illustrations can make a text more complex. Both books tell part of their stories in full-page illustrations, eschewing text in favor of visuals. These two works rely heavily on the visual elements to bring the reader into a full understanding of the story, as the images tell part of the story not conveyed fully in the words of the text. This use of illustrations increases the complexity of these texts, given that these images must be decoded in addition to the words in the text.

These types of books not only require a level of textual literacy but also a high degree of visual literacy, making them possibly more complex than books with only text. Consider, too, the widely popular format of graphic novels. With very few words, these books would often rate a very low reading level quantitatively; however, their reliance on images make them quite complex. A good example of this is *Maus* by Art Spiegelman. In this graphic novel, the complex visuals are integral to the understanding of the complex themes of guilt, survival, race, and luck that this work conveys. We could argue that *Maus* is just as complex as a text-only book such as *The Hiding Place* by Corrie Ten Boom because the graphic novel requires high levels of both textual and visual literacy. In any text that features illustrations, we must determine if their function is merely illustrative or if they are integral to the story and thus add a layer of complexity to the work.

Audience

For whom was the text written? What perspective/bias does this audience type entail? Whom does the text best fit, and is this different from the intended audience? Why is there a difference?

When qualitatively analyzing a text, we should consider the audience of the text. We don't mean the reader as an individual (which we will do when we consider the reader dimensions of text complexity) but rather the generalized audience to whom the work is aimed. Stories naturally lend themselves to a certain type of audience that authors and publishers consider as they produce works. This, as we noted earlier, is one of the defining characteristics of young adult literature, in that we often consider books to be young adult because they are marketed to that audience. Considering the intended audience gives us an overall impression of complexity, since books targeted at older readers will likely feature more sophisticated syntax and use of figurative language and literary devices, automatically making them more complex than books aimed at a younger audience.

We can determine for whom the text is written in several ways. First, we can use the age of the main character as a determining factor. Most books will match an intended audience's age plus or minus two years: If a main character's age is 16, we can assume the intended audience is from 14 to 18. Second, publishers will often give books their own designation, including age groups or grade levels. Looking in publisher's catalogs, in professional review sources, or on their websites can give a general indication of the audience the publisher is targeting. (Listings on Amazon.com or other bookseller sites will often provide this information as well.)

Sometimes we see that there are certain perspectives or biases that come with an audience type. Works of children's literature are often looked down upon as less complex because of the young audience at which they are aimed. While we might prefer that these biases not affect the production and distribution of works, the fact is that they do. So as we consider audience, we must be aware of any bias from the author or the publisher's marketing, as this may affect our assessment of the book. In addition, there are often books that are marketed at a certain age level, but close analysis suggests a different audience. A fine example of this is the book *Fanny's Dream* by Caralyn and Mark Buehner. A picture book marketed to young children, this book's theme is much more suited to adults as the main character of the story is dealing with marriage and family issues that few children would understand. While this book's marketing might target it to a less sophisticated audience, its themes and presentation make it much more complex.

Levels of Meaning

Is there a central question that the author is trying to answer or give perspective on? How many inter-pretations does that central question allow for? How dense are the concepts in the text?

Narrative has been used since the beginning of time to convey meaning. Consider ancient peoples sitting by their fires, telling stories that explained their world and showed people how to behave. Myths, legends, and folklore gave the people the context they needed to build their cultures and to find meaning in life. Today we may tell stories for different reasons, but narrative, by its very structure, still holds multiple layers of meaning and potential interpretation. The more layers of meaning possible in a text, the more complex we would consider it to be.

In judging a text's complexity, then, we must determine the central theme or question the author is trying to address. If this central issue is clear and unambiguous, perhaps even didactic or preachy, then this text could be considered less complex. If, however, the central question is more ambiguous and open to multiple interpretations, then we have a more complex text. To see how levels of meaning impact a book's complexity, compare *Double Love* (the first book in the Sweet Valley High series) by Francine Pascal and Kate William to *Stargirl* by Jerry Spinelli. The central theme of both is friendship and fitting in; however, their complexity is vastly different. In *Double Love* the central question is whether the sisters will come to terms over the boy they both like. This issue is unambiguous and progresses to a single, predictable outcome. In contrast, *Stargirl* takes the central question of friendship and spins it many ways. The subquestions and ideas that Spinelli addresses progress as his main character, Leo, finds the eccentric Stargirl's uniqueness interesting. When the popular crowd adopts Stargirl, Leo watches from the sidelines, but when her popularity plummets, he is one of the few to stand by her. Trying to help, Leo works to help her become "normal" but soon finds that friendship is often about looking beyond perceptions and accepting people as they are. Without a doubt Spinelli's central questions that lead us and his characters to a deeper understanding of friendship are multilayered and open to many levels of interpretation, making it the more complex of the two works.

Most texts will also address other issues not always explicitly related to the central idea; the more issues explored in a book and the more densely packed the concepts, the more complex a text may be, depending on how extensively they are treated. If we consider a book like *Stargirl* with the essential question: Can love cross boundaries?, this can take us down any number of avenues including discussions of where boundaries are, how love is developed and kept, how differences define us as humans, and when the odds one faces are insurmountable. We suggest that a book like this that treats a number of themes in significant ways will be more demanding for readers.

When exploring these layers of meaning, we suggest considering three important elements of a text: theme, conflict, and connections.

Theme

How many themes are present, and how are they connected? Does the theme represent a universal issue or need? Is the theme blatant or didactic, or is it more subtle? How is the theme constructed and revealed to the reader? What subtleties does the author use to express theme? How does the theme tie the whole work together? How dependent are interpretations of theme on elements like plot, character, or setting?

We use the term "theme" to refer to a story's central meaning. Most works of complex literature will express many interconnecting themes at once; in fact, stories that have only one theme most often present a blatant moral message that is didactic and not very interesting to read. We have moved far away from the moralizing stories of the 1800s that explicitly state a lesson to be learned, to the stories of today where multiple ideas and viewpoints are expertly woven into the entire text in an authentic way.

The most adept authors take several interconnected themes and subtly construct them using the elements of plot, setting, and character to slowly reveal their ideas and issues to the reader. This type of integrated theme ties a work together in complex ways that allow readers to come to their own conclusions about what the author is trying to say. Integrated themes also most often represent universal truths since the ideas that transcend space and time are the most complex issues we face; works that address these timeless themes will most certainly be complex as well. For example, *The Hunger Games* by Suzanne Collins shows us how an author can use the elements of plot and character to subtly create a complex book with integrated themes. Using the plot element of a fight to the death coupled with a reluctant heroine, Collins addresses issues of societal violence, voyeurism, the sanctity of human life, one's ability to choose, political oppression, and the power of relationships—to name just a few. It is these interconnected themes that makes Collins's work so popular and also what makes it complex.

Looking closely at not only the complexity of the theme itself, but also the structures and elements the author uses to create that theme, can show us how complex a work is.

Conflict

What conflict is evident in the story? From what source does the conflict stem? How does the source of conflict affect the meaning or theme of the story? How does the conflict tie the whole work together? How dependent are interpretations of conflict on elements like plot, character, theme, or setting?

As forces, objects, or characters encounter one another in a narrative, inevitably there is conflict. In fact, conflict is what most often keeps a reader interested in a story, and the conflicts of a story can influence a text's complexity.

Conflict can come from a variety of sources; it can be man-against-nature, man-against-man (or against-self), or man-against-society. The source of the conflict can have an effect on how complex the story is. Conflicts of man-against-nature may be less complex because the main outcome of these conflicts is simply survival. In Gary Paulsen's *Hatchet*, for instance, Brian's conflicts lie with the elements of nature around him—his survival is dependent on his learning to find food and shelter and to protect himself from the elements. While this conflict takes on different forms (the moose in the lake, for instance, or the fierce storm that destroys his shelter), the conflict is rather narrow in its scope.

On the other hand, man-against-society conflicts can be much more complex since society represents a broad spectrum of possibilities that can affect the resolution of the conflict. In Ally Condie's *Matched*, Cassia's conflict with the Society and its officials is a complicated one that has connections to her parents, her sibling, and even her own standing and status. In addition, this external conflict parallels her own internal indecision about the romantic feelings she has for two boys, conflicting feelings that the Society would have her forget or ignore. This societal conflict has deep roots and extends into multiple areas of Cassia's life and the narrative.

There can obviously be multiple conflicts in a book, and the more forces that come to play and the more connected these are to other elements of the story, the more complex a text will be. In looking at conflict we must not only consider the central conflict but any additional issues that may relate to it. As we noted with theme, here we must also consider how a story's conflicts inform the work as a whole. How the author uses conflicts to connect the other elements in the work will impact the work's complexity.

Connections

What connections can be made between this book and a reader's broader world experiences? What connections can be made between this and other texts, both narrative and informational? Does the text make allusions to other texts? How much does the meaning of the text rely on these allusions and knowledge of other texts?

Consciously or unconsciously, authors build into their stories elements that will connect with their readers and with a broader literary tradition; the more connections, the deeper the possible layers of meaning. Every reader will need some type of background knowledge to fully understand a book; the more these connections demand of a reader, the more complex a text will be. For example, given their historical settings, books like Hesse's *Out of the Dust* or Anderson's *Chains* require background knowledge about the Great Depression or Revolutionary America, knowledge that not all readers may bring to these texts. A text like Fleischman's *Whirligig*, while it can be enjoyed on its own narrative merits, gains increased meaning if the reader is familiar with the archetypal hero's journey; seeing the main character's cross-country narrative in connection with mythical archetypes deepens the meanings afforded by the text.

Keene and Zimmerman (2007) outline three types of text connections readers make: text-to-self, text-to-text, and text-to-world. Readers might naturally make connections with themselves, given that the self is familiar territory for them. But books that, in order to make sense of the text, require readers to make connections to other books (in the form of allusions or other intertextual dependencies) or to the world around them (geographically, historically, culturally) are likely to be more complex. Adept authors make their work richer and more complex by bringing in a variety of outside connections and subtly constructing them using the elements of plot, setting, and character as they slowly reveal their ideas and issues to the reader.

Not only do these connections impact the reader, but they will also impact our instructional choices, since it is often our job to help readers make these connections, especially when they may not make them on their own. It is also our job to help readers gain the skills they need to then make these connections on their own. A book like Chris Crutcher's *Running Loose*, with its contemporary high school setting, demands little specialized knowledge beyond what high school readers are likely to bring with them. Thus, from a pedagogical perspective, a book with fewer connections like this one will require less intervention from us as professionals. On the other hand, there exists a wealth of connections we must or can make for a book like *Out of the Dust*, connections to the Great Depression oral histories, photographs of the time period, and other original documents or informational texts. These instructional demands can imply a text is more complex.

Structure

Every narrative, no matter how simple or complex, has a similar structure, consisting of the basic elements of fiction that go into creating a whole work. Each of these elements is important to consider individually since the way authors use these different devices informs the work's complexity. However, as we consider structure we must also consider them in concert with the other elements. No work will stand on just one element alone. As with theme and conflict, we will always ask ourselves how this individual element integrates with all the others. It is only by looking at the work as a whole that we will be able to see the entire picture of complexity.

In addition, as we consider each element we should also consider how these elements play out in different genres; specific genres will often use different literary elements to different effect. For example, in a romance, focused primarily on the characters and their actions, the plot may be the conventional boy meets girl, boy loses girl, boy gets girl back. However, the characters may be more sophisticated because the author focuses on showing their inner feelings and ideas. On the other hand, a fantasy may use setting to more effect since the world in which the action takes place plays a big part in how the story is created. How the author uses figurative language to describe this imaginative setting may be what brings a new depth to the age-old theme of good versus evil. The complexities of an unfamiliar setting will add complexity to the text.

While all genres will use all the elements, each one has its own conventions and standards; this is why we believe that we should be very careful in comparing complexity measures across genres. If we compare a romance to a fantasy, one may come up lacking; if, however, we compare one romance to another, it becomes much easier to see levels of complexity within that genre. While this is not always the case, and very good comparisons can be made across genres, we must note that these differences can change our view of a book's complexity. This is especially true when we are working with genres with which we are less familiar. If we have fewer titles in our repertoire, we may not be able to make as accurate a judgment of a work's complexity as we could otherwise. Building wide genre expertise, not only with young adult books but with children's books as well, is the best way to combat this potential challenge.

Many of us will already be schooled in each of these structural elements and adept at recognizing how they work together to inform a work of fiction. We know that many of the following points will be familiar to our readers. However, we feel that analyzing these structural elements in a context of evaluating complexity requires us to consider their particular attributes individually.

Setting

Is the setting familiar or unfamiliar? Does the story take place in more than one time or place? How often does the author switch between settings? How many details does the author use in describing setting? How dependent are interpretations of setting on elements like plot, character, or theme?

The details of when and where a story occurs make up the setting, and in fiction we can see a range from very familiar settings to the very unfamiliar. Understandably, texts with settings that are more familiar are usually going to be less complex than those with unfamiliar settings.

While most books have a single setting that dominates the narrative, not all books stay within these narrow confines. A book might move among school, home and work settings; these may all be within the same city or town, but the author may use different locations within them. These simple changes in location are expected and often less complicated than other settings. Sometimes these changes can be more radical, including stories that feature changes in location such as someone traveling to another country or having two different narrators from different locations telling their stories. Changes in the time period can also range from a character time traveling between eras to the narration of different characters in different times. Whatever the type of change, novels that have significant changes in setting will tend to be more complex than those that represent one location or time period.

In addition to the complexity of time and location, it is also important to note how the author describes a setting. Often, books with very commonplace settings will have fewer details describing the setting, and those with complex settings will have greater detail. The depth of description used is a good indicator of how complex a setting is intended to be, but we must also note that this also relates to the use of style and tone, which we will discuss in detail later. Laini Taylor's book *Daughter of Smoke and Bone* uses a wide variety of sensory details to bring depth to the book's two settings: real-world Europe and an otherworldly location. This duality of location makes this book's setting complex on its face, but the depth of detail the author uses to bring the setting to life increases the complexity. By using literary devices and figurative language to describe her setting, Taylor brings a deeper context to her work that engages the readers' senses and demands more attention from them, thus raising the complexity.

Plot

How is the plot constructed? How many plot lines does the story follow? How explicit is the plot? Does the plot follow a conventional chronology, or does it jump around in time? How identifiable is the climax? Are there numerous climaxes that build to a central resolution? Does the story resolve in a predictable way, or are there twists and surprises? Does the end resolve satisfactorily, or are there points left open? Do these points lead to a sequel, or is this a stand-alone title? Does the plot contain any contrived or artificial elements? How credible is it? How dependent are interpretations of plot on elements like setting, character, or theme?

How an author portrays the sequence of events that tell a story can greatly affect a work's complexity. Straightforward, chronological plots that progress from one moment to the next, telling events in order, tend to be less complex as they require less of the reader. However, stories that features multiple plot lines or nonlinear presentations of the plot make more significant demands on the reader. In addition, stories told in fragments or with "missing" pieces that require the reader to make inferences to fill in the gaps will be more complex.

Complex plots can make characters, motivations, and conflicts more difficult to understand since readers must piece together parts of the puzzle as they read. *Strings Attached*, by Judy Blundell, tells the story of Kit Corrigan, a teen girl trying to navigate love and life as she works to make it as an actress in 1950s New York. Many of Kit's experiences and decisions are impacted by past events, things that happened not only to her but to members of her immediate family. To show how all this impacts Kit's current experience, Blundell intersperses chapters outlining events in the present with those retelling events from the past. But there is no pattern to how these chapters are integrated, and the only indication of time change is a simple statement of the month and year at the beginning of each chapter. This gives the novel greater complexity since all the characters in the novel appear both in the present and the past, forcing the reader to pay close attention to the time changes to keep the events and personalities straight. The reader is only able to see the full picture of Kit's life by integrating both present and past events, adding a significant layer of complexity to the book.

Some works feature multiple plot lines, usually connected in some way but not always explicitly so. A fine example of multiple, related plot lines is Louis Sachar's *Holes*, which tells two different stories that come together in the end though a shared genealogy of the characters. Another type of complex plot is one that is episodic in that it takes short bits of story and tells each individually. These types of episodic plots are especially complex when they do not tell the story in chronological order but skip around in time, place, or character to show how the individual episodes relate to the whole theme. In Paul Fleischman's *Whirligig*, for instance, we read about Brent Bishop, a young man who kills a girl while driving drunk and must travel across the country building whirligigs as restitution. His story is interrupted by chapters representing episodes in the lives of characters who never interact with or cross paths with Brent but who are influenced at some future time by the whirligigs that he builds. These fragments are connected, but not with chronological or even personal connections, and thus require significant interpretation by the reader to build into a coherent tale.

One other level of complexity comes as we consider how many climaxes a work has. If a book builds from significant exposition to climax several times throughout the novel, the level of complexity is higher. These types of novels also usually display lots of twists and turns in the plot; we read something at one point in the book, only to have our understandings contradicted or supplanted by later events or information. The constant movement of plot elements in this type of novel keeps readers on their toes, as they must constantly be changing their interpretation of the story. A nice example of how multiple climaxes can lead to twists and turns in the plot is in *The Last Thing I Remember* by Andrew Klavan. We start with Charlie escaping from an unknown facility with no memories of the past. He finds help and we come to a climactic moment when the cops come for him, only to find that it is a year later than his last memory and he was convicted of murder. After he escapes again, the exposition starts anew, leading us to another climax where Charlie must confront what he knows to keep a diplomat from being murdered. This plot contains extreme twists and turns; as readers we think it is only a day later than Charlie's last memory, but soon realize actually it is a year later. He seems to be a good kid, but then we find out he was convicted of murder. Jumping from one element to the next with significant plot changes gives this work a higher level of complexity.

The trend toward sequels is very dominant in young adult literature today, and when a book continues on into other volumes, the complexity of the story can be increased. While we must consider each volume individually to determine complexity, we cannot negate the fact that additional volumes in a series give the story a more complex arc than we see with a stand-alone novel. Books with sequels will often feature cliffhanger endings and unresolved conflicts or plot sequences. *The Last Thing I Remember*, introduced above, is one such novel; while the immediate threat is conquered, we end the novel knowing nothing more than a few sketchy elements about the year that Charlie has lost, and he is being chased once again by the cops. Books that leave the reader hanging or those that do not resolve except though sequels can be more complex than stand-alone novels.

Character

How many characters are in the book? How many could be considered significant characters? Is the protagonist a complex or multilayered character rather than a stereotype or flat character? How much emotional or physical change does the protagonist experience over the course of the novel? Are additional characters complex or flat? How close to real life representations are the characters? Do they represent cultures, races, colors, or ideas that are outside of the perceived norms of a particular population? How realistic are the relationships between characters? Are these portrayed in authentic ways or glossed over? How much imagination/prior knowledge is needed to connect to or understand character depictions? How many details does the author use in describing the characters? How dependent are interpretations of character on elements like plot, setting, or theme?

The players in any story are one of the most vital components of fiction that impact a work's complexity. Our first consideration should be the sheer number of characters in the work. Whether they are considered main or minor characters, the more characters we must keep track of, the more complex we consider the text. We must also consider characters' roles in the work. If minor characters are only there to add texture, then the work may be less complex than if a minor character exists, for example, to serve as a foil to the main character.

It is important to determine how authentically the author portrays these characters. The more an author works to portray authentic characters in a text, the more likely those representations are to add complexity to the text. In a fictional world, a character who shows the depth and range of a real person is going to be more complex, and texts become even more complex when this holds true for both major and minor characters. On the other hand, an overreliance on stock characters or stereotypes that are contrived, artificial, or commonplace may lead us to view a book as less complex. For example, consider Jessica, the main character in Wendelin Van Draanen's *The Running Dream*. A competitive runner, Jessica loses her leg in an accident, causing her to remake her life and dreams. Jessica is a complex, authentic character, exhibiting a range of typical teenage emotions, from anger to guilt to frustration, but as Van Draanen describes her challenges, she takes the character far beyond that. The range of emotions Jessica feels as she grieves the loss of her leg and searches for ways to redefine herself makes her a complex character and increases the complexity of the book.

We must also consider whether characters represent the diversity that surrounds us. We should consider works that have characters of other cultures, races, or ideas as higher on the complexity band for two reasons. First, when we have characters that represent different ideologies or world views, other story elements such as conflict and theme are bound to be influenced, making the text more complex; you cannot represent multiple perspectives without adding to the complexity of a novel. Secondly, characters that are outside the normal experience of a reader will make that work more complex for that reader, requiring that readers expand their understanding or activate some prior knowledge to fully comprehend the characters. As in real life, diversity just makes the world more complex, and so it is with novels.

In examining characters, looking to the level of detail used can help assess complexity. Often books with stock characters will have fewer details since the author is relying on the reader's understanding of an already held stereotype to "fill in" details about the characters. On the other hand, texts with complex and deep characters will have greater detail since the author has to show us more about these people. Also, authors must use details to make the relationships between the characters clear. If we are to understand how major and minor characters interact, the author must use complex details to show us their relationships. These layers of detail, while they can help make characters and relationships more complex, also make the text as a whole more complex by placing additional demands on readers as they try to retain and interpret what an author shares.

Finally, dynamic characters who exhibit change—in the form of physical, social, or emotional development—will be more complex than flat characters who remain static over the course of the story. The more dynamic the characters in a text, the greater the complexity will be. These character changes are also usually tied to conflicts in the text, normally the motivating factor behind changes, and certainly may be tied to the themes of a book. The more interconnected these changes are with other story elements, the more complex a text will be.

Point of View

What point of view (omniscient, first-person, third-person, etc.) is the story told from? Is it told from more than one point of view? How diverse is the point of view, and how connected is it to a reader's experience? What age group or developmental level does the point of view express? Does the point of view make sense? Does the author maintain an appropriate point of view throughout the book, or does it change for reasons other than the natural progression of characters and ideas? How dependent are interpretations of point of view on elements like plot, setting, character, or theme?

Through whose eyes the author tells the story can affect the work's complexity since the choice of point of view dictates the amount and the kind of information that the writer shares.

This in turn will affect how the reader experiences and interprets characters, plot events, conflicts, and even themes.

Because so much of the effect is dependent upon how the author executes the point of view, judgments about point of view and complexity can be quite challenging. For example, an omniscient point of view that tells us every little detail can become didactic and thus be less complex; however, a more artful use of omniscience to juxtapose the thoughts and motivations of multiple characters can make a work much more complex. In a similar vein, the use of a first-person narrator obviously limits what the author can reveal about other characters, which can place a higher inferential demand on the reader. A first-person narrator also must be evaluated for reliability, however, and with more postmodern young adult novels being written today, such a choice could increase the complexity of a text substantially. In Geraldine McCaughrean's *The White Darkness*, for instance, the narrator (Sym) is a deaf teenage girl who carries on a fantasy relationship with Lawrence "Titus" Oates, an Antarctic explorer who died on Richard Scott's doomed 1911 expedition to the South Pole. Through a series of unlikely events, Sym herself ends up in Antarctica with her uncle, a man obsessed with the theory of an Antarctic entrance to a hidden Inner World. As readers, we are not sure just how much Sym knows about the underlying motives of her uncle and the true nature of their journey, which begins as a seemingly innocuous vacation to the south of France. Her own relationship with the long-dead Oates and her obsession with all things Antarctic call into question numerous times her reliability as the story's teller, making this a complex text.

One thing that is clear is that a book told from more than one point of view will be more complex. Just as more plot lines and more characters add to the complexity, so does the addition of more points of view. Having two or more characters comment on the same events in a story increases the complexity of a text by presenting differing interpretations that the reader must sort out. For example, in *Flipped* by Wendelin Van Draanen we get both Juli's and Bryce's perspective; as we progress over time we see how both characters are reacting to the same events. We also are given more insight into both characters as we get their emotional points of view as well. Because we see two sides of the same story, readers are called upon to be more engaged in the story as they sort out and reconcile both characters' experiences to determine the true nature of the narrative.

Another thing to consider is when points of view in a text are outside of the normal experience of a reader. When readers must take themselves outside their normal experiences, they are required to expand themselves or activate some prior knowledge to fully comprehend a text. The more diverse the points of view represented in a text, the more complex that text is likely to be.

A final factor to consider is how the point of view expressed matches up with the intended audience of a work. If the point of view expressed is very childish and the intended audience is young adults, this work may not be of the highest complexity. At best, a work's point of view should match or exceed the intended audience while still maintaining believability for the work to be considered complex enough for the readers we are targeting.

Language Conventions

When we considered quantitative readability formulas, we found that these formulas only looked at the semantic and syntactic dimensions of language; in a qualitative review, it is the way authors use these dimensions that influences the complexity of a text. How authors select their words, how they combine them into sentences, and what this creates in a holistic sense is something that no computer can measure. Words and sentences not only convey surface meaning, but the artistic use of language conventions allows us to find deeper, more substantial meanings in the simplest of words. An author's use of these stylistic elements is essential for us to consider; here we outline two main categories of language conventions: style and tone, and literary devices.

Style and Tone

What style and tone does the author use? How does that style or tone affect other parts of the work such as its organization? For what effect is that style or tone being used? What details does the author use to convey the style, mood, and tone of the work? Is the author's style or tone consistent throughout the book, or does it change? How and why does this change take place? Is the change logical and consistent with the other elements, or is it unpredictable? Does the book contain dialect or other specialized or archaic language usage, and to what extent is this language used?

The style and tone an author selects for a work can have a strong impact on its complexity. Narrative style can cover the range from conversational to elevated, and tones can range from playful to formal to angry. A conversational style is likely to be less demanding than an elevated style, and some tones will be more identifiable for teen readers. These judgments are not necessarily clear-cut, so we must consider what style and tone is used, for what purpose it is used, and what effect it has on the work as a whole.

Authors are very conscious in selecting a style and tone for their work. Not all options will be useful in all situations, so selecting the best one for that story is important. The result of this selection can impact the complexity of the work. If the author has selected a less complex tone such as one that would contain lots of references to popular culture, but he or she uses that tone in an ironic way, then the text will be much more complex than the simple tone designation would have us believe. Rae Mariz's dystopian novel *The Unidentified* is an example of this. Mariz portrays a future world where commercialism dominates most social interactions: students attend schools sponsored by corporations where they create new products and participate in market research, hoping to become sponsored by corporations themselves. While the book is filled with references to a futuristic-but-easily-recognizable pop culture, the underlying tone is one of suspicion, and the book turns a critical (and sophisticated) eye on the troublesome possibilities of a world steeped in commercialism.

Style choices can impact the organization of a text, increasing its complexity. For example, epistolary style will create a text that is organized in the form of letters; this style may make more demands on a typical reader than a traditional prose style. A journalistic or dramatic style can also impact a text's organization, and genre conventions can also affect style and tone choices. A text based in the tradition of steam punk science fiction, for example, will tend to blend the style conventions of heroic adventure contained within a historical setting, characterized by a suspenseful tone.

As we considered in our previous discussions, it is important to note the details the author uses to convey their style and tone. Works with more details that bring depth to these elements will certainly be more complex than those that only rely on limited description or a reader's previous experience with other works in that same style. Paying attention to changes in style can also be very important; significant changes in style and tone without any reason or purpose can mark a work of poor quality. However, artistically applied changes throughout a text can bring great depth and complexity to a work.

One last important element to consider when looking at style and tone is how these choices affect the syntax they used. While some of these syntax issues are measured when computing the quantitative measures we spoke of in chapter three, we should also consider them from a qualitative perspective. The syntax of *When You Reach Me* by Rebecca Stead, for instance, is dominated by simple sentences; on the other hand, *North of Beautiful* by Justina Chen

Headley has more syntactically complex sentences. While both address themes relating to family, the first might be considered less complex and the second more complex due to each author's use of syntax. Another stylistic choice that affects language use will be the introduction of conventions such as dialect or archaic language. In Moira Young's *Blood Red Road*, for example, she uses a very raw southern dialect to portray the postapocalyptic society and to convey the main character's lack of education and experience. Phrases like "ain't bin" or "against th'other" give this work a very raw tone that is perfectly suited to its setting and character but their use also raises its complexity.

Literary Devices

What literary devices does the author use? How frequently are these devices used? How integral are these devices to the meaning of the text? How sophisticated or complex are these literary devices? For what effect are these literary devices used?

The use of devices and figurative language in literature is something that most of us have had drilled into us since we started school. Sophisticated use of these devices will always make the work more complex. These devices should be familiar to most professionals as we've been trained in how to identify them and understand how they are used; for convenience, a brief summary of the major devices is included in box 4.1. For teens, these devices may be less familiar, and their use in literary texts will make more demands on them; even for skilled readers, some of these devices will take closer readings to detect. Some devices (like a simile) are pretty straightforward, but others (like an extended metaphor) can be harder to follow and make sense of. Determining the frequency and effect of these devices will provide us with a clearer view of a work's complexity.

In *Marcelo in the Real World*, for instance, Francisco Stork introduces the motif of music early in the book, as Marcelo is undergoing brain scans to explore the nature of the "internal music" that he often hears in his mind. Later, when Marcelo visits the home of his coworker, Jasmine, this motif is extended into a metaphor comparing the difficult decisions Marcelo must make about helping an accident victim to playing the right notes in a piece of music. Marcelo, throughout the rest of the book, grapples with this and other difficult decisions with consequences for those he loves and continually refers to his desire to play the right notes, to sound the right tone. While grasping this metaphor isn't vital to a superficial understanding of the book, recognizing it helps readers sympathize and understand Marcelo's inner motives and conflicts. Its artful integration in the book raises the book's complexity.

Knowledge Demands

What background information or prior knowledge is necessary to comprehend this text? What does the author assume readers already know? Are there parts that could be confusing? What level of intervention/preparation would need to be done for/with the reader to clear the confusion? How explicit is the author in giving the reader content knowledge? How much is implied that the reader will already know?

Reading is not an isolated act, texts do not exist in isolation, and readers will always bring their own experiences and ideas into the mix. As Keene and Zimmerman (2007) contend, readers make a variety of connections to a text; sometimes these are complex connections, so evaluating them is essential if we are to determine a text's complexity. In his work *Readicide: How Schools Are Killing Reading and What You Can Do about It*, Kelly Gallagher brings this point to the fore in his analysis. He contends that there are some texts that, while perhaps syntactically simple, cannot be understood without the context knowledge necessary to do so. He gives many examples, including a paragraph written at a very low reading level that is difficult to understand unless you have specialized knowledge of baseball. Many of you may have

Box 4.1 Common Literary Devices

Metaphor and simile	Comparisons that contrast two things and imply that one thing is another. Simile uses like or as, while metaphor does not.
Idiom	An expression whose intended meaning differs from its literal meaning.
Pun	Contrast between two words that sound the same but have distinct meaning.
Personification	Assigning human characteristics to animals or inanimate objects.
Symbolism	Utilizing an object to stand for another idea, action, or element.
Irony	A statement that conveys the opposite of what would be expected.
Sarcasm	Use of tone to express the opposite of what is stated.
Hyperbole	Excessive exaggeration.
Rhythm and meter	Emphasis of speech.
Rhyme	Combination of words that sound alike.
Assonance	Repetition of similar or identical vowel sounds in words that are close to each other.
Alliteration	Repeated sounds in words that are near each other or beginning several words together with the same sound.
Repetition	Repeating the same word or phrase for emphasis.
Onomatopoeia	Words or phrases that seek to reproduce an actual sound.
Motif	A repeated pattern or structure that connects to a work's themes.
Parable	A brief story that represents a moral or religious concept.
Allegory	An extended metaphor with symbols that have both literal and figurative meanings.
Allusions	A reference to an outside event that may be historical, biblical, or literary.
Caricature	An exaggerated description that distorts a character.
Foreshadowing	A preview, either subtle or overt, of upcoming actions or emotions.
Symbol	A concrete noun that is used to represent an abstract idea.

experienced this same phenomenon such as we did when we worked with a student on a second-grade reading level who was devouring a bike repair manual that was beyond his expected level, but he was aided in the reading by his extensive knowledge of bicycles.

Examples like these show us that what a reader brings to the text can be just as important as what the text has to offer when we determine complexity. Generally, if a text requires a great deal of background knowledge that would come from either cultural, literary, disciplinary, or other sources outside of the text, the text will be considered more complex. The tricky part of this dimension is that what a text demands will vary from reader to reader, since no two readers will have the same background or prior knowledge. We have to make these decisions based on general understandings of our students as a whole, and our experience as teachers plays a significant role in this.

Sometimes authors will provide needed background knowledge explicitly in a text, but other texts may rely more on the reader to fill in needed details. As we consider this dimension in evaluating complexity, it can be helpful to think about how much instructional intervention we'd need to provide our students in order for them to fully comprehend a text. Books that would require more intervention would generally be more complex. Since no two readers will be alike, as we consider books holistically, these dimensions will very much be contingent upon individual classrooms and applications. We will address this topic further in the next chapter when we explore dimensions of the reader in greater depth.

Conclusion

Just as Gray and Leary (1935) outlined in their study, there are a number of variables that impact the complexity of a text. The three-tiered model fully captures these dimensions through a qualitative analysis, and by applying the essential questions outlined here, we can make more meaningful evaluations of a book's complexity. We believe that without considering these variables we will never be able to have a full picture of the relative complexity of a text. This is why the authors of the CCSS clearly state that the qualitative measures should override the readability scores. However, a text is not the only player in this game of teaching and learning we are trying to win. The readers themselves and the tasks we use are also significant players. In our next chapter we will focus on these dimensions and how the match between readers and tasks can influence our perceptions of complexity.

Bibliography

Gallagher, K. (2009). *Readicide: How schools are killing reading and what you can do about it.* Portland, ME: Stenhouse Publishers.

Gray, W. S., & Leary, B. E. (1935). *What makes a book readable: With special reference to adults of limited reading ability, an initial study.* Chicago, IL: University of Chicago Press.

Keene, E. & Zimmerman, S. (2007). *Mosaic of thought: The power of comprehension strategy instruction.* (2nd ed.) Portsmouth, NH: Heinemann.

School Renaissance Institute. (2000). *The ATOS[TM] Readability Formula for books and how it compares to other formulas. Report.* Madison, WI: Wisconsin School Renaissance Institute. (ERIC Document Reproduction Service No. ED449468). Retrieved May 6, 2011, from EBSCOHost ERIC database.

Chapter 5

Reader and Task Dimensions of Text Complexity

Up to this point in our discussion we have considered just the text. The implication here is that the linguistic structures (quantitative dimensions) and the literary structures (qualitative dimensions) are the elements of a text that influence meaning and complexity. This view is solidly based in the perspective of formalist or new critical literary theorists who believed that the focus of literary criticism should be on analyzing the features inherent in the text. Their purpose was to isolate the text from any historical, biographical, or cultural context, making their interpretations dependent on the text alone. This view discounted not only the author's intention in creating the text but also the reader's personal reaction to it.

To a certain extent formalists have a valid point in that the form and structure of a work make it what it is; with few exceptions, a text's structure cannot be changed once it is published, so we can analyze these structures to create meaning. However, even as new criticism began to permeate teaching methods in universities, theorists began to question the way formalists isolated the text. Trotsky (2005), for example, contended that formalist theories are flawed because they neglect to consider those who write and read literature. These criticisms of the formalist views led to the development of new avenues of critical thought, among them the Marxist ideas of Trotsky (2005) and the reader-response theories of Rosenblatt (1995). These theorists recognize that other elements are essential in the process of making meaning with a text. As educators, we also accept the premise that a text cannot be fully separated from its origins, readers, and uses. The creators of the CCSS also seem to accept this premise since the last portion of the three-tiered model of text complexity relates to readers and tasks, two elements that bring meaning from outside the text.

In adding these dimensions, the CCSS changes its theoretical frame from the solidly formalist view of the first two elements to a view that is grounded more in reader-response theories. We feel it is important to understand this change in theoretical underpinnings because it greatly affects our interpretation of the dimensions. Viewing complexity though a formalist frame offers us a concrete view through which we can analyze texts, one that we have outlined in the previous two chapters. However, when we consider the reader and task, the structure this frame gives us is much less concrete, and it changes how we define text complexity.

Reader and task elements are much less concrete than the others because of the basic fact that every human being is different, making it impossible to articulate every situation for every individual, so here we are only able to make generalizations. By their very nature generalizations are less concrete, so most of our work done in applying this dimension will lie with individual professionals who have knowledge and experience with individual students and individual classrooms. This is one reason why the CCSS only gives a cursory discussion of the reader and task dimensions. They often rely on teachers' judgment, experience, and knowledge of their students and their content area to provide context for these dimensions (appendix A, p. 4). In this context we are pleased to see the authors of the common core recognizing the valuable contribution that teachers provide in making important decisions about the role readers and tasks play in making meaning in the classroom. We also agree that teacher expertise and experience are critical factors in assessing readers and creating classroom tasks. We would suggest, however, that even though individual application is essential with these dimensions, a discussion of generalities is well worth the effort as it can help us grasp more fully what we mean when we talk about readers and tasks.

The application of a different theoretical foundation also changes how we define complexity. A text is essentially going to be more or less complex all on its own; adding the readers and task dimensions into the mix does not change the inherent complexity of a text. What it does change is the relative complexity of the text as defined by the reader's ability to comprehend the text and the relative complexity of any task's knowledge demands. Conducting an analysis of the quantitative and qualitative structures of the text will deliver a certain level of complexity. However, this analysis can be lowered or raised depending on the demands placed upon it by the characteristics of a reader or a task.

For example, the novel *Wisdom's Kiss* by Catherine Gilbert Murdock uses a variety of forms to convey its story, from letters to encyclopedia entries. In an analysis of the text alone we would place this text at a level of about 10th grade. If we then apply the reader dimension, we find that the complexity of this text will increase if we are dealing with readers who have had very little experience with varying literary formats. If we are working with 11th- or 12th-grade readers who lack this experience, we might consider this novel as appropriate given this additional complexity. If we consider the task dimension, we might find a situation where the teacher has developed a strong curriculum that gives students deep knowledge about different formats. In this situation, the knowledge requirements of the texts are better met, and thus the text's complexity may be lowered as well. With this additional support, the text could easily fall into an eighth- or ninth-grade band. So depending upon the reader's needs and the tasks used with this text, it could potentially meet the complexity standards for some students and classrooms from grades 8–12.

This leads us to the conclusion that when we consider the reader and task dimensions, we focus less on determining the complexity of the text itself and more on finding the right match for our readers and instructional tasks. To apply the reader and task dimension, we must carefully select texts that fit with the capacities of our students and the structures we use to teach them, as this is the only way to fully define the text's complexity. This idea relates to Vygotsky's (1962) concept of the zone of proximal development, suggesting that we need to design tasks and situations where students are met at an appropriate developmental level. When a task is too simple or too complex, optimal learning does not take place; instead, we seek to place learners in tasks that are a stretch for them but that they can meet with the help of a more capable expert. As teachers, we can serve this role, supporting students in their skill development by providing texts and tasks that meet their needs. The idea is to find the perfect textual match for every reader and task.

Paying close attention to our readers and the tasks we use in the classroom is not a new idea for teachers. As professionals, the things we have outlined above will be no surprise as we always strive to match students' interests to specific texts, knowing that they'll be more likely to read about settings, characters, or themes that they find relevant. We also know that certain texts are well suited to specific tasks. To teach students about making inferences, for instance, a good teacher will carefully select a text that requires such skills of students and allows for an authentic context in which to develop those skills. Evaluating the reader and task dimensions, then, is a critical component to giving us a full view of how complex a text is and to making the best matches to our students and their needs.

Building on the limited information offered in the CCSS, we now wish to add additional depth to our understanding of these elements. We begin by looking at the reader, to consider what kind of readers we hope to develop as a result of their experiences in our classrooms or libraries. Then we'll consider what kind of readers we're actually faced with, after which we'll discuss how the reader's aptitude reconciles these two issues. At the end of the chapter, we'll turn our attention to dimensions of the tasks we ask students to complete with these texts.

Reader Dimensions of Text Complexity

Envisioning Independent Readers

What kind of readers do we want our adolescents to become? How do we want our readers to behave in the future? What behaviors or skills are exhibited by an independent reader who can tackle complex texts? How will this text and my use of it create these behaviors or skills? How does a consideration of these skills in light of who my readers are create a more complex text?

Encompassing all the outcomes and benchmarks of the CCSS is the intent that students will be prepared to do complex college- and workplace-level reading independently. If independence is the overarching learning outcome for our students, we must first build a vision of what an independent reader looks like. Here we consider the future, not the present; a clear picture of where we are heading will help shape our purposes more clearly. Understanding this future will also help us to build a self-fulfilling prophecy, as it were, in that if we see our students becoming strong independent readers, then the texts we select and the tasks we create are more likely to help them develop skills and behaviors they will need. For us, independent college- and workplace-ready readers are those who read independently and select their own books; who read for pleasure; and who, when given assigned reading in a work or school setting are able to engage with new texts confidently using skills they have mastered. These are the kinds of confident reading behaviors we must build in students. Let's take a closer look at these and other important reader behaviors.

- *Readers have developed lifelong reading habits.* The ability to enjoy reading as a fundamental, lifelong skill is one of the most basic behaviors of a reader. Readers use their free time to read, they engage with a variety of texts throughout their lives, and they turn to texts and reading for pleasure and information. This is not something they do solely because they are forced or assigned to; they have developed habits and beliefs that make them readers for life.
- *Readers know how to select their own materials to match personal interests or tasks at hand.* Readers know how to navigate the world of texts. They know how to use libraries, bookstores, and other information repositories to gain access to the texts they need. They know that texts vary, and they know how to select texts that match their personal interests, information needs, and reading abilities.
- *Readers evaluate their reading based on their own interests and other universal criteria.* Readers know how to decide if a text fits their needs. This is especially true of informational texts in that they are able to identify whether or not a text will give them the information they need. They use methods to decide if the text is factual or has bias, and if its content can be trusted. Readers also know how to evaluate texts read for enjoyment. They know if these texts fit their reading interests and needs, and they know how to abandon texts when they are not matching these needs.

- *Readers understand the purpose of reading and realize that it can be for pleasure as well as information.* We read for many reasons: to get information, to inform opinions, to educate ourselves, and to enjoy stories and ideas. Readers understand all these reasons to read, and they know how to find and evaluate texts to fit all these needs.
- *Readers read widely, including things that are below their level and things that are above their level.* Readers will read a great variety and understand that reading widely is important; this suggests that they will read things that would be considered below their level as well as things that are above it. Even readers who read complex texts independently will encounter texts well above their level, but because of their skills and experience they will be able to select, evaluate, and navigate even the most challenging texts.
- *Readers have a positive attitude about reading and are willing to tackle all kinds of texts and stick with harder texts longer.* One of the most important characteristics of readers is that they have a positive attitude about reading. They do not see reading as a chore or obligation, and they find innate pleasure in the act itself. Readers also have a strong sense of self-efficacy in that they believe in their own reading competence. Since they are confident with their abilities, readers are willing to tackle all kinds of texts. If a text is difficult, readers who think positively about reading and their own abilities are more likely to have the motivation to stick with it for a longer period; they often have more successful experiences with the texts they read because they work through the challenges to get to the benefits.
- *Readers understand how format and genre make meaning and know how to identify important parts of the text.* Through their experience, readers naturally build the knowledge of how the structure of a text gives it meaning. They understand that certain packages or formats carry certain types of information and may be directed to certain audiences; they also understand how the text is organized within that format and how to navigate through it. For example, an independent reader would understand that a newspaper carries current local and national news and would know how to use the different sections to find articles of interest. Readers also understand the conventions of genre. For example, they understand that the genre of fantasy relies on the imagination, but that historical fiction represents a more accurate reality. They are familiar with a variety of genres and use this knowledge to make connections among them, their reading, and the world, as they select, evaluate, and comprehend their reading.
- *Readers use comprehension and recognition strategies fluently.* Readers rely on a variety of comprehension strategies. They use strategies such as comparison, summarizing, visualization, inference, predictions, drawing conclusions, word identification, context clues, and questioning. These strategies are a natural and basic part of their approach to a text; in fact, the best readers don't really have to think consciously about their use.
- *Readers monitor their understanding and make adjustments as necessary.* Readers are constantly monitoring their understanding of a text, and they know how to make adjustments in their reading strategies to help resolve problems in comprehension. For example, they know how to identify critical parts of a text or when to reread to increase their comprehension; they know when to speed up or slow down their reading, often based on the purpose they have in reading. They also know when to abandon a text entirely and how to search out a replacement text when needed.
- *Readers actively make connections between their own experiences and a text, between a text and other texts, and between a text and the world.* In order for reading to be the kind

of experience that helps us learn and grow, we must be able to apply the reading to other contexts and use it to inform our opinions; this fundamental skill is one emphasized by the CCSS. The connections we make can also bring greater purpose to literature. We love the books that connect to us in some way, such as when we see a character like us or find a plot element that reminds us of our own experience. Making these connections while reading helps us to find books we love; these books, in turn, help us to understand the intangible yet powerful reasons we read.

- *Readers share their reading and their passion for reading with others.* Talk to a reader and she will often want to talk about what she is reading. Readers light up with excitement when they talk about books they love, and they are interested in what other people have to say about what they have read. They are often part of in-person or online communities that engage in talk and writing about reading.
- *Readers know how to respond to literature.* Readers are skilled at responding to literature because they know how to analyze their reading, connect their reading, and share their reading experiences. They have learned how to talk, read, and write about reading. Being able to respond to literature helps readers feel more confident in school or social situations where responding to reading is a critical part of success. Good readers know how to think critically about what they read, how to ask probing questions that question underlying assumptions or mis- or underrepresented perspectives.

We contend that the type of independent college/workplace-ready readers the CCSS envisions will be readers who exhibit each of these behaviors. Our job then is to find the best match among text, reader, and activity that will allow us to create the independent readers we describe above. No two readers will start in the same place with their reading ability, so as professionals we must begin where they are and provide the necessary scaffold to take them to where we want them to be. The texts we choose will play a large role in this process, so as we look at our readers we must include as part of our complexity analysis an indication of where individual texts can take them. For example, with a reader with less self-efficacy, we might match them with a text that connects to and expands their own interests because it will allow them to not only make connections with a text but also to have a positive experience with it. A book like *The Berlin Boxing Club* by Robert Sharenow, for instance, is a qualitatively complex text; however, if we are aiming this text at a group of readers who like boxing, this complexity is lessened given that these readers better meet the knowledge demands of the text. This coordination between text and reader matches this text to reader interests at an appropriate complexity level, allowing us to use this text in our classrooms to build independent reading behaviors. This match happens because a book so closely linked to a reader's interests is the kind of text that allows them to find those very important personal connections that help readers to understand why reading is pleasurable. In addition, they also are more likely to be able to respond to it and share it with others more confidently. So here, then, we have a text that is not only complex in and of itself but also one that allows us to build the complex skills necessary for an independent reader.

The Adolescent Reader

Having considered what our readers will look like in the future and how the texts we use impact the skills we are trying to foster in our readers, we now focus on the present. We often tell our university students that one of our main goals as professionals is to find the right book at the right time for the right reader. While we will outline much in this book that will help you in this effort, there are also many other professional resources that you can turn to if you feel you need more information. Teri Lesesne's book *Making the Match: The Right Book for the Right*

Reader at the Right Time, Grades 4-12 (2003) is a fine example of a resource that guides us though the process of matching individuals with suitable texts. There is no doubt that matching readers and texts can be a big challenge, especially when you consider that no two individuals will react to a text in the same way given the different personalities, experiences, and knowledge they bring to a text. Ultimately, the best judge of an individual reader's needs is an individual professional who works with him or her. The more experience you have, not only with your students but with the literature they read, the more you will be able to find just the right match for each individual and the curriculum you are covering.

So while we cannot talk about the individuals you will encounter in your classrooms, we are able to make some generalizations about adolescents that impact our ability to match readers to just the right text at the right level of complexity. Considering adolescent development, issues of individual makeup and experience, and the reader's aptitude can give everyone a general construct to apply when considering the present needs of our readers. From there it is up to us as individual teachers to work to understand the demographics and diversity in your own classrooms and tailor your own resources to meet the needs of your individual students.

Adolescent Development

What developmental concerns (physical, cognitive, emotional, and social) impact our readers? How will these affect an adolescent's learning and, consequently, our teaching? Which of these developmental issues are important for us to take into account when selecting texts?

Adolescence is defined as a period of life that begins with the onset of the biological changes associated with puberty and ends when an individual has established himself or herself as an adult; this period most often occurs between the ages of 12 and 20. During this period, individuals undergo a variety of very profound changes—physical, emotional, intellectual, and social—that redefine their identities and roles in the society in which they live; during this time, they also make decisions that can influence the rest of their lives. Although this has not always been the case, we understand today that adolescents are not the same as adults. Research has shown that important areas of the brain, including the prefrontal cortex which controls higher-order thinking skills, are not fully developed until about age 30 (Weinberger, Elvevag, & Giedd, 2005; "Understanding," 2011). These fundamental neurological differences make teenagers very different from adults.

Developmental psychologist Erik Erikson's (1968) theory of psychosocial development sees the development that occurs during adolescence as a series of psychosocial crises that individuals must resolve. During each of these increasingly more complex crises, individuals struggle to achieve individuality and learn to function in society. Erikson sees the need to form a sense of identity as one of the key developmental challenges for this period of life. Core tasks that adolescents attend to while building this sense of identity require them to develop their own sense of mastery, autonomy, sexuality, intimacy, and achievement. In the end, all developmental tasks of this period of life all revolve around the task of identify formation.

While there are many events that lead to an adolescent growing into an adult, Havighurst (1972), extending Erikson's work, outlines eight specific developmental tasks that are important parts of adolescents' specific identity formation. These tasks include creating mature relationships, defining one's gender role, accepting one's body, finding emotional independence, preparing for adult life including marriage and a career, and developing a moral code that defines responsible behavior. Each of these developmental tasks moves individuals toward the formation of their own unique, adult identities.

During adolescence, these tasks are accomplished in a complex environment of constant change. The first changes of adolescence are the complex biological transformations that are associated with puberty. The extremes of physical development beginning in adolescence not only affect teens' physical appearance but also greatly impact their sense of self-esteem and their sexual identity. Hormonal shifts associated with puberty also spark complex emotional changes. In addition, adolescents are undergoing complex psychological changes; the adolescent brain develops the ability for increasingly sophisticated and elaborate information processing skills ("Understanding," 2011; Weinberger, Elvevag, & Giedd, 2005).

Adolescence also encompasses a time of extensive emotional transition as youth learn to view themselves and their roles in a more autonomous manner. The teenage years are often characterized by many conflicting and negative emotions as teens face a great deal of pressure from many fronts. As adolescents develop, they must confront these emotions and find their independence from the adults in their lives, both emotionally and physically. Adolescents are also undergoing great social changes as they redefine themselves within social groups, prepare for their future roles in society, and reach new levels of interpersonal intimacy. During this time, social problems can become more complex, which can cause conflict for teens as they encounter the stress of expectations from peers, adults, and other institutions that do not always coincide with one another (Steinberg & Sherk, 2006).

So why are these developmental issues important for us to consider in the context of identifying text complexity? It is because consideration of these issues becomes integral to our search for the best text-to-reader match. Without a thorough knowledge of our teen readers' developmental needs, we will struggle to make a good match. Young adults are very responsive to the world around them, and they most often want to read books about issues that are relevant to their experiences and concerns. We have found that finding texts that match a reader's developmental needs is one way to ensure that a reader will connect with and ultimately gain meaning from a text. Young adult literature has a unique ability to connect with teens since, as Donelson and Nilsen (2005) note, the same transition to adulthood they are experiencing is at the thematic core of most young adult fiction. Since they see themselves developmentally reflected in the pages, young adults are drawn to works of young adult literature. When readers are drawn in this way to a work, their interest and motivation are more fully engaged, a state that readies them for learning tasks that meet the CCSS standards.

The use of young adult books as part of the overall design of our readers' curricular experiences allows us to address other important developmental concerns. As teens develop cognitively, they need to have opportunities to form their own opinions and to develop a moral system of responsible behavior. Books that thematically connect to teens' experiences will help readers to have these opportunities and to gain meaning from them. Teens also need a safe environment to "test" their identities as they try out a variety of emotional responses to complex situations. Books can provide this safe zone, but only if they feature characters that reflect a teen's own identity and concerns, even if they face challenges the reader may not. Adolescents also enjoy engaging with their peers, which makes them also more motivated to engage with a text when it is something that their peer groups also enjoy.

We contend that young adult literature will nearly always better meet the developmental needs of adolescent readers. We find that many works of the canon currently taught are so removed from modern teens' developmental needs that they cease to be of real use. We frequently encounter teachers who strive to teach their favorite classic, but year after year find students hating the experience. This is due, we suggest, to the fact that the themes and characters of the books they try to teach are so far removed from their students' developmental needs that teens find them irrelevant. And when teens' developmental needs don't match their reading, we often find resistance from readers who are trying to forge an independent identity. As we evaluate a text, we must consider that a text that is developmentally beyond our readers' capacities will likely be too complex for them. Since we are also sure to find texts that are developmentally below our readers' expectations, it is up to us as professional teachers to find that precise balance that allows an individual reader to be matched with an appropriate text.

Individual Makeup and Experience

What role do race, gender, socio-economic status, and cognitive capabilities play for our individual readers? How do these considerations affect the reader? Is the text something that teens will find appealing? Is the text appropriately complex for the readers we are targeting? What experience or knowledge does the text require of the reader? Do my students have this experience or knowledge without my intervention? How much intervention is necessary?

In addition to general developmental needs, there are important individual issues we must consider. These issues can be divided into two areas. First are considerations of individual makeup; these factors are physical in nature in that they are the biological or social constructs that are placed upon individuals, including elements such as race, gender, socioeconomic status, and cognitive capabilities. Second are considerations of individual experience; these factors are more psychological in nature and have to do with the experiences that an individual has encountered over his or her lifetime. These individual characteristics will vary greatly from classroom to classroom. We encourage professionals to get to know the diversity of their students' situations as this information will provide them with what they need to know to match texts to the individual demands of their students.

Considering both the physical and psychological makeup of a reader is important because it is these factors that impact the types of knowledge demands a text places on the reader. For example, socioeconomic background can make a work more complex when we consider books such as Walter Dean Myers' *Lockdown*. This novel recounts the story of a young man in a juvenile detention facility, a setting that may be unfamiliar for many teens, making the book more complex because of the cultural background knowledge the text requires. This is not to say, of course, that just because a student does not have familiarity with this setting that he or she cannot or would not appreciate this book. All teenagers, regardless of their background, have experienced events and encountered ideas that will help them to empathize with a wide variety of the complexities of life. The best young adult writers, in fact, tap into universal concerns and emotions in their characterizations that are likely to appeal to a wide variety of readers, no matter how closely matched they may be to the characters in the book. Our purpose here is to explain factors of complexity, so the fact remains that the closer the match between a reader's and fictional character's makeup, the less complex a book may be for that reader.

Our job as professionals is to consider readers and the experiences they bring to the text as we seek books that sit at an appropriate complexity level for that reader's experience. Every text will demand a certain knowledge level from its readers, inherent in the text itself and based on how it is constructed and presented. For example, when a text is set in a historical period, it may demand of the reader some background knowledge, or if a book is built on certain genre conventions, it may be necessary for the reader to have experience with that genre in order to comprehend the work. So while readers bring their own experiences, the text will also require something of readers; if readers lack the knowledge and experience required from the text, then the text is going to be much more complex. One author recently had an experience of this nature with the book *The Boneshaker* by Kate Milford. The author had very much enjoyed the text, but upon using it in the classroom found the class completely confused by it. She quickly discovered that this was because the text required a lot of background knowledge related to the folklore of Lazy Jack Tales and of Goethe's *Faust*. The text's characterization and thematic content required that the reader have this background and, because the author had it, she found this book to be interesting and teachable; however, her students lacked such knowledge and thus found the text far too complex to be of any use in the activities she had designed.

Research has also shown that texts that require a large amount of previous knowledge are more complex since these demands have a significant impact on what readers can comprehend (Gallagher, 2009; Irwin & Davis, 1980). One of the major problems with many of the exemplar texts in the CCSS outline is that they can require significant amounts of previous knowledge to read them. If this knowledge is not present, then teachers must spend large chucks of classroom time bringing students up to speed. This can cause great stress for students, who must struggle to not only understand the reading so they can apply it to classroom learning but also gain the necessary background information at the same time.

Even with the most expert instruction, there are still many who will be unable to gain the knowledge they need to fully comprehend the texts. This is why students often turn to shortened, simplified, or notational overviews for reading. If students are not reading the text itself but turning to easier alternatives, then we have lost not only the purpose of our instruction but the purpose of the CCSS as well (Broz, 2011). How can we say students are reading increasingly complex texts if they are not even reading them in the first place? On the other hand, because they are contemporary, address the point of view of a modern teenager, and connect powerful, timeless themes from the outset, the majority of modern young adult literature does not require the large amounts of previous knowledge required by many classics. And even if the book is outside of most experience such as a historical novel or a novel on an unfamiliar topic, modern authors are adept at foregrounding salient points to help us bring a vision of what the context is without having to build large stores of background knowledge to do so.

We must also keep in mind that there is only a certain level of frustration that readers will put up with. If readers are required to know or develop too much background knowledge to make sense of a text, their level of frustration rises, making them unwilling to even read the book let alone engage with it in a meaningful way. There is a balance point here where we must determine when a work is going to tip the scale over the edge for our readers. Some required knowledge helps increase the complexity and can make the reading a learning experience—something we want our students to engage in. However, if we tip the scales too far the other way, the work is just out of reach.

Especially as we move to the higher grade levels, finding this balance becomes a much more challenging task. For example, the CCSS offers *Alice's Adventures in Wonderland* by Lewis Carroll as an exemplar text at the fourth- and fifth-grade level. This text, like most of the other exemplars offered, requires little previous knowledge and scaffolding; students need only understand creative word play, something they have probably experienced with Dr. Seuss, and some of the conventions of fantasy journeys, which they get in books like *Harry Potter*. Also, many of them will have seen the ubiquitous Disney movie version that gives them some experience with the characters and plot.

Moving down the list to the ninth grade, however, we find the exemplar text of Homer's *The Odyssey*. Here the knowledge base required is of epic poetry, translated language, Greek mythology, politics of the ancient Greek isles, ancient inheritance and succession laws, mariners customs and sea travel, ancient Greek history, and the events that led up to and after Troy, among many other topics. Very few, if any, of our students are going to come to the reading with the ability to comprehend this text without a lot of intervention. While many could read *Alice* without significant intervention, very few could read *The Odyssey* without significant support. So we ask ourselves: Why not choose instead *As Easy as Falling off the Face of the Earth* by Lynne Rae Perkins? In this novel, Ry accidentally misses his train and has many complex adventures to get home. With a modern setting and a teenage point of view, this novel requires less prior knowledge and scaffolding. At the same time, however, it embraces the same themes as we find in *The Odyssey*, such as perseverance, respect, and loyalty. Taking on the hero-journey structure, this novel is complex in the qualitative sense, containing multiple perspectives, multiple levels of meaning, and sophisticated symbolic language. A novel of this type, offering the complexity, structure, and themes of the classic but with more approachable knowledge demands better suited to our students' experiences and makeup, would be a much better choice to create the learning environment that will help our students reach the anchor and grade-specific standards for the CCSS.

The Reader's Aptitude

The next logical question in this exploration of the reader now becomes: How do we help the readers we have today become the readers we (and society) want them to be tomorrow? The standards set forth in the CCSS are designed to be indicative of these end goals, and they provide (purposefully, we believe) little direction on how to lead students to those goals. In this section, we hope to illuminate some considerations about texts and readers that we ought to reflect on as we make decisions related to meeting these goals.

Most significantly, we feel that professional teachers and librarians should be actively and purposefully involved in helping match appropriate texts to readers. If we can be successful at this, we can help student-readers develop the skills and behaviors they'll need to become the readers we want them to be. Our experience and plenty of research have led us to identify some criteria we ought to consider in making these decisions: interest, experience, and motivation. These are all things that the reader brings to the book, and, while they can be influenced by outside forces, if they are not already inherent in the reader, it becomes much more of a challenge to find the right text to help build independent readers. As we make our text selection, it is critical to consider how the texts we select will build on our readers' interest, motivation, and experience, but also how to build on their developmental needs to foster and strengthen the factors that help them become lifelong readers.

Interest

Will this text be of interest to my readers? How can I capitalize on my student's interest to build the ideal learning environment?

One sad thing we know about today's adolescents is that they are less likely to be readers (Bauerlein, 2010). They find reading less interesting, making them more likely to turn to other avenues for entertainment and information. Part of our job as professionals is to reenergize their interest. As Lenters (2006) notes, studies show that the most common factor cited for teens' reluctance to read is lack of interest in what they are given to read. Wilson and Kelley (2010) found in their study that only 10 percent of good readers indicated that English language arts was their favorite class and not all enjoyed what they read in class because the material was not connected to their reading interests. Reeves (2004) contends that one of our biggest problems is that the secondary school curriculum is so full of books written by adults addressing adult concerns that there is no space for books that are connected to their developmental needs. In addition, Smith and Wilhelm (2002) found that boys who exhibited literate behaviors outside of school resisted school reading, in part, because it was assigned and forced on them and seemed unrelated to their lives outside of school.

Study after study has shown that teens react negatively to many teacher-assigned books, mainly because they are just not interested in what their teachers ask them to read. Some even go so far as to say that the fault for the reading problems of today's teens lies with teachers who assign novels that don't take into account the reading interests of teenagers (Bushman, 1997; Santoli &Wagner, 2004). We find that this may be an extreme assumption, but even if not all the fault lies with traditional practices, we can certainly make the case that a lack of connection to teens' interests can easily lead directly to students' reluctance to read.

We have seen many examples of teens who will read a book that is far above their reading level because they have interest in it. One older teen in our experience read at about a second- or third-grade level but was plowing through J. K. Rowling's <u>Harry Potter</u> series. They certainly took him a long time to finish, but he stuck with them because he loved the world that Rowling had created. If a book relates directly to their lives, addresses themes that are immediately important to them, and portrays characters that are near their own age, teens are more likely to find a connection with it and want to read it. This positive connection is critical because it allows us to construct a learning environment, that fulfills our duty to the CCSS and helps encourage the behaviors of the independent reader.

We must say that providing reading of interest to modern teens is not about rejecting important works of literature, nor is it about simply catering to what might be considered the shallow, unrefined interests. It is, however, about finding the best possible tools to create the best possible learning environments. Readers stick with complex texts because something in the text speaks to them—some character, some conflict, some theme. Likewise, if a text is relevant and appealing, our students are likely to stick with it, even if it's complex. This phenomenon is what has allowed us to observe students in our lower-grade classrooms immersed in Orson Scott Card's *Ender's Game*—a fairly complex text perhaps better suited to older readers—because they found the story and characters so relevant and compelling. We cannot create independent, college-ready readers if we continue to allow tradition to lead us away from works that are of most interest and relevance to the teen readers we are trying to reach.

Experience

What outside experience or knowledge does the reader bring to this book? How can I capitalize on my students' previous experiences in life and with other texts to build the ideal learning environment?

Something magical happens when we find a text that is just right for us. Teachers often think that because they love a text or have had a positive experience with it, the students they teach will have the same experience. This, however, is not always the case; every person will bring his or her own life experiences and prior reading experiences to the text, and these will automatically color any text he or she reads. We have had many experiences with teachers who have had a very personal connection to a text but when teaching that text find their students have no connection to it. You may have also had the experience where you loved a book, but when your friends read it, you find that they do not like it. These simple examples show, as Rosenblatt (1995) and Bleich (1975) contend, that what a reader brings to a book is just as important as what the text has to offer. Since we don't read in a vacuum, everything we read is impacted by our previous experiences and knowledge. Being able to comprehend a complex text depends, then, as much or more on our ability to understand the context of the text as it does on our ability to decode the individual words.

The reader's own experience is one element that will often provide an entry to a book and keep a teen reading until the end. For example, the daughter of one of the authors found a connection to a book recommended to her by her English teacher, *The Curious Incident of the Dog in the Nighttime* by Mark Haddon. She came home from school, curious whether her dad thought she would enjoy the book. Having read it himself, he could tell her that although it was a book written for adults, it was popular with a lot of teenagers (it won the Alex award from YALSA, an award recognizing adult books that appeals to teens). He cautioned her that while it dealt with the story of a young boy with autism and was very well written, some of the language was strong and some of the content may not be what she was used to reading. She ended up reading the book and enjoying it. Now, she is not autistic herself, and so at first this book might not seem to tap into her own interests; at the time she read the book, however, she had just finished a group project where she had worked with an autistic boy. This experience did pique her interest, and, in part, she read the book because of its exploration of autism.

This teen usually prefers to read books by authors such as Wendy Maas or Wendelin Van Draanen; in fact, the last book she had read before reading Haddon's was Van Draanen's *The Running Dream*—a book that she absolutely loved. Like the protagonist in *The Running Dream*, she is a runner and an athlete and had much else in common with the main character. The books that she usually reads feature protagonists and situations that are closer to what she is familiar with in her lived experiences. However, a book like Haddon's allowed her to explore a world that she was unfamiliar with and wanted to know more about. In discussions the author had with his daughter about this book, it became clear that she found connections to Haddon's autistic main character and to his quest for his mother. Even though the book's characters and settings may have been removed from her immediate experience, she still found relevance in the themes and ideas explored by the novel.

This example shows that connections made through reflected experiences as well as expanded experiences are very important to teens. But in order to stick with a book, in order for the book to have a meaning for teens, they still must be able to relate to the characters, the themes, even the conflicts of the book. *Harry Potter* certainly explores settings and faces conflicts that our teens will never literally experience for themselves. But Potter's feelings of inadequacy, his doubts about his role in the society of wizards, his efforts to prove himself—these are elements that are very familiar to many teens and speak to their experiences. As teachers and librarians helping students make choices about their reading, we should recognize that one-to-one matches of experiences and book content may not happen, but that good matches will provide teen readers with relevant characters and themes while at the same time allowing them to explore unfamiliar territory. Finding the balance between texts that speak to the experiences the readers already bring and those texts that require them to build entirely new experiences is the challenge we must address for each of our readers.

Motivation

What motivational factors should I consider when selecting texts? Will my students be motivated to read this text? How can I capitalize on my students' reading motivations to build the ideal learning environment?

The psychological concept of motivation is very complex, and even after decades of research and philosophizing, it is still often difficult to determine what motivates people to read or not to read or what motivates them to enjoy one text over another. We do know that motivated readers choose to read more, have higher reading achievement, and enjoy their experiences with books a great deal (Ulper, 2011; Wilson & Kelley, 2010). Also apparent from the research is that a lack of motivation can prevent us from engaging in tasks; for poor, reluctant, or struggling readers, their lack of motivation for reading means they tend to do less of it than most other groups of students (Allington, 2012). And even if a person is generally motivated, this may not carry over to all times and situations. So for even the most proficient and motivated reader there can be a lack of motivation to read even the most simple text if he or she fails to see that it will serve a useful purpose. A text that's too complex for this reader will only exacerbate this problem. As professionals we can use these understandings to our advantage by selecting texts and creating conditions that will be the most motivating to our students.

We have all seen those great movies where a dynamic teacher motivates a class to greatness. In our experience, we have seen teachers who will never be lauded on the big screen, but whose passion and love for literature motivate their students to tackle even the most complex texts. However, a teacher's passion can only go so far, and if we could tap into students' own motivations, we might have a better time of it. Professionals, then, must not rely on their own passion alone but find things that both they and their students are motivated to engage in; this combination makes for the most ideal teaching and learning conditions.

Without a doubt, using young adult literature in the classroom can be motivational for both teacher and student. Studies have shown that both engagement with reading and motivation to read increase when adolescents read young adult novels. They have also clearly shown that students will choose to read young adult books over the works traditionally included in the canon (Bushman, 1997; Scherff & Groenke, 2009). These results suggest that young adult books will be significantly more motivational to students than any other book and that reading these books can help students build the intrinsic motivation they need as independent readers.

Sadly, we often encounter professionals who don't always pick the types of books that engage and motivate their readers. We often discount the types of reading that many teens like to do, disregarding their books in favor of those we feel more worthy. When we do this we are not only discounting students as individuals but also discounting what may be their own intrinsic connection to reading. Student engagement offers the best route to independent reading, and if we discount teens and their reading though these actions, we may never be able to engage them enough to create college-ready readers. As instructors of literature today we have so many choices of books that can engage readers that we must keep in mind that selecting the right texts can be a powerful motivating tool.

The good readers we outlined earlier are essentially those readers who have developed lifelong literacy habits; an important part of our job is to create environments that help nurture these habits. One of the most significant ways we can build these habits is to match the right reader with the right text. We often tell our students that a nonreader is just a reader who has not found the right book yet. If we find the right book that matches a reader's developmental needs, individual makeup, and capitalizes on their interest, motivation, and experience, we have addressed the reader fully in our complexity analysis. When a reader finds the right text, it is then easier for teachers to move past the text itself and engage in the complexities of it required by the CCSS; we are better able to interpret words, analyze structure and theme, and create critically engaged readers when we do not have to spend time initially motivating students to read or providing scaffolding for overly complex forms. As the CCSS considers the reader to be fundamental to our choice of complex texts, all professionals should look closely at their readers to determine which texts are going to be the right ones. We contend that since all of our readers are young adults, when considering the reader dimension, young adult texts will always be the best choice not only for the CCSS as a whole but for our students as individuals as well.

Task Dimensions

How will the tasks I select impact the complexity of a text? How will my tasks provide the necessary scaffolding for my students' comprehension of a complex text? How can I make connections or expand the connections that a reader makes from a book to their world with the tasks I select? How will my pedagogy support or detract from the outcomes I expect?

There is no doubt that much of our professional training has been directed to helping us create the types of classroom and learning experiences that the task dimension of the CCSS refers to. We have had courses on how to create lesson plans and units, we have observed other teachers, and we have studied books and journals that show us new techniques. We have the foundations that are necessary to show us how to select a text, design a thematic unit, build assessments that test our students' knowledge, and take a standard, create a learning outcome, to finally select activities that express that outcome. With the implementation of the CCSS, this process will not significantly change; it is only the standards that we seek to meet that are different.

In our view, task dimensions are fully dependent upon one's overall theory of pedagogy. That is why in part two of this book we will fully outline our own application of the model of inquiry learning. We will show how this model can be used with complex young adult texts in conjunction with the CCSS standards to plan for and create ideal learning environments. So for this part of the discussion we are not going to outline the things you could glean from your training or the rest of this book. Instead, we would like to outline some important general guidelines that we should take note of when considering the task dimension of the three-part model of text complexity.

A text's complexity level can change depending on the type of task used   In a classroom, we do not engage with a text in isolation, and a text's level of complexity may change depending upon how the text is used in an instructional situation. For example, if we choose to use only excerpts of a text, even the most complex text can be made less complex. If we choose to use a book for whole-class, assigned reading, because of the makeup of the class we may be forced to choose a book that will not be as complex as we would like for some readers. The essential questions we pose as we create a unit as well as the focus and complexity of each individual task we use in any unit can significantly impact the complexity rating of a text. If we select a complex theme such as forgiveness, for instance, even a less complex text can rise to higher levels of complexity when we consider it within the context of that complex theme. We cannot assume, then, that every text will hold its complexity level across time and situations. Here, our professional experience is very important as it is only though a deep analysis of each text and task situation that we can match the right texts to the right situations with the appropriate level of complexity.

Scaffolding will be necessary at times for all readers   Any professional is aware of the great diversity of adolescents that enter our classrooms each year; from such diversity comes the challenge of a range of skill levels in any given set of students. From those who are confident to those who need support or are struggling, no two readers will be alike, and, as we've discussed earlier in this chapter, no two readers will also have the same experiences to engage the knowledge demands of every text. Because of this, all readers will need support and scaffolding of texts at one time or another.

The CCSS takes special note of struggling or reluctant readers' need for support, but even the most competent readers will need intervention at one time or another. The building of reading skills is not a linear process, and as even the best readers move to higher complexities they are bound to need help. As we design tasks, we should ensure that we provide the necessary scaffolding and background knowledge for students. Since high levels of frustration can prevent readers from being motivated to read, we need to ensure that the right information is given at the right time so that the text is at a complexity level that will not send readers out of their comfort zone.

The task of scaffolding so that the readers' experience and the knowledge demands of a text match can be accomplished in many ways. For us, however, one of the best ways to do this is to make connections. We have found that the more connections we can make to an individual text—to the reader, to other texts, to the world, and outside experiences—the easier it is to engage readers in a text and provide the necessary scaffolding. This technique will help us address the knowledge demands the text makes on the reader by providing much-needed context and support. This process of making connections also raises the rigor of our instruction. The more connections a text has, the more depth and complexity we can achieve in our instruction. What we want here is to have texts engage in conversation with one another, the world we live in, and the reader. If we begin to expand the texts to encompass this broader context, we are automatically making the text and our instruction of it more rigorous. Especially when we are teaching a text that requires a lot of background knowledge, having two texts that speak to the same theme or situation can provide the support our students may need. Many of us have been doing this for some time as we make connections between young adult novels and other canonical texts. However, complex young adult books may need scaffolding, and techniques such as pairing two young adult books or reading nonfiction texts alongside a novel will be successful ways to develop understanding.

In addition, we can also respond to the call of the CCSS to include more informational texts by making connections between fiction and nonfiction. Integration of nonfiction works that represent other disciplines is one of the best ways to build experience and fulfill knowledge demands. The kind of integration we are looking at here may not really be a new way of thinking, but if we contextualize it according to the CCSS demands for increased levels of informational texts across the content areas, it opens up all kinds of possibilities. As we put all kinds of texts together, including even multimodal texts and other nonbook formats, we are better able to create the scaffolding environments our students need as well as encourage the behaviors that will lead to independent reading.

Critical analysis of our pedagogy is necessary to ensure that we are fostering independent readers   In its overview of the research, the authors of the CCSS state that evidence has shown that current pedagogies have not done enough to build college-ready, independent readers. Their contention is that not only do we need to look at the texts we use to make them appropriately complex, but we also need to critically analyze our pedagogy to ensure that we are creating the type of readers our society needs.

As teachers, we often consider the positive benefits of teaching techniques, but we can fail to realize what the negative consequences can be. Just as doctors do, we need to have as our motto: "Do no harm." This suggests continually examining our techniques critically to determine any potential negative outcomes and whether the positive outcomes outweigh the negative. For example, we may assign the whole class to read a single text together. While there are many potential positive outcomes to this approach (such as opportunities for collaborative work or more efficient support from the teacher), we also need to consider that assigning books may have some negative effects as well: Assigning books does not help students build necessary habits of learning to choose books for themselves, and assigned books may not match well with readers, thus perhaps dampening motivation or interest. This can also lead to a lack of enthusiasm for reading itself, which does not foster the conditions that build lifelong readers.

One of the authors finds these elements so negative that she no longer assigns whole-class reading, instead using a genre approach with guided questioning around thematic units so that all students get to choose every book they read in her classes. With this technique she finds that she reaches the diverse needs of students and allows for differing tastes and ideas. She has also found that discussions are deeper when there are lots of examples to draw on, her class is more enthusiastic, and her students are reading more than ever as they discover new books that their peers are passionate about. This may be quite a radical approach for many, and we acknowledge that it may not work for everyone. However, we emphasize that no matter the approach, it is imperative that we take a critical look at our methods. If we look critically at the reasons for a pedagogical choice, such as assigning whole-class reading, we may find the positive outcomes outweigh this negative or that the only way to achieve one outcome is through a certain technique, so it must be used. When our choices may be constrained, our critical eye will help us consider how to build something else into our curriculum that helps our students build the skills and habits that may not be fostered by other techniques.

No matter what pedagogy, activity, or task we choose, there will always be a weighing of positive or negative potential outcomes. For us, fundamental to this process is looking closely at the behaviors of real readers. We then must ask ourselves if these are the habits exhibited by these readers in our classrooms. If our own readers are not exemplars of the types of readers we are trying to build within the context of the CCSS, then we need to find activities and tasks that do build these habits. We will meet the expectations of the CCSS if our pedagogy:

- Helps students learn to love to read by building, lifelong reading habits
- Teaches our students how to successfully select, evaluate, and navigate texts
- Helps them to apply comprehension and vocabulary strategies independently
- Helps them to develop their own tastes and abilities
- Gives them authentic applications of texts and broadens their experiences
- Shows students how to synthesize their experiences and how to make connections between their own experiences and their reading

We contend that we are not doing the best that we can if our pedagogy is filled with excessively complex texts that have no applicability to today's teens and are further dried out by picking them apart only to complete exercises that look like busywork. Sadly, we seem to be building readers like the young women one author encountered in one of her courses who indicated to her with great pride that she had never read a book for pleasure since fourth grade. Or another freshman student who needed hours of intervention to help him write a two-page personal response to a scholarly article. Now is the time then to critically analyze our pedagogy and approaches to ensure that we are building the best environments that will help us fulfill the criteria of the CCSS. In this atmosphere of change we encourage you to take a few risks and try something new. We have certainly found that our application of the CCSS has taken us out of our comfort zones as well.

Conclusion

We have looked at each of the dimensions for analyzing text complexity according to the three-tiered model of text complexity. For us the exciting thing is that this model allows us to articulately defend and use a great variety of texts in our classrooms, including young adult literature. Now with a full vision of what the model is and how its different elements work together to provide us a comprehensive definition of complexity, our next step is to apply our knowledge to the evaluation of individual texts, a process that we will model for you in our next chapter.

Bibliography

Allington, R. L. (2012). *What really matters for struggling readers: Designing research-based programs* (3rd ed.). Boston, MA: Pearson.

Bauerlein, M. (2010). The new bibliophobes. *Educational Horizons, 88*(2), 84–91.

Bleich, D. (1975). *Readings and feelings: An introduction to subjective criticism.* Urbana, IL: National Council of Teachers of English.

Broz, W. J. (2011). Not reading: The 800-pound mockingbird in the classroom. *English Journal, 100*(5), 15–20.

Bushman, J. H. (1997). Young adult literature in the classroom—or is it? *English Journal, 86*(3), 35–40.

Donelson, K. L., & Nilsen, A. P. (2005). *Literature for today's young adults* (7th ed.). Boston, MA: Pearson/ Allyn & Bacon.

Eccles, J. S. (2004). Schools, academic motivation, and stage-environment fit. In R. M. Lerner & L. Steinberg (Eds.), *Handbook of adolescent psychology* (2nd ed., pp. 125–153). Hoboken, NJ: Wiley.

Erikson, E. (1968). *Identity, youth and crisis.* New York: Norton.

Gallagher, K. (2009). *Readicide: How schools are killing reading and what you can do about it.* Portland, ME: Stenhouse Publishers.

Gallo, D. R. (2001). How classics create an aliterate society. *English Journal, 90*(3), 33–39.

Havighurst, R. J. (1972). *Developmental tasks and education* (3rd ed.). New York, NY: David McKay Co.

Irwin, J. W., & Davis, C. A. (1980). Assessing readability: The checklist approach. *Journal of Reading, 24*(2), 124–130.

Lenters, K. (2006). Resistance, struggle, and the adolescent reader. *Journal of Adolescent & Adult Literacy, 50*(2), 136–146.

Lesesne, T. (2003). *Making the match: The right book for the right reader at the right time, grades 4-12.* Portland, ME: Stenhouse Publishers.

Piaget, J. (1955). *The language and thought of the child.* New York, NY: Meridian Books.

Reeves, A. R. (2004). *Adolescents talk about reading: Exploring resistance to and engagement with text.* Newark, DE: International Reading Association.

Rosenblatt, L. M. (1995). *Literature as exploration.* New York, NY: Modern Language Association of America.

Santoli, S. P., & Wagner, M. E. (2004). Promoting young adult literature: The other "real" literature. *American Secondary Education, 33*(1), 65.

Scales, P. C., & Leffert, N. (2004). *Developmental assets: A synthesis of the scientific research on adolescent development* (2nd ed.). Minneapolis, MN: Search Institute.

Scherff, L., & Groenke, S. (2009). Young adult literature in today's classroom. *English Leadership Quarterly, 31*(4), 1–3.

Smith, M. W., & Wilhelm, J. D. (2002). *Reading don't fix no Chevys: Literacy in the lives of young men.* Portsmouth, NH: Heinemann.

Steinberg, L., & Sherk, S. D. (2006). *Adolescence.* In J. Wilson, & K. Krapp (Eds.), *Gale encyclopedia of childrens' health: Infancy through adolescence* (pp. 32–36). Detroit, MI: Gale.

Trotsky, L. (2005). *Literature and revolution.* Edited by William Keach. Chicago, IL: Haymarket Books.

Ulper, H. (2011). The motivational factors for reading in terms of students. *Educational Sciences: Theory and Practice, 11*(2), 954–960.

Understanding adolescent brain development. (2011). In A. L. Sutton (Ed.), *Adolescent health sourcebook* (3rd ed., pp. 21–26). Detroit, MI: Omnigraphics. Retrieved Jan. 8, 2012 from Gale Virtual Reference Library.

Vygotsky, L. S. (1962). *Thought and language.* Edited and translated by E. Hanfmann and G. Vakar. Cambridge, MA: MIT Press.

Weinberger, D. R., Elvevag, B., & Giedd, J. N. (2005). *The adolescent brain: A work in progress.* Washington, DC: The National Campaign to Prevent Teen Pregnancy. Retrieved from: http://www.the nationalcampaign.org/resources/pdf/BRAIN.pdf.

Wilson, N. S., & Kelley, M. J. (2010). Are avid readers lurking in your language arts classroom? Myths of the avid adolescent reader. *Reading Horizons, 50*(2), 99–112.

Chapter 6

Applying the Three-Tiered Model of Text Complexity

Introduction

The practical application of the three-tiered model of text complexity to classroom situations now leads us to concretely apply the model to the evaluation of individual texts. We have formulated an approach for articulating the complexity of different aspects of a text around our own structure. However, we realize this process can happen in many ways, and in fact, many districts have already created their own formats. While we feel the format we give is more comprehensive and provides a better vision than those based on the limited points of the CCSS, we encourage individuals to adapt our ideas and applications to any format required by their own organizations. In addition, while our main purpose here is to analyze young adult literature, this format could be used to defend all types of books including adult novels or even classic works. No matter how you use, change, or apply our format, we hope that it will provide you with the basics you need to not only analyze but defend the complexity of a variety of books for use in your classrooms.

Many may just be able to judge works on a more basic or cursory level; however, we feel that in order to apply the CCSS it is imperative to do a comprehensive analysis of work. A comprehensive overview of a text is an essential part of the planning process for individual teachers. In order to select the right texts for the right readers so we can provide the perfect scaffold to bring students to progressively higher levels of text complexity, we must fully understand the entire text. Since every text has strengths and weaknesses, a comprehensive view of a text will help us to pinpoint the strengths of a text so we can then match those strengths to the right reader and the right tasks. We also believe that conducting a compressive analysis is important for collaboration and communication. A comprehensive analysis will be a collaborative tool that cooperating teachers can easily use to find points of agreement or disagreement around texts. These forms can also be used to communicate concretely to other teachers in different content areas or to administration or governing boards in very specific terms the complexity of any individual title. Using this complete analysis as a basis for defending the texts we select will help us to demonstrate our professional expertise and help others see the strength of young adult literature.

Box 6.1 Likert Scale For Middle and High School Complexity

Lower Complexity	Midrange Complexity	High Complexity

1	2	3	4	5

Analysis Form

To facilitate our comprehensive analysis, we have developed an analysis form that is designed to complement the structure we have outlined in the previous chapters. To that effect there are three main sections to the form: quantitative, qualitative, and reader and task. The quantitative section provides space to record the results of a variety of quantitative readability measures; we encourage you to include as many or as few measures you see as needful. In the qualitative and reader and task sections, we have pinpointed the various sections that address the essential questions we asked in the previous chapters. For each section we provide a space to record answers, notes, and ideas about those questions. The important things to record here are those issues that are of any importance in making the text more or less complex.

In these sections we have also provided a column for a numerical rating. We find that while narrative is fine, we also want a shorthand way to convey the relative location of a text on a complexity scale for each section. Given the fact that Likert scales are very common and give us a quick notation of where an item falls on that scale, we chose to add this notation into our form (see box 6.1).

We assume that all the books we look at will fall into the complexity band for middle and high school students; our rating, then, is not based on a vision of a complexity from preschool on up but a vision of grades 6–12. When we give a book a rating of one (1), we do not mean to suggest that this book is not complex, but rather that on the 6–12 band, it will fall on the lower end, making it more complex on a 6th-grade level but not a 12th-grade one. Also, this rating is not meant to provide a numerical consolidation that can be added to achieve an overall score for the book; it is simply meant to be a shorthand notation that explains the narrative. We found the application of the Likert scale to be useful for two reasons. First, it allows a quick skimming of the form, so you or others can focus on important points without having to read the entire text. Second, it allows us to clearly see which individual areas have stronger indications for complexity. This is especially important as we plan curriculum since in this process we will want to match books with tasks. In this matching process, books with higher complexity in one area will be more suited to an instructional focus in that same area, and our shorthand rating allows us to see this quickly. If our instructional focus is theme, then a book rated high with a 4 or 5 in theme under levels of meaning will be particularly appropriate for a task that delves into thematic construction.

At the end of the form we have included a box for overall assessment. This box will allow you to summarize your findings and give a comprehensive recommendation for complexity. This section can also be used to indicate what grade levels you may feel this text will be appropriate for. In appendix A we have included a blank copy of the form for you to utilize in your own analysis.

Analysis Models

To more fully communicate how the principles we have outlined and the form we have created can be applied to young adult literature, we will model the process for you with the analysis of six young adult books. This process certainly has an element of subjectivity to it, and we know that others may judge the texts differently and come to different conclusions than we have. You will note that both authors completed this process for a set of books, so even the differences in the way we two individuals approached the process can be seen in our examples. However, we hope that this process will help you get inside our heads a little as we show you how we look at and analyze books. Certainly these examples can provide a pattern for your own analysis of other texts, but we also encourage you to use these examples to communicate with others a strong argument for the complexity of these titles. While we could have conducted this analysis on an extraordinary number of books, we focused our selections on more modern titles of young adult literature; we also selected our own exemplar titles to cover a wide range of genres. We further sought to include a wide range of interest designations, trying to include boy-friendly books and books from multicultural perspectives, for instance. In addition, these books represent a range of complexity levels that will be appropriate for both middle and high schools.

To assist you in connecting these ideas to the common core, we offer in some parts of our analysis various Common Core anchor standards that apply to the situations we are speaking of. While the grade-level standards can be more specific, we have chosen to only represent the anchor standards in an effort to remain more open about grade levels to which these could apply. When necessary to express the standards, we use a code. The letter indicates the type of anchor standard (R=Reading; W=Writing; S=Speaking; L=Listening), and the number after the letter correlates with the number 1–10 of the anchor standard. So, for example, an R1 indicates reading anchor standard one, which revolves around making inferences and addressing areas of uncertainty.

American Born Chinese by Gene Luen Yang

Quantitative Dimensions of Text Complexity

Lexile	GN530L (2–3 text complexity grade band)
ATOS	3.3 (3rd Grade) Middle-grade+ interest level
Flesch-Kincaid Grade Level	5.2 (5th Grade)
Coleman-Liau	8 (8th Grade)
SMOG	6.5 (7th Grade)
Gunning Fog	7 (fairly easy to read)
Dale-Chall	7.79 (9–10th Grade)

Qualitative Dimensions of Text Complexity

Format

	Comments	Rating
Size	The book is 6″ × 8.5″; graphic novels come in many sizes and there really isn't a standard size or set of sizes for these books. It has 240 pages, and while this is on the lower end for novel length, it is on the higher end for graphic novels, so this is the standard by which it should be judged.	3
Font	The font in this book is designed to mimic handwriting, a common choice in graphic novels. It is consistent throughout the novel, with the same font being used for dialogue/thought bubbles as well as narrator boxes. Words are bolded more frequently in graphic novels to show emphasis, and this book is no exception. The font uses only uppercase letters, another element common to the graphic novel genre.	4
Layout	The book follows the standard layout conventions for the graphic novel—with frames (containing images and text) and gutters (the blank space between frames) arranged in sequential order. The number of frames per page will vary as the sizes of frames vary. The "reading" of these frames poses a challenge to readers unfamiliar with the genre of the graphic novel.	5
Construction	Like most graphic novels, this is printed on high-quality paper to allow the color and drawings to be sharp and vivid. All of the visuals in this book are in color.	3
Organization	The story is organized through the use of panels displaying images and accompanying text boxes to reveal dialogue, thought, or narrative commentary. This is, of course, quite different from the way novels or short stories are typically organized, and that means a greater degree of complexity for *American Born Chinese*.	5

	Comments	Rating
	In addition, the three plot lines present throughout the story (see below for more information) play into the organizational scheme. The three lines are clearly distinguished (until the end of the novel) by separating them in the book—not into chapters, but into separate sections demarcated by a separate page with a small icon in red (a monkey, Jin, or Chin-Kee, depending on the focus of the section). In addition, a unique Chinese icon appears along the top of each page in each section—one icon for each of the three main story lines. Finally, each section makes use of a subtly unique color scheme. While these cues help clue the reader into the focus of each section, especially relating to the setting and main characters, the organization is still necessarily complex.	
Illustrations	Illustrations are critical to this kind of text. While words still convey dialogue, characters' thoughts, and narrative commentary, much information is contained in the visuals that accompany the words. Characters' reactions, events in the plot, and contextual information about setting will all be conveyed almost exclusively through images. This makes this novel more complex in a unique way, as readers must make many inferences from the visual images rather than relying on the words in the text. In addition, readers must learn to "read" the visual sequence of panels in this novel. Attending to the way panels are organized and the gutters that indicate separation between panels is crucial to understanding which panels should be read in which order. Subtle clues in the sizes of panels and their arrangement can have significance within the context of the story. And subtle visual clues (such as the "laugh track" accompanying some of the panels featuring cousin Chin-Kee) are meant to convey important meanings to the reader.	5

Audience

Comments	Rating
ATOS places this book on a middle-grade+ interest level, although our experience suggests a wider range of interests, up through and including older teens. Booksellers indicate that this work is for ages 12 and up, and review sources indicate ages 13 and up, 15 to adult, as well as 12 to 18. The characters represent a variety of age ranges: one is in middle school and the other is a little older teen. These measures seem to fall all along the same lines, indicating that the text is aimed at middle school teens ages 13–15. The intended audience and the audience that will enjoy the text are very compatible.	3

Levels of Meaning

	Comments	Rating
Theme	The theme of the book is largely about finding one's own identity, especially in terms of embracing one's roots. While this may seem to be more applicable to immigrant or ethnic minority readers, there are clear parallels for all of us. Everyone has elements of their background that they might have reason to feel ashamed of, and the conclusions that Danny/Jin reach in the book can apply to a wide range of readers. This theme is explored first through the Monkey God, who wants to throw off the limitations of being a monkey and rise above them; only when he realizes that he can be proud of this aspect of himself does he find happiness and satisfaction. A similar progression is played out for Danny/Jin, and reinforced by the visit of Chin-Kee and his interactions with Wei-Chen. The final confrontation with Chin-Kee and the revelations that follow seem to put Danny/Jin on a healthier path.	3
Conflict	Given the three story lines, the conflicts range appropriately. For the Monkey God, the conflicts seem at first to be largely external: he is fighting for recognition and equality among the other gods. As his journey progresses, though, it becomes clear that the conflict is internal as he struggles to come to terms with his own identity. For Jin (or Danny, the name for his Americanized self), the conflicts follow a similar pattern. Early on, it seems he's largely in conflict with external cultural forces as he tries to fit in to American society. As time passes and we see Danny—the representation of Jin's embracing of American culture—the conflict shifts to be more internal as Jin/Danny fights against the heritage and culture he has worked so hard to abandon (partly embodied by the stereotypical Chin-Kee). The conflicts in the book are sophisticated and not clearly seen on a casual read. They represent common, almost archetypal conflicts presented in a host of immigrant stories and are, as such, authentic in their multiple layers and shifting nature.	3
Connections	As many of us have felt left out or have experienced the need to fit in and the sacrifices we might make to do so, there are many straightforward connections to make to this story. Other immigrant stories (many of which could fall into the informational text category) and even other stories about teens who don't fit it would make appropriate connections to this book. Another obvious connection would be to the original Monkey God myth from Chinese folklore, as it informs heavily the first part of the book.	3

Structure

	Comments	Rating
Setting	The setting of the Jin and Danny story lines in the book is modern and the action of the story takes place in mostly recognizable settings. The infusion of Asian culture will be unfamiliar to some students, but shouldn't be a stumbling block for comprehension or enjoyment of the book. The monkey god story line has a far different setting, of course, with more mythical elements. Some familiarity with the original legend might be helpful, but Yang has provided enough background and clues within the telling of the story that this shouldn't prove too challenging for most readers.	3
Plot	There are three story lines followed in the book, seemingly unrelated at first. The book opens with a retelling of an ancient Chinese myth about a monkey who acquires supernatural powers by studying the Tao, challenges the gods, and is buried under a mountain of stone as punishment; later he accompanies a monk on a journey collecting sacred texts. This narrative is threaded between two other stories—again, seemingly unrelated—about a Chinese American boy named Jin Wang and an American boy named Danny who has a Chinese cousin. The one narrative details Jin's awkward (and often unsuccessful) attempts at trying to embrace American culture and fit into American teenage social groups; the second details Danny's embarrassment at his cousin's strange cultural habits. The three narratives come together at the end of the novel as we find that Danny and Jin are the same person—Danny is the typical American boy that Jin wants to transform into, abandoning his Chinese culture and heritage. Chin-Kee reveals himself as the Monkey King, sent to help Jin/Danny embrace his cultural roots and identity. These narrative threads are challenging to follow as the story progresses, and this sophisticated technique adds a real layer of complexity to the book. The resolution at the end actually encourages a second reading through, since events and dialogue mean different things in the context of what's revealed by the novel's ending. Complex parallels between the monkey's journey to self-discovery (via accepting his monkey nature) and Jin/Danny's own evolving sense of identity may not be clear from the first read.	5
Character	The main characters in the novel are the monkey god from Chinese legends, Jin Wang/Danny, cousin Chin-Kee, and Wei-Chen (a boy who emigrates from Taiwan). Minor characters include some high school students, including love interests for Jin/Danny (Amelia/Melanie) and Wei-Chen (Suzy Nakamura). Jin/Danny is perhaps the most important character in the novel, and he is painted in complex and authentic strokes. His inner	4

(continued)

	Comments	Rating
	conflicts about culture, identity, and fitting in are realistically portrayed and explored in satisfying depth. This treatment is both aided and complexified by Yang's choice to portray these conflicting sides as separate people. The monkey god provides an important foil for Jin as his portrayal mirrors Jin's, but he shows an example of the path to self-realization through accepting those parts of us we can't change. Yang modernizes the ancient Chinese legend, giving the monkey a "modern" attitude and resistance to the status quo and to those who do not want to accept him for who he is. Wei-Chen also provides something of a foil as he shows another, less satisfactory, path to dealing with the challenges that Jin faces. Their renewed friendship at the end of the novel suggests important developments in Jin's character. The cousin, Chin-Kee, presented in Danny's story line is an embodiment of all the American stereotypes of Chinese people and culture. He speaks with a strange accent, eats strange food, and boldly shares unusual or potentially offensive ideas. The fact that he's such an embarrassment to Danny symbolizes Jin's own struggle with what he sees as embarrassing about his Chinese heritage. While Chin-Kee might seem a simple, flat stereotype, he is actually a complex feature of the text in the way he mirrors Jin's perception of his heritage.	
Point of View	The points of view represented in the story vary based on the narrative thread under focus. Yang's decision to divide Jin/Danny's two points of view into separate characters actually helps consider them in isolation. But once we discover that these two are one and the same character, some reconciliation of the two views is necessary. The introduction at the end of the story of the monkey god's point of view, which serves in part to tie together the disparate threads of the book, forces even more synthesis on the reader. These multiple points of view provide additional complexity for the text.	4

Language Conventions

	Comments	Rating
Style and Tone	Since the book consists primarily of dialogue, with the small exceptions of some narrative during the Monkey God's tales, the style is largely a conversational one, which makes the text itself relatively less complex. The visuals also must count here toward complexity, though, and the color schemes used in the different stories and even the "laugh track" employed during the Chin-Kee stages make for a more sophisticated style.	4

	Comments	Rating
Literary Devices	Given the dominance of dialogue, there are few instances of figurative language in the text, a common literary device. The Monkey God story provides a clear analogy to Jin/Danny's story, however, even though this doesn't become clear until later in the book. Chin-Kee also serves as a symbolic character, representing Jin/Danny's struggles with his culture in the light of his seemingly conflicting desire to embrace American culture. These uses of literary devices, although few, are pretty sophisticated.	4

Knowledge Demands

Comments	Rating
This book represents some significant knowledge demands for readers. Aside from the clear demands of reading a visual text that relies as much on colors and composition as it does on words, there is also the use of multiple story lines to deal with. Readers will need to keep track of these story lines and, eventually, see how they come together in meaningful ways at the same time as they're learning to attend to visual elements.	4

Reader Dimensions of Text Complexity

Envisioning Independent Readers

Comments	Rating
Independent readers need to be able to read more than traditional print genres, and the graphic novel format of this book can help them develop some important skills in visual literacy. In addition, the presence of the "gutter" (the blank space in between frames in a graphic novel) requires inferential thinking (R1), an important skill that independent readers must develop. The three interconnected story lines in the book also can help students develop skills in keeping track of multiple threads and making connections between them. Finally, independent readers read widely, and about a variety of others' experiences, which this book allows them to do in a motivating context.	3

The Adolescent Reader

	Comments	Rating
Adolescent Development	Adolescents are on a quest for their identity—a major part of what it means to be an adolescent is to shape that eventual adult identity through formative experiences in teenage years. Such is the case, too, for Danny/Jin and even the Monkey God, as they seek to assert themselves and establish a role in the larger society. These issues explored in the text are very relevant to most teenagers in this stage of life, but perhaps even more so for older teenagers who are about to step more formally into an adult world.	3

(continued)

From *Integrating Young Adult Literature through the Common Core Standards* by Rachel L. Wadham and Jonathan W. Ostenson. Santa Barbara, CA: Libraries Unlimited. Copyright © 2013.

	Comments	Rating
Individual Makeup and Experience	Some individual students will find more to identify with in Jin/Danny or Wei-Chen because they too are immigrants or even from minority backgrounds; the book may be less complex to them. However, many students can sympathize with Danny's awkwardness, making the issues the book explores relatable and thus less complex to the majority of students.	3

The Reader's Aptitude:

	Comments	Rating
Interest	The visual elements of the text are likely to appeal to a wide range of teenagers, as evidenced in part by the rising popularity of this genre. The mythical elements of the Monkey God will appeal to a generation that's been fascinated by the Lord of the Rings and Harry Potter series, and the search for identity that Jin/Danny embarks on is one that most readers can relate to, even if they haven't been immigrants in the strictest sense of the word.	3
Experience	While a good number of students who read this book are unlikely to be first-generation immigrants, that should not stop them from connecting their own experiences with fitting in or feeling on the outside of social groups to Jin/Danny's problems. In terms of reading a visually complex text like this one, some of our readers will have experience, but the vast majority probably won't. This does add to the book's complexity, as we've outlined above.	3
Motivation	For some readers, motivation for reading a text like this may be lacking, given that they see "comic books" as a lesser form of literature. Others will find high motivation for a book like this because of its connections to the comic book tradition. We expect that the majority of readers would find the book at least initially compelling given its uniqueness and the draw of visual images in general. The story itself, though, with its clear connections to teenage issues, should motivate even reluctant readers once they get a taste of it. In addition, the "mystery" factor of how the three story lines will eventually unite may motivate other readers.	3

Task Dimensions of Text Complexity

Comments	Rating
Clear tasks associated with this text would be teaching skills in visual literacy; analyzing and interpreting the text's use of colors, the composition of individual frames, and the arrangement of frames will all be part of helping students comprehend the graphic novel. Since these are skills that are likely unfamiliar to most students, we should consider this text more complex. Common core connections include looking at content presented in diverse formats (R7) and analyzing the structure of the text (R5). In addition, this text provides an	4

Comments	Rating
opportunity to analyze how characters change and how events and conflicts work together to make that change (R3), consistent with the expectations of the common core. The nature of any of these tasks is likely to be more complex given the graphic novel format.	

Overall Assessment:

Comments
This text has a wide range of applicable bands. It would easily be used in any of the 8–12 grade complexity bands. Graphic novels are an exploding genre right now, and *American Born Chinese* represents some of the best writing that's being published in the genre. We live in an increasingly visual world, and our students need to be able to read visual images and texts as critically as anything in print. Having them read this book allows us to expose students to a wider variety of texts and teach them some skills that will be important for them as teens and adults. The thematic elements of the story are like icing on the cake—they are so relevant to our own students and explored in such a creative way that this book will likely be a favorite for many readers.

The Berlin Boxing Club by Robert Sharenow

Quantitative Dimensions of Text Complexity

Lexile	880L (4–5 text complexity grade band); Ages 14–18
ATOS	5.7 (5th/6th Grade) Middle-grade+ interest level
Flesch-Kincaid Grade Level	5.4 (5th Grade)
Coleman-Liau	8 (8th Grade)
SMOG	5.4 (5th Grade)
Gunning Fog	7.1 (fairly easy to read)
Dale-Chall	7.9 (9–10th Grade)

Qualitative Dimensions of Text Complexity

Format

	Comments	Rating
Size	The dimensions of the hardback edition are 8 ½″ × 5 ½″, which is typical for a novel. It has 404 pages, putting it on the higher end but not at the highest end of the spectrum, making this number fairly typical of a book of this type.	3
Font	No font type is indicated; however, the overall font is of a readable quality that is typical of many fonts used in novels. The majority of the font is standard throughout, but there is a significant use of an italic font as well. This font is used to differentiate German words used in the text. It is also used to set off a whole story that the main character is reading from outside the text. It is also used to indicate titles of works that are quoted. The author uses this font change in the same way one would use it to cite titles in a text but also uses it to show the change in context for things that are added by giving the reader clues to the foreign language and text additions.	3
Layout	Layout is as expected. The text block is typical, with ample margins and space between the lines. The text is spaced out so it is not densely packed, making it easier to read.	2
Construction	The paper and binding are of typical of a hardback book. The book is available in hardback, paperback, and as an e-book. This indicates that the publisher is committed to the title at a high level of quality.	2
Organization	The book is first organized into three parts that cover a span of years. The middle part (which covers three years) is the largest; the first (two years' coverage) and the last (one year coverage) are about equal. Each part is introduced with a quote from a historical	4

	Comments	Rating
	document. In the parts, the remainder is organized into unnumbered chapters. Each chapter is introduced with a title that foreshadows content in that chapter. While this arrangement into parts and chapters is standard, the author uses them in an unconventional way that indicates the time progression This nonstandard use of traditional organization raises the complexity level of the work.	
Illustrations	The novel contains line illustrations. The main character of the work aspires to be an artist, and these drawings come from him. They are cartoons, caricatures, and maps that he has drawn as part of his daily life. Thus the illustrations support the text by bringing visual images that are part of the story. However, they also add depth as they provide context to the character development, and especially in the case of the cartoons they provide outside commentary on the text by showing feelings that the main character does not express in the text.	4

Audience

Comments	Rating
The Lexile level indicates ages 14–18. ATOS puts it at a middle-grade+ level, which indicates upper grades such as eighth. Review sources indicate grades 7–10 and grades 6–9, and ages 11–18. The main character is 14, but because of the realities of war that he is dealing with, he often acts with insight and courage that could be considered beyond his years. There are other teen characters in the book as well as adult characters that support the main character. However, the point of view is entirely with the main character, so his age seems best in determining audience. The book does contain some rough content and frank descriptions of life during wartime, so this certainly would not be a book for a very young audience. Overall, the target audience seems to be ages 14 and up.	3

Levels of Meaning

	Comments	Rating
Theme	There are strong themes of the individual versus society in this book. Karl is placed in the middle of the Nazi campaigns even though he has never considered himself to be Jewish. The rights of an individual when a society is against them are an important part of how Karl looks at the world. There are also strong themes of growth in the book. As Karl goes though the events, he grows from a boy into a man. This growth is paralleled with his gaining strength through boxing, so there are good correspondences here between theme and character portrayal. There is also a strong theme that addresses the nature of courage. There are characters who show courage and those who don't, and they are not always	4

(continued)

From *Integrating Young Adult Literature through the Common Core Standards* by Rachel L. Wadham and Jonathan W. Ostenson. Santa Barbara, CA: Libraries Unlimited. Copyright © 2013.

	Comments	Rating
	the ones you would expect. These main themes are interconnected and provide good. potential for studying how themes shape characters and vice versa.	
Conflict	The main conflict is man versus society as Karl and others fight the Nazis. There are also man-versus-man conflicts. Karl has conflicts with his mentor Max as well as with his boxing rivals in the ring. These small conflicts support and foreshadow the broader societal conflict. This leads to internal conflict as Karl tries to figure out where he fits in this world and what he can do to protect himself and his family.	4
Connections	There are many direct text-to-world connections in this novel. As it is based in a historical time period, much of what is discussed is historically accurate. There are connections to real people such as Max Schmeling and to real boxing matches. Generally, both fiction and nonfiction on the war or the trials of the Jewish populations under the Nazi regime are easy matches to this novel. There are also great text-to-self connections as Karl's point of view is spot-on as a teenager. As he feels many of the same insecurities that teens feel, teen readers will be able to connect with him and to see his vision during these hard times. There are also great connections here for individuals who enjoy boxing.	4

Structure

	Comments	Rating
Setting	The novel is set in Berlin, Germany, 1934–1938. This setting will have basic familiarity with most students. The author does not spend a lot of time discussing the setting separately but lets the setting come out naturally as the plot progresses. Thus he uses only necessary details to describe the setting. While the individual locations in and around Berlin vary in the novel, the main location stays the same throughout. The setting by its nature has an impact on the main character and his emotional progression in the story as he grows from a boy to a man.	2
Plot	The plot is constructed to follow the exact timeline of the years it covers. The story progresses from year to year with no changes or flashbacks. However, the indication of time change is very vague. The novel covers a span of about five years, but the only indication of this change is at the beginning of the parts where the years are indicated. This gives the plot a natural flow that mimics real life, since the days and years seem to meld into one another very naturally. However, it adds to the complexity as one must pay attention to these markers to identify time. There are numerous small climaxes, such as Karl facing bullies and losing love, that build to a final climax, and the family's need	3

	Comments	Rating
	to escape. The progression is quite predictable, although the character and frame make the novel innovative and fresh. The ending offers a resolution but again, following a real-life pattern, we don't tie up all the ends. We don't know what happens to everyone as some are left behind and no information is given. This may be disconcerting for some, but it is this that makes the novel believable.	
Character	There are many characters in this book. Karl is the main character and dominates throughout. His family (father, mother, and sister) and his mentor Max are the next most dominant. There are many other characters that Karl interacts with who play minor roles. Karl is a multilayered character who progresses naturally though the novel. He is well drawn, and the emotions and reactions he has to the situations he is in are consistent with his characterization and the teenage point of view. There is a nice diversity of characters. We encounter many Jewish and German characters but also minorities such as a gay character and a character who stutters. These characters bring depth to the novel and allow Karl to grow in his understanding about the negative effect the Nazis have on a number of differences, not just religious differences. Characters are naturally described throughout, and only those details needed to describe them are used.	4
Point of View	The story is told from Karl's first-person point of view. While Karl's view alone does not embrace diversity, the fact that he encounters diverse characters brings in other points of view and allows him to change his own perspective. Karl's point of view is clearly a teenage one. His concerns are self-focused at first, but then as events progress, he becomes more outwardly focused. This is a natural teenage progression, and the characters and setting are made more approachable and realistic because of this authentic portrayal.	2

Language Conventions

	Comments	Rating
Style and Tone	The style of the text is very approachable. While the author uses details and devices to describe each structural element, they are not used to excess. While the text is richly told, it is not overdone. The author uses a combination of long and short sentences and relies on dialogue as well. This may be one of the reasons for the low quantitative ratings. The tone of the story is optimistic. Karl	2

(*continued*)

From *Integrating Young Adult Literature through the Common Core Standards* by Rachel L. Wadham and Jonathan W. Ostenson. Santa Barbara, CA: Libraries Unlimited. Copyright © 2013.

	Comments	Rating
	faces many challenges, but he is not jaded by them. The tone brings out his courage and strength in an approachable way.	
Literary Devices	The text uses typical devices such as simile and metaphor.. Again these are rich, innovative, and interesting, but they are not overdone, making the text very approachable. An important device the author uses is symbolism. He builds his character to look to other Jewish boxers and superheroes as symbols of courage and the power to overcome evil. These symbols are important to the main character and to the understanding of the theme of the story.	3

Knowledge Demands

Comments	Rating
The text is very self-contained. The context is very explicitly detailed for the reader, so not much information needs to be added before this text could be understood. Even those entirely unfamiliar with the events of the war would most likely be able to understand this title. However, as this is unlikely, everyone will most certainly bring the basic background knowledge needed. One of the strengths of this text is the possibility to take basic background knowledge and build it into something more. Most people will not know of the issues of race and boxing nor of the Schmeling/Louis fight that had much to do with issues of race relations and racial superiority. These themes and ideas, while touched on in the text, could be greatly expanded in a classroom setting.	2

Reader Dimensions of Text Complexity

Envisioning Independent Readers

Comments	Rating
There are strong text-to-self and text-to-world connections with this book. As such, it could be used to show readers how to make those connections. This text also has great potential to show readers how to respond to texts through written and multi-modal forms. Because readers are drawn to care about Karl and his struggles, they will find connections that will lead to enjoyment and engagement with this text and thus to things that will build important independent reading skills leading to lifelong habits. Also, because of the strong teen point of view and the addition of the boxing action, this text will have connections to struggling readers that can lead them to insights into how to read a text for pleasure.	3

The Adolescent Reader

	Comments	Rating
Adolescent Development	Karl's character delves into many typical developmental tasks such as building identity, developing autonomy, and defining a moral code. Despite the fact that readers will most likely never have experienced exactly what Karl experiences, they will be able to see themselves reflected in him. Karl's authentic progression from boy to man will also help teens to see outside themselves and to build new understandings of their own development.	4
Individual Makeup and Experience	Despite the historical and geographic context, this book has a universal appeal. Karl is a strong male character that will appeal to a broad base of both boys and girls. The approachable writing style makes it suitable for a variety of reader ability levels. This text will be appealing to many and matches the developmental level and interest level of the age group of readers it is targeting.	2

The Reader's Aptitude

	Comments	Rating
Interest	The historical setting will provide an avenue of interest to many readers. Also, the typical teen point of view will make this book of interest to a wider audience. The unique interest point for this book will be through the boxing angle. Those teens who enjoy sports, including boxing, will find connections to this element that they may not be able to find with other historical novels of the same period.	3
Experience	As noted, the knowledge demands for this title are low, but because of the time period we can expect that all readers will bring some background to the text that will help them understand the context. The boxing parts of the text are well described, but those with boxing experience will most likely find more depth there than those unfamiliar with the sport.	2
Motivation	A combination of historical fiction and sports literature, there are many avenues that can connect to a variety of readers' interests, helping them to be motivated to read this text. The main character is very interesting, and readers will be easily drawn into his world. Thus they will be motivated to continue reading to see how he grows and faces challenges. Also, because he represents a teen at a solid developmental level, teens will also be motivated by the connections to themselves to see the text though to the end.	3

Task Dimensions of Text Complexity

Comments	Rating
This text shows strong integration of its structural elements, and as such, it would have strong connections to reading anchor standard two when used with activities that show how the relationship of literary elements progresses over the course of a text to create theme (R2). For task connections, however, this book's strongest links are to the history it presents. There are numerous nonfiction texts that could be paired with this title (*Hitler Youth* by Bartoletti, for example) (R8, R9). There are also numerous other fictional novels that could be used in conjunction with this one to apply reading anchor standard 10, which calls for us to analyze how two or more authors write about the same subject using two or more texts from the same time period. There is also great potential to lead students into writing tasks by having them do short research projects on the war or on the sport of boxing (W7). There is also potential here to find topics for argumentative writing exercises as well that are drawn directly from the issues in the text (W1).	4

Overall Assessment

Comments
The qualitative measures of this book vary widely, and for the most part they don't match the intended audience of this work. The measures that indicate an 8th- or 9th-grade level are the most accurate given the analysis of other elements. The theme, content, conflict, and point of view of this book also put it clearly as an age 14 and up book, placing it also more on an 8th- or 9th-grade level. The complexity of the conflict and theme that are well integrated with the other structural elements as well as the unique organizational aspects make this a middle-grade title. The character is very approachable, and this book will connect well with reader interests and developmental needs from about ages 13–15. When used along with nonfiction texts to bring depth to this work and its historical context, this text could certainly be used in a lower grade level. Also, its approachable character and strong connection to boxing could make this a high-interest title that would appeal to older readers at a lower reading level. These lower- and higher-band uses aside, in general this book seems to fit best at an 8th–9th-grade band.

 From *Integrating Young Adult Literature through the Common Core Standards* by Rachel L. Wadham and Jonathan W. Ostenson. Santa Barbara, CA: Libraries Unlimited. Copyright © 2013.

Clay by David Almond

Quantitative Dimensions of Text Complexity

Lexile	490L (2–3 text complexity grade band)
ATOS	3.2 (3rd Grade) Middle-grade interest level
Flesch-Kincaid Grade Level	2.3 (2nd Grade)
Coleman-Liau	4 (4th Grade)
SMOG	3 (3rd Grade)
Gunning Fog	4.5 (easy to read)
Dale-Chall	5.50 (5th–6th Grade)

Qualitative Dimensions of Text Complexity

Format

	Comments	Rating
Size	The softcover version of the book measures 5″ × 8″, making it similar in size to reader's paperbacks and not mass-market paperbacks. This suggests the publisher wants the book to be seen as more sophisticated reading. The book is 247 pages long.	3
Font	The font is a standard serif font, easy to read. A sans-serif font of a larger size is used for chapter titles.	2
Layout	The book features wide margins, with page numbers in the left and right margins rather than at the top or bottom of the page. This presents less text on each page, making for faster reading of each page.	2
Construction	Standard paperback construction. The paper is of a medium quality.	2
Organization	The book is organized into four parts with chapters within each part. There's nothing unusual about the organization, although the four parts mark major changes in the tone/events of the story line. The book also features a reader's guide at the end, suggesting that the publisher finds the book complex enough for purposeful study.	3
Illustrations	No illustrations.	×

From *Integrating Young Adult Literature through the Common Core Standards* by Rachel L. Wadham and Jonathan W. Ostenson. Santa Barbara, CA: Libraries Unlimited. Copyright © 2013.

Audience

Comments	Rating
ATOS indicates this book is at a middle-grade interest level, booksellers indicate ages 12 and up, and review sources show this title is for grades 6–9. The protagonist of the story is a 13-year-old boy, and middle-grade readers will likely be at the low end of the audience for this book; issues of budding romance, friendship conflicts, and bullying are likely to appeal to those readers. However, the issues of death explored in the narrative, the ideas of creation and artistry and science, are more likely to be noticed by and mean something to older readers. The magical elements of the book might initially appeal to those who have found appealing books like the <u>Harry Potter</u> series, but the darker elements portrayed in *Clay* are more closely aligned with the later books in that series and may be more appropriate for older readers. So although we have a younger protagonist, he's portrayed as a more mature and complex figure, lending him appeal to older readers. This is a difficult book to pigeonhole for audiences, then, as it could have a range larger than readability scores or interest and grade levels might indicate.	4

Levels of Meaning

	Comments	Rating
Theme	The predominant theme in the book is about man's potential for evil and how we wrestle against our darker natures. Issues of good and evil are treated extensively in the book, but they're given a concrete nature in the form of Davie and his struggles between wanting to create something, to do something special with his life and with the potential he has to cause harm to someone else. The tension caused by this struggle is not a theme that's typically explored in this depth in young adult literature which makes this work very unique.	5
Conflict	The conflicts in the book begin as fairly straightforward problems: Davie and Geordie are bothered by a gang of bullies, they fight about Davie's attraction to a girl, and they seek to make a little extra money in their role as altar boys. Things blossom quickly into more substantial conflicts, though, as Stephen Rose moves into the neighborhood. His power to instill life in inanimate objects (either in a figurative way through his artistic abilities or in a literal way that only Davie seems fully aware of) introduces a serious conflict between moral visions of the world and ideas of good and evil. Even the simpler conflicts of, say, the bullying take on new significance in light of this. Davie also faces some internal conflicts, both as he experiences the first glimpses of the power, which cause him to question his sanity, and as he sees how the power might be used to bad ends, which causes him to question his motives and the morality of their actions.	5

From *Integrating Young Adult Literature through the Common Core Standards* by Rachel L. Wadham and Jonathan W. Ostenson. Santa Barbara, CA: Libraries Unlimited. Copyright © 2013.

	Comments	Rating
Connections	The motifs of creation, art, and science explored in the book provide connections to texts like Mary Shelley's *Frankenstein*, a connection alluded to when Davie's family watches the movie and he himself experiences some emotional changes. Readers can also make connections to Davie's experiences with bullies and with first romantic relationships. None of these connections is crucial to understanding the text, but they do add layers of meaning. In exploring the potential for evil in each of us and the philosophical idea of evil, the book also connects to a number of classic books and informational texts written on similar themes.	4

Structure

	Comments	Rating
Setting	The book is set in a contemporary time period, which will not pose a challenge for readers. The spiritual setting, where the Catholic church, its practices and beliefs, plays a strong role in some of the conflicts and events—may pose some challenges for readers unfamiliar with the faith. The elements of Catholicism are drawn into larger explorations of good and evil and the power of creation, which give the text a more complex setting. Being set in Felling, in Northern England, introduces complexities of language, with the characters speaking in a dialect that Almond captures brilliantly, and vocabulary, with the boys regularly using words like *nowt*, *prat*, and *bliddy*. The dialect in this area of England is closer to Scottish than anything else. This all contributes to a powerful sense of place but will make the text more complex for readers unfamiliar with the dialect.	5
Plot	The plot is straightforward, with most action taking place in a single time period and presented in chronological order. There are mysteries about the past of Stephen Rose that are alluded to throughout the book, but the most complicating element of the plot is certainly the "magical" power that Stephen and Davie possess that brings inanimate things to life. While teen readers are certainly willing to suspend disbelief and believe in such fantastic possibilities, the darker nature of this power and its placement in an otherwise conventional and realistic setting are likely to generate some questioning and reflection about this. The connections made by Almond between this power and the conflicts and themes of the book increase the text's complexity.	3
Character	The protagonist, Davie, is superbly drawn and a very complex character. He starts the tale as a rather unassuming boy who is mischievous but genuinely decent. As events unfold, he wrestles with internal questions about good and evil, about his own desires to see the local bully out of his life, and about his romantic feelings for a neighborhood girl. He starts to glimpse his own potential	5

(continued)

	Comments	Rating
	power and the power of his beliefs, and this sets him on an uncertain path. By the end of the book, Davie feels a real sense of his lost innocence, and the things he's experienced have changed him fundamentally. His relationship to Stephen is very complex, as he goes along with Stephen's wishes at the same time as he's doubtful about the other boy's motives. Stephen Rose, the boy who comes to Felling under mysterious circumstances, is a similarly complex character, although it takes time to understand this. He is enigmatic, not the least because of his amazing talent to craft lifelike statues that are beautiful and terrible at the same time. As Davie comes to learn more about him and his supposed power, he is drawn into Stephen's world, a world that is very ambiguous. But he also learns more about the sad and unfortunate circumstances in Stephen's history. Stephen's character allows for a multilayered treatment of the nature of humanity, of evil, and our potential to harm others. The other characters in the book are largely flat characters, exhibiting no change over the course of the book. The priest, Stephen's aunt, and Davie's parents play minor roles.	
Point of View	The story is told from Davie's point of view using first-person narration. This allows us to get inside Davie's mind as he wrestles with these complex issues. But it also raises the question of the reliability of the narrator; the suggestions of Stephen's powers of hypnosis also cast some doubt on the narration that Davie gives. This point of view allows us to fully explore issues of good and evil and true motivations at the same time as Davie considers them. It's a very appropriate point of view, but one that leaves us with more questions than answers by the end of the book.	4

Language Conventions

	Comments	Rating
Style and Tone	The tone of the book is unusual for young adult texts, and is characteristic of Almond's books—part of what, in our opinion, makes him such an interesting young adult writer. Initially, we might classify the tone as dark, and this seems fitting because the book does explore issues of death, abuse of power, and more mature conflicts. However, much of this exploration is what we would consider metaphysical—generating questions and encouraging thoughtful reflection about the issues. Never is violence or darkness glorified or glamorized in the book, but it is dealt with in honest ways that reveal the complexity belied by simple good-evil classifications.	4

From *Integrating Young Adult Literature through the Common Core Standards* by Rachel L. Wadham and Jonathan W. Ostenson. Santa Barbara, CA: Libraries Unlimited. Copyright © 2013.

	Comments	Rating
Literary Devices	One of the complex devices that Almond uses in the book is the metaphor of art as a creation force. Laid out for the first time in the art class that Davie is in with Stephen Rose, it's further developed when Stephen looks for a specific kind of clay, and when Davie recalls creating animals out of modeling clay as a young child. These allusions to the power of art to create life and evoke emotion take on more ambiguous tones when Davie and Stephen create Clay, and the metaphor of art and creation underlies all of this. There is a lot of ambiguity about what's real and imagined in the book (typical of Almond's writing), and he may be using the clay man as a metaphor for Davie and Stephen indulging their darker desires and taking action on them in the real world. The allusions to hypnosis, the fact that many of the events in the book take place at night, and Davie's own wondering about whether events might have taken place in dreams adds weight to this possibility. If the story is meant to be an allegorical representation of man's struggle with inner darkness, it's a sophisticated treatment of such for a young adult book.	4

Knowledge Demands

Comments	Rating
The dialect spoken by the characters, the vocabulary used, and the elements of Catholic faith and practice embodied in the narrative will make some demands on readers. We assume that some readers will be familiar with Catholicism, but few (in the United States at least) with the Northern English dialect; some support will be needed for all readers who encounter this book. Additionally, the exploration of metaphysical issues of good and evil, of morality, and of the connection between art and creation will make significant demands on most readers. These things are worth exploring, and Almond lays them open in a way that encourages deep exploration, but they do make demands on the reader both in terms of background knowledge and of interpreting meanings.	5

Reader Dimensions of Text Complexity

Envisioning Independent Readers

Comments	Rating
The sophisticated treatment of deeper philosophical and metaphysical issues in the book can spark serious thoughts for students, helping them see a purpose for literature beyond simple entertainment or escape. The number of potential text-to-world connections that could be made both with the events and the themes of the book should help students see how reading can bring us into a large discourse about important issues. The complexity of the text allows for practice with meaningful reading behaviors, such as forming inferences or questioning the text (R1); reading this book can help students become more independent and proficient in these skills.	4

The Adolescent Reader

	Comments	Rating
Adolescent Development	Part of an adolescent's maturation is his or her recognition of the self as an actor in the broader world, one whose choices can have an impact—positive or negative—on others. That idea is carefully explored in this text, and as such provides a meaningful way to discuss this issue with teens. While the book also explores issues of friendship, romance, and fitting in with others—all of importance to teens at this stage of their development—the issues of death and the power one individual can have over others are more central to the narrative.	4
Individual Makeup and Experience	On its surface, a book about a boy in Northern England who creates a living man from clay may seem to be completely unrelated to most of our readers; and there's much here that will be unfamiliar to our students. The issues of friendship and first romance present in the text are explored only peripherally, although they suggest that Davie might find help by connecting to others. His philosophical and metaphysical wrestlings may be connected to the kinds of questions teens ask about issues of good and evil, especially those with religious backgrounds or who are more socially aware. Older students are likely to find more of relevance here than younger students.	5

The Reader's Aptitude

	Comments	Rating
Interest	This book will not be of interest to all readers, as it explores some things that aren't commonly addressed in young adult literature. However, there are certain readers for whom the book will be a significant read and could perhaps usher them into reading texts that deal with broader, metaphysical issues like those in the book. Students who show an interest in these issues will probably find the book of greater appeal.	4
Experience	Readers who have been bullied or who have difficulty fitting in with others will likely identify with Stephen Rose, and their experiences will color their view of him. Those who have questioned some of the accepted "rules" of right and wrong in their lives will also likely connect with Davie and his thoughtful consideration of morality. Readers with a religious background can also relate to the underlying issues as well as characters in the book, and those experiences will likely inform their understanding and interpretation of the thematic elements.	4
Motivation	Again, not all readers will find the motivation to read a book like this. Initially, the idea of creating a man from clay may be of interest to readers who enjoy fantasy or magic in their books; the direction of this book moves quickly to more metaphysical	4

Comments	Rating
concerns and may no longer be of interest to those kinds of students. However, the brilliant characterizations and the knuckle-biting plot will likely draw in even readers who are not interested in the philosophical issues being explored.	

Task Dimensions of Text Complexity

Comments	Rating
There are numerous opportunities afforded by this novel to explore other, informational readings about the issues of good and evil and the nature of humanity. (Recent books like *The Better Angels of Our Nature* by Steven Pinker and related columns by David Brooks in the *New York Times* are some possibilities.) (R2). Historical events like the Holocaust, Stalin's dictatorship, and Pol Pot's regime could also be explored in the context of questions raised by this book (R9). Exploring texts on bullying and responses to bullying could make more concrete connections, perhaps more relevant to students' immediate lives (R1). Common core standards for informational texts could be met with these pairings. Additionally, the book could provide opportunities to build background knowledge in Catholicism, in the Protestant-Catholic conflict, and even in dialects of English. There is much that is unsaid in this book, and so making inferences (R1) is a critical behavior for comprehension; tasks centered around teaching that skill would be very appropriate for the study of this book.	4

Overall Assessment

Comments
The quantitative rankings of this book are very low. The complexity of this text makes it more suitable to higher bands, so its qualitative rankings will override all other rankings. *Clay* is an unusual book given its impressive exploration of deep philosophical issues, issues that have been explored through millennia of human existence. It leaves us with no real answers—as works treating these issues often do—but it raises important questions that, as adults and as a larger society, we must wrestle with. For these reasons, the book is well worth studying and discussing. Additionally, its strong characterizations (especially of Stephen and Davie) and engaging plot make it a compelling read. There are many instructional possibilities with this text, and it could form the anchor for a number of meaningful units. This work would be suitable for the 9th–12th-grade bands.

From *Integrating Young Adult Literature through the Common Core Standards* by Rachel L. Wadham and Jonathan W. Ostenson. Santa Barbara, CA: Libraries Unlimited. Copyright © 2013.

The Pirates of Turtle Rock by Richard W. Jennings

Quantitative Dimensions of Text Complexity

Lexile	1210L (9–10 text complexity grade band)
ATOS	7.8 (7th/8th Grade) Middle-grade interest level
Flesch-Kincaid Grade Level	9.4 (fairly difficult to read)
Coleman-Liau	11 (11th Grade)
SMOG	9.1 (9th Grade)
Gunning Fog	11 (hard to read)
Dale-Chall	8.61 (11th–12th Grade)

Qualitative Dimensions of Text Complexity

Format

	Comments	Rating
Size	The hardback edition measures 8 ½" × 6", which makes it fairly typical for a novel. It has 152 pages, making it on the shorter end of a novel. Overall the look of it is very small, indicating more of a children's book than one for an older audience. However, that is deceptive as the content is very complex, so this book represents an atypical application of size.	2
Font	Font is listed in the front cover as New Century Schoolbook, which is one of the more readable fonts. The font is consistent throughout the book; there is no variation.	1
Layout	The text has a standard layout. It is presented in the center of the page block with 1" margins all around. This makes the lines of a standard length, and the spacing between the lines is standard. The layout is entirely as expected.	1
Construction	According to publishing sources, this book was only published in hardback. This shows the publisher was committed to this title. However, the book was originally published as a weekly installment in a magazine. This construction makes this story unique. It gives it an interesting flow of plot, and it also makes some great connections to other older serialized publications.	3
Organization	The organization is standard, with paragraphs and chapters only. The chapters are not numbered but instead have narrative titles that reflect a topic that foreshadows some of the action in the chapter.	2
Illustrations	No illustrations.	×

From *Integrating Young Adult Literature through the Common Core Standards* by Rachel L. Wadham and Jonathan W. Ostenson. Santa Barbara, CA: Libraries Unlimited. Copyright © 2013.

Audience

Comments	Rating
The ATOS interest level is Middle Grade. Book reviews indicate the level to be grades 6–9. Other publishing information indicates ages 10 and up. The main character Jenny is age 16. A secondary character of the Pirate Coop DeVille is also a teenager, but his "profession" as a pirate as well as his actions and decision-making processes age him. There are also three main adult characters, and we get some of their point of view throughout the novel. We believe that the text was written for an audience of 9th graders and up. Despite the book reviews, this book seems ill suited to a 6th-grade level because of the main points of view and the complex style. The complexity of the text is much more suited to an older audience.	3

Levels of Meaning

	Comments	Rating
Theme	This short novel covers a variety of themes that emerge authentically from a well-constructed story. Foremost is a discussion of the role that fate or chance plays in the lives of humans. This theme is shown through the progression of presumably random events that come together to create the whole story. The author makes some subtle references to this theme throughout the novel. The overarching theme of fate is also connected by a theme of alienation. The main character is feeling restless in her life and is alienated from family and friends, but then fate takes her on an adventure that engages her in the world again. The main character's progression also brings forward themes of developing self-awareness, gaining wisdom from experience, and how to manage chaos. All these themes tie the work together as much of it is represented in random episodes that on the surface do not look like they connect, but with this background they do. This makes the interpretation of theme fully dependent upon understanding all the other elements such as plot and characters.	4
Conflict	The main conflict of the book lies with its main character, Jenny. She is dissatisfied with life and wants an adventure. The conflict then stems from the alienation she feels with her own life; she is not connected at all to her family or to the boy who has a crush on her. When the Pirate shows up, she is able to expand outside herself, but she then comes to find she is pretty satisfied with her life. This conflict is integral to the themes of the story. As the book has an underlying mystery there is also conflict between the characters. Much of this conflict is expected, such as DeVille and his crew who conflict with police and other authorities. Also, expected conflict comes between the two boys vying for Jenny's attention. However, there are some unexpected	3

(continued)

	Comments	Rating
	forms of conflict when we encounter some scheming professors and when Jenny's mad uncle tries to help out but keeps forgetting what he remembered. These sources of unexpected conflict add to the unique nature of this text and make it more complex.	
Connections	This novel has many text-to-self connections. Jenny is a typical teen who, like many, is dissatisfied with life and is looking for new adventures. This general malaise for current life conditions is something that many teens will resonate with. There are limited text-to-world connections as this novel is very grounded in the explanations of a particular event with an individual character focus. However, there are some connections to ecology and keeping our planet healthy. There are also subtle connections to the creation of art and how this impacts the world. Because of the context of the mystery there could also be some connections to ancient stone carving such as Stonehenge or the Easter Island Moai. There are several text-to-text connections that can be made, including to classic books like *Treasure Island* by Robert Louis Stevenson. You could also make character connections to other young adult books like *Pirates* by Celia Rees or *Bloody Jack* by L. A. Meyer. Also, because this work was published as a serial, you could make other connections to serial publications like those of Charles Dickens. Because the text was published in this form, you could make great connections to thematic short story collections such as those on body image in *Does This Book Make Me Look Fat?* edited by Marissa Walsh. It is also possible to make media connections though the recent *Pirates of the Caribbean* movies or the many retellings of the Treasure Island story.	3

Structure

	Comments	Rating
Setting	The book is set in Kansas-by-the-Sea, Florida. The use of a variety of figurative language techniques brings this setting vividly to life for the reader. While the trappings of Florida are real, the town is not. The author has created a whole culture and structure around this fictitious town that makes it very believable and realistic. This "real" place gives the overall setting a slightly surrealistic feeling as the reader knows through the trappings and plot elements that this really could not happen in a real-world setting. There is a brief mention at the beginning and throughout of a historical past that impacts the mystery the main characters are trying to solve, but other than this the story remains in the same time and general	3

From *Integrating Young Adult Literature through the Common Core Standards* by Rachel L. Wadham and Jonathan W. Ostenson. Santa Barbara, CA: Libraries Unlimited. Copyright © 2013.

	Comments	Rating
	place throughout. Where the setting excels is in the author's descriptions.	
Plot	On the surface, the plot is very simple. Jenny meets Pirate Coop DeVille, and together they go in search of a long-lost treasure. However, this simple reduction does not do the plot justice. As the progression of events unfolds, the author switches point of view constantly, and this makes the plot much more complex. This technique also brings up a number of subplots, such as with Jenny's father and mother and their dissatisfaction with their work and with Jenny's mad uncle who has led an extraordinary life that constantly comes back to play a part in the overall plot. The plot does not convey a simple mystery but a complex interweaving of events that come together to show how the fates connect peoples' lives. This makes the themes discussed above very integral to the plot and its progression; the construction of the novel's plot makes the theme happen.	3
Character	Jenny is the main character. She is a typical teen, and the description of her is at a basic level. A secondary character, who is described in somewhat more detail as he and his experiences are less familiar, is the Pirate Coop DeVille. The characters of Jenny's mother and father are more of stock descriptions of parents. However, the other adult character of Jenny's uncle, like DeVille, is more complex since he and his experiences are less familiar. There are also many secondary characters, including a talking parrot that adds levity to the story, DeVille's crew, some interfering professors, and another potential boyfriend for Jenny. Each of these characters add color and uniqueness to the novel. As each of these characters play a role in the story and we get some of the story told from each of their points of view, this makes the character dimension more complex than most novels.	3
Point of View	Throughout the novel the author changes point of view many times. We get information on the thoughts, actions, and feelings of all the major and minor characters at one point or another. This makes the book very complex. Another level to the complexity of this novel is that the author often changes the point of view at random in the chapter. While it may seem arbitrary, these changes are expertly connected to the overall theme and context of what the author is trying to convey making the element of point of view and theme integral to one another.	4

Language Conventions

	Comments	Rating
Style and Tone	The overall style of this novel is elaborate. The author uses many long sentences. These often contain a litany of examples and	5

(continued)

From *Integrating Young Adult Literature through the Common Core Standards* by Rachel L. Wadham and Jonathan W. Ostenson. Santa Barbara, CA: Libraries Unlimited. Copyright © 2013.

	Comments	Rating
	descriptions, but the author executes them so well that they are interesting and vivid to read. The author also uses extended descriptions that bring depth to the characters and the setting. He uses unexpected comparisons that are fresh and innovative. In addition, the author also uses metafictional techniques, as he frequently calls attention to himself when he comments back to the reader about the events and sometimes offers advice. The tone of the novel is sarcastic and comedic, and at times it has the feel of a farce. However, this is balanced by the very serious nature of the themes and the realism of the characters. This makes the book hard to peg as it crosses genre boundaries with its style. It is not humor, but it is very humorous; it is not fantasy, but it has that sense of other worldliness. The author uses the style to great effect to bring together this interesting balance that makes the book very intriguing.	
Literary Devices	This work uses to great effect numerous literary devices and forms of figurative language. There are many examples of metaphor, simile, analogy, hyperbole, foreshadowing, imagery, allusion, idioms, etc. This book excels in this area. It does have some pop culture references, but they are expertly woven in to expand upon the other figurative language used and bring this book's use of these devices to an approachable level that is still skillfully rendered and ripe for study.	5

Knowledge Demands

Comments	Rating
While the style and tone of this book is very elaborate, it does not demand elaborate knowledge from the reader. The author's use of a familiar current setting does not demand any historical knowledge from the reader. The characters and plot are also familiar and would require very little previous knowledge. Also while the author's style, tone, and use of literary devices is complex, they are so well tied into the rest of the novel that they do not require any previous experience or knowledge to fully appreciate them on a level of craft or to understand the humor that they bring to the novel.	2

Reader Dimensions of Text Complexity

Envisioning Independent Readers

Comments	Rating
This text will be a strong match to teen readers' personal interests, and with its strong style and use of literary devices it will be a good one to help students learn evaluation skills. The text is unique in its use of humor and language, so it is in a form that not many teens will have encountered before. This makes it useful in helping teens understand different genres and forms of texts. Because of its	4

Comments	Rating
complexity it will also be a good text to have students apply comprehension strategies as they monitor their understanding of the plot flow and complex language.	

The Adolescent Reader

	Comments	Rating
Adolescent Development	The strong voice of the main character, who is also trying to develop a sense of mastery and achievement, will resonate well with teens. Themes that connect to the developmental tasks of defining mature relationships, finding emotional independence, and developing a moral code are also present here.	5
Individual Makeup and Experience	This text will be appealing to a variety of teens. The main character is a girl, but there are also many boy connections with the pirate characters. The socioeconomic status is middle class; however, this does not play a big role at all. There are limited viewpoints of race, but this does not necessarily play a big role, nor will it hinder any one group's enjoyment. The text requires very little of the reader as far as background they would need to bring to it.	2

The Reader's Aptitude

	Comments	Rating
Interest	This text will be of interest to a wide variety of readers. With mystery, realism, and romance all put into one package, the cross-genre approach of this book will be appealing.	3
Experience	Experience with other pirate stories or with humor and satire will be helpful for students here. Or if they don't have that knowledge, it will be a great way to build that knowledge.	3
Motivation	This text has high motivation as the story and characters are interesting and progress well. Readers will be drawn in. The developmental connections will also bring them into the text.	4

Task Dimensions of Text Complexity

Comments	Rating
This novel would provide a good start to the study of language. It offers many strong examples of figurative language and innovative language use. Any activity or unit focused on these issues could use this book as their foundation. This novel would also provide a great foundation for the study of structure creating theme (R2). It could also be used to great effect on units on inferences (R1). There are many other connections with other fiction texts as noted above, or you could add it	4

(continued)

Comments	Rating
to a thematic unit about fate, even one connected to the mythological fates, or to one about discovering your place in the world. You could also make strong connections to nonfiction texts about ancient stone carving or pirates as well as media depictions of the same themes. (R7, R9)	

Overall Assessment

Comments
The quantitative and qualitative assessments of this novel match nicely. This book clearly has a complexity level of 9–11th grade and will have uses throughout that band. In the 9th grade it can be used to study the complexity of the plot and theme. It also gives an approachable introduction to figurative language. At the 10th- and 11th-grade bands it can certainly be used for more elaborate study of literary devices and author style. This novel, while the format is deceptively simple, is structurally complex and reaches the requirements of the higher levels of complexity very easily. It also connects well to that same age group and has a variety of complex uses for these older grades, making it a perfect fit in many situations for the 9th–11th grade.

This Dark Endeavor by Kenneth Oppel

Qualitative Dimensions of Text Complexity

Lexile	690L (2–3 text complexity grade band); Ages 11–14
ATOS	4.9 (4th/5th Grade), Upper-grade interest level
Flesch-Kincaid Grade Level	5 (5th Grade)
Coleman-Liau	7 (7th Grade)
SMOG	4.9 (5th Grade)
Gunning Fog	7.3 (fairly easy to read)
Dale-Chall	6.68 (7th–8th Grade)

Qualitative Dimensions of Text Complexity

Format

	Comments	Rating
Size	The hardback edition of the books is a typical 8″ × 5″ format. The hardback edition has 304 pages, putting it in the middle range for this type of novel.	2
Font	Standard serif font is used throughout the book; there are no real variations in fonts.	2
Layout	The text is laid out in a standard format, with relatively common margins and blocks of text.	2
Construction	Being a hardcover book, the binding is of solid quality and the paper is of higher quality. The flyleaf is designed to look like a classic novel, complete with simulated water or smoke damage. The book is also available in e-book and audio editions.	2
Organization	The book is organized into chapters. Most chapters cover related series of events, but some do span multiple days or longer time periods.	2
Illustrations	No illustrations.	X

Audience

Comments	Rating
The Lexile indicates this book is for ages 11–14, and the ATOS indicates an upper-grade interest level. Review sources indicate ages 12 and up and ages 13–18. The fact that the main character is 16, combined with the ATOS interest level designation, puts this work at a higher level than most audience indicators show. The content of the work is more sophisticated, and we suggest this book is aimed at high school readers, ages 14 and up. Some of the content present in the book is also better suited to older teen readers.	3

Levels of Meaning

	Comments	Rating
Theme	The most dominant theme in the book is the perils of the pursuit of knowledge and of power over nature, similar to the themes found in the original *Frankenstein*. The knowledge that Victor pursues is alchemical or slightly fantastic rather than purely scientific, but the theme is made more complex by the fact that Victor initially pursues the learning for the sake of his twin brother's health. Once the brother has regained his health, however, Victor continues to pursue the elixir of life, suggesting that it is the power that comes from that knowledge that he's most interested in. A secondary theme is sibling rivalry, most concretely displayed by the two twins' jousting for Elizabeth's affections. Victor explores his growing attraction to her in authentic but honest ways, and he resorts even to deception in his efforts to attract her attention. This is a complex treatment of a theme that is not often seen in young adult literature.	3
Conflict	Related to the primary theme, one of the major conflicts in the book is that of man versus nature. Kurt's struggles with his illness push Victor to investigate the "dark" arts of alchemy, a pseudo-science with the object of understanding nature's deepest secrets and powers. The quest to find a solution to Kurt's illness spawns conflicts between the children and their father, a man who once practiced alchemy but has since disavowed it. Their quest also brings them into eventual conflict with Polidori, a rogue alchemist who helps them discover the secrets of the elixir of life and then betrays the Frankenstein children. The conflict Victor experiences in his quest to heal his brother is an understandable one that touches on sibling relationships. A further conflict arises between Victor and Kurt over their adopted sister, Elizabeth. Both have romantic feelings for her, but she is not interested in a romantic relationship with Victor and spurns his advances while accepting Kurt's. These conflicts are multilayered and complex, especially as seen through the eyes of Victor.	4
Connections	An obvious connection is to the original *Frankenstein* by Mary Shelley. By giving some history to and exploring the developmental years of Victor Frankenstein, Oppel brings the Frankenstein story to a new generation of young readers. A reading of the classic after *This Dark Endeavor* could certainly be enhanced as Oppel tries to be faithful to the characterization of Victor Frankenstein that Shelley gives. The book has other connections to the tradition of Gothic literature. Set mostly in a sprawling estate with dark corners and hidden passages, as well as the brooding terror of the quests	3

	Comments	Rating
	Polidori sends Victor and Elizabeth on connect this to the strong tradition of Gothic writers and books like Shelley's *Frankenstein* or Stoker's *Dracula*.	

Structure

	Comments	Rating
Setting	As with most Gothic tales, this is set in an earlier day, probably late 18th or early 19th century. It takes place mostly in the Frankenstein castle, a vast estate with plenty of secrets. Other events take place in underground caves, dark forests, and the alchemist's laboratory—all suitably Gothic locales. The physical location will likely be familiar to students who have seen versions of the Frankenstein or Dracula stories. The Frankenstein parents are portrayed as modernists, more sophisticated than the household help or local villages. It's suggested that Victor and Kurt's father has eschewed the arcane explorations of his youth for modern science. This puts the young Frankensteins (especially Victor) in something of an unusual place as they are curious about the mysteries of nature and the truths that may lie behind the superstitions that govern the lives of many at the time.	3
Plot	The plot is straightforward, with events occurring within a small window of time, the few months of Kurt's illness. There are twists and turns aplenty, mostly provided by the alchemist Polidori and the quests he sends the youths on for ingredients of the elixir of life. But these do not create an overly complicated story line.	3
Character	There are a fair number of characters in the book, although the Frankenstein children (including Elizabeth) and their friend Henry are the most significant figures. Of the other characters, Polidori, the alchemist the children consult in seeking the elixir of life, plays a more major role than the parents, and is definitely more complex. Other characters, such as the parents or the household staff, serve largely functional roles, providing a foil, in the father, to Victor's thirst for arcane knowledge, or some minor help along the way, as in the case of the nursemaid.	3
Point of View	The story is told in first person, with Victor serving as the narrator. This gives readers an inside look at his motivations, most importantly when it comes to the quest for knowledge—a quest that starts out in the hope of helping his brother but takes on a different shape once Kurt recovers. The use of Victor to narrate makes sense, of course, but also raises the important question of	4

(*continued*)

	Comments	Rating
	his trustworthiness. We can see through his justifications about deceiving Elizabeth in hopes of attracting her attention, and we begin to question the root motives for his pursuit of the elixir. Oppel does not thickly veil this, but it does provide the text with more complexity to have Victor telling the story.	

Language Conventions

	Comments	Rating
Style and Tone	Oppel's book is written in a Gothic style, purposefully mimicking the syntax and word choice of the original *Frankenstein*. The style can seem stiff or formal at times but is not unwieldy or overly complicated. Readers will notice a clear difference, though, between this book and other young adult literature set in modern times.	4
Literary Devices	The book, as should be expected, makes use of many of the Gothic tropes: the secret passage in the Frankenstein mansions leading to a library of forbidden knowledge, the trap door and elevator in Polidori's laboratory, the mysterious potion and its arcane ingredients, characters with mysterious pasts and motives. While these are unlikely to present challenges to readers, given the widespread use of such tropes in a variety of genres today, they do add to the complexity of the text.	4

Knowledge Demands

Comments	Rating
While the connections to Gothic literature and especially to Shelley's *Frankenstein* are significant, a reader who is unfamiliar with these in depth will not likely be hampered in comprehension. The writing style that Oppel adopts, mimicking traditional Gothic writing, may place some unique demands on readers. The locations of the setting, while cast in Europe, are described in enough detail that they should not pose a stumbling block to readers. This is, on the whole, a very accessible book about the origins of the Frankenstein mythos.	3

Reader Dimensions of Text Complexity

Envisioning Independent Readers

Comments	Rating
Independent readers draw from a variety of texts, and the unfamiliar elements of this book will help teens experience something familiar (the inner conflicts of Victor, his feelings for Elizabeth, his rivalry with his brother) in unfamiliar contexts (alchemy, magical potions, arcane ingredients). These readers also are skilled at making connections between texts, and the book provides ample chance for that to	3

From *Integrating Young Adult Literature through the Common Core Standards* by Rachel L. Wadham and Jonathan W. Ostenson. Santa Barbara, CA: Libraries Unlimited. Copyright © 2013.

Comments	Rating
both Gothic classics and to modern reflections on the progress of scientific knowledge and its unintended consequences. There is something here, too, that helps students take their first steps into a larger literary tradition of *Frankenstein* and similar books exploring these issues.	

The Adolescent Reader

	Comments	Rating
Adolescent Development	Teens are likely to be most drawn to books that represent familiar settings, conflicts, and story lines. The recent popularity of paranormal romances suggests that they are also looking to explore different settings and story lines, especially as they transition to becoming more adult in their tastes and choices. This book offers just such an alternative for these readers, and provides some familiar elements (especially in terms of emotional content and the character of Victor) in a unique setting. Adolescents are also starting to recognize the influence they might have on the world around them, how their choices can have consequences beyond just themselves. This is very much the experience of Victor in the story, as his thirst for knowledge, which begins in the hopes of curing his brother but clearly moves beyond that, may have real consequences for those around him—both positive and negative. His growing knowledge (witness his excitement at the formula that allows him sight at night) gives him increased power and influence in the world around him—a feeling that teenagers also experience, especially as they near adulthood. This story provides a meaningful way to explore some of these things for teen readers.	3
Individual Makeup and Experience	Students who are familiar with the Frankenstein story will probably find something special in this book, as they know a bit about how the larger story arc ends. Seeing its beginnings in these pages will be of particular interest to them; knowing what eventually happens will certainly color the way they interpret events in this book. Those with a more general experience with this genre will also see things in the book through a slightly different lens, as they'll get glimpses into motivations and rationales for the "mad scientist" kind of character.	3

The Reader's Aptitude

	Comments	Rating
Interest	With the recent resurgence in books with supernatural elements, there is a natural interest in a book like this, connected as it is to another famous "monster" story. The Gothic elements are likely to	3

(*continued*)

	Comments	Rating
	appeal to a certain group of teenagers, but may in fact turn off others who find these supernatural elements less interesting. Oppel's characters, given their age and their own maturity, are more likely to be of interest to older teens. As such, this book has a likely less broad appeal than young adult literature set in more modern, familiar contexts.	
Experience	Few (if any) of our readers are going to have experience with arcane ingredients and life-giving potions, but their experience with these and other Gothic elements in movies may help ease access to this text. Readers with siblings (even twins) will likely relate to the elements of sibling rivalry in the book, and their own experiences will likely color their response to these elements. And the romantic element, with Kurt and Victor vying for Elizabeth's affections, will resonate with many readers; Victor's unjust rejection (in his view, at least) may also connect with readers' feelings of being misunderstood or underappreciated. In spite of the seemingly unfamiliar setting and plot, there is plenty here to connect to most teens' experiences.	3
Motivation	The mysteries of the book and its plot are most likely to draw readers in, as is common with Gothic literature. The twists of the plot, the mysteries about the older Frankenstein, the adventure of gathering ingredients for the potion—all of these make for an exciting tale that will be hard to put down. The familiar conflicts and entanglements will relate to teen readers as well.	3

Task Dimensions of Text Complexity

Comments	Rating
A primary task associated with this book would be analysis of the point of view (R6) that Victor presents in comparison to other views on the events of the novel. This is fairly complex work, as it requires us to take on the perspective of someone other than ourselves, which can be challenging for teen readers. Tasks could also explore the way Victor changes over the course of the novel as a result of events and his interactions with those event and other characters (R3). This book could also be the entry point for a larger discussion about the pursuit of knowledge (especially scientific knowledge) and how that might have unintended consequences (R2). Issues relevant today could include cloning, genetically engineered food, gene tests on embryos, stem cell research, and a whole host of other issues. These are complex issues and would require some significant time and background knowledge to explore completely.	4

Overall Assessment

Comments
The quantitative rakings of this book are very low. They do not accurately reflect its overall complexity, so the qualitative rankings of this work should override other rankings. Oppel's book represents a trend in young adult literature toward moving away from contemporary setting and familiar story lines, a move that we fully applaud. By tapping into one of the most familiar stories in English literature, this book both opens the door to reading and enjoying a classic text but also to re-seeing that text in new ways. It sheds light on characters and events that we all think we know about, and provides important insights into scientific pursuits at the same time. By not presenting overly complex connections to the original tale, this book remains an accessible gateway to explore significant themes. Overall we would place the text in the 9th- and 10th-grade complexity band.

Wisdom's Kiss by Catherine Gilbert Murdock

Quantitative Dimensions of Text Complexity

Lexile	1280L (9–10 & 11-CCR text complexity grade band); Ages 14–17
ATOS	8.8 (8th/9th Grade) Middle-grade+ interest level
Flesch-Kincaid Grade Level	8.5 (9th Grade)
Coleman-Liau	10 (10th Grade)
SMOG	7.1 (7th Grade)
Gunning Fog	10.5 (hard to read)
Dale-Chall	7.85 (9th–10th Grade)

Qualitative Dimensions of Text Complexity

Format

	Comments	Rating
Size	The hardback edition is 5 ¾" by 8 ½", a typical size for a hardback book. This edition has 284 pages, putting it in the middle range for number of pages.	2
Font	This novel uses a variety of fonts. The book notes that it uses Abrams Venetian, Centaur MT, Clois Oldstyle, and Perpetua. Some are simple and readable; others are flowery with lots of broad strokes. Some are also in italics; others are underlined or bolded. Differing font styles are tied to the organization of the work. The author uses the change of font to indicate different points of view as well as different ways of telling the story. The variety and uses of fonts make this work very complex.	4
Layout	The layout varies. The author tells the story in the form of diaries, memoirs, encyclopedia entries, letters, biographies, and a stage play. Each of these is given a different layout. The text block is more dense, with longer lines in the encyclopedia entries and biographies. The block is spread out with shorter lines in the diaries and the stage play. The layout is tied to points of view and formats, adding to the complexity of this work.	4
Construction	The hardback edition is constructed in a typical pattern with quality binding and paper. The work is also available in e-book and audio editions, showing the publisher's commitment to this title.	2
Organization	The book begins with an introduction and is then divided into four parts. The introduction and parts are set off with full-page spreads with patterned details around the edge. In the parts, the	3

 From *Integrating Young Adult Literature through the Common Core Standards* by Rachel L. Wadham and Jonathan W. Ostenson. Santa Barbara, CA: Libraries Unlimited. Copyright © 2013.

	Comments	Rating
	work is divided into "chapters" by the inclusion of the various formats. Statements in a particular font and style show the reader what format is coming; for example, the diary entries are introduced by a complex font that tells us whose diary it is. These font/style indications stay the same throughout the book for each type of information source. Because of this the organization is logical and consistent; however, it still requires the reader to pay close attention to the changes in order to follow the text.	
Illustrations	No illustrations	×

Audience

Comments	Rating
The Lexile range indicates this book is for ages 14–17. The ATOS interest level indicates this work to be at a Middle Grade+. Booksellers indicate this book to be for ages 12 and up. Review sources indicate grades 7–12 as well as grades 6–9 and ages 8–12, 10 and up, and 11–15. The characters are of differing ages, from teen to adult. The main female character is a teenager. The unique presentation of the work adds to the difficulty in pinpointing an audience as evidenced by the broad range of ages and grades indicated in the review sources. With this information and with a reading of the text, it seems this book is aimed at an audience of about ages 14 and up. However, it could go up even into the adult range.	3

Levels of Meaning

	Comments	Rating
Theme	This work is strongly connected to traditional fantasy genres, so the themes it represents are typical of those genres. There are themes that revolve around seeking adventure and then being put to the test to see if the character can succeed. This connects to the traditional hero journey pattern. As in fairy tales, honesty and cleverness are rewarded and evil is punished, so in the end the main characters are transformed into better versions of themselves. While these themes do not address groundbreaking issues, they are certainly universal, as fairy tales have addressed them for centuries. As the genre of the work is integral to the story being told and the themes build from this, the theme ties the work together through its genre.	3
Conflict	The work revolves around nine central characters who each have their own type of conflict to address. From conflicts of being in love with the wrong person to conflicts arising from political ambition, the broad scope of the conflicts is integral to the story. The author also uses all these conflicts to expertly tie all the characters and plot elements together. The plot starts by addressing the conflicts individually but then the whole cast of	5

(continued)

	Comments	Rating
	characters comes together to address their own conflicts and a larger political conflict in a very satisfying manner. The conflict is what builds the themes and allows us to see who is good and who is evil. Each conflict is dependent on the characters and plot, so their interpretation and resolution is dependent upon all the other elements.	
Connections	While some readers may find text-to-self connections with the characters' search for identity and love, the strongest connections with this book are text-to-text. As the text harks back to traditional fantasy, it connects well with this genre, in particular the tale "Puss in Boots." The use of different formats from diaries to encyclopedias also provides text-to-text connections with a variety of genres to show how different forms convey different information.	3

Structure

	Comments	Rating
Setting	The story is set in a fictional kingdom, Montagne. While this setting is unfamiliar, because it harks back to traditional fantasy and is reminiscent of typical medieval historical settings it becomes more familiar than a purely fantastic setting would be. The story stays in one kingdom; however, the characters travel between different parts of the kingdom, and other kingdoms are referenced. With no map provided as might be typical of a fantasy, these changes and references to other places could pose a challenge for many readers. The author uses good details to describe the setting, however, helping the reader be immersed in it even if they may not entirely know where they are.	4
Plot	The plot is intricate. To begin, the story follows plotlines revolving around the nine main characters. These plotlines converge as the story continues so that everyone is finally involved in only one main plotline. With the use of a variety of formats to tell the story, the plot continually jumps around in time and place. Oftentimes these formats come from a time that is further in the future, so they tell of information that happens well after the present time period of the story. The final climax is very identifiable, and it builds throughout as individual conflicts build to climaxes and then are resolved. In the book there are many twists and surprises that are completely resolved, so there will be no sequel. Some elements may seem contrived because of their connection to traditional fantasy; however, they fit the story well and their use along with the rest of the intricate plot elements gives them a fresh and interesting perspective.	4

	Comments	Rating
Character	There are nine main characters in the book. As each plays a significant part in the story and many portions of the story are told from their point of view, each of them is multilayered and interesting. Even the one nonhuman character (a cat) is well drawn and plays a significant role. There are also minor characters that come and go, but each of these adds a great deal of color to the story. In the fantasy world the author creates, these characters represent a wide range of cultures and socioeconomic levels that also adds depth to the story. All the characters are portrayed in authentic ways, so not much prior knowledge is needed to understand the character depictions. As with all the elements, the author uses many details to describe the characters, as each is connected to the other structures of plot and theme.	4
Point of View	The story is told from a variety of points of view. Some are first person, others third, still others are omniscient. The change of setting between the present and the future also adds an interesting depth to the point of view. As some information is given that would not be available to characters in the present time, the author is allowed to provide different commentary on the story than would be allowed if only one time period was used. The various points of view add to the depth of the characters and support the plot as well, so point of view is very integral to the building of all the other elements.	4

Language Conventions

	Comments	Rating
Style and Tone	The style of the text is based in traditional fantasy and builds on these traditions. With the varying points of view, however, the style also varies depending on who is speaking and the purpose of the text (is it informative, as the encyclopedia entries, or is it personal, like the diary entries?). The depth of description also varies with the changes in point of view. The author uses a vide variety of vocabulary words, many of which will be outside the normal experience. The tone of the majority of the work is toward lighthearted adventure and fairy-tale romance. The author uses description and dialogue conventions that support this tone even when the action is heightened, so the overall sense of the story remains hopeful and fun.	4
Literary Devices	The author uses extensive vocabulary, which also builds on her use of a wide variety of literary devices. The author uses motifs and symbols that are typical of traditional fantasy contexts. Much of the story draws on the hero journey archetype, although with the varying viewpoints the direct links to the pattern are	4

(continued)

	Comments	Rating
	somewhat diluted. Metaphor and similes that are interesting and unique are also used. These devices are certainly not the focus of the text, so they do not stand out, ensuring that they meld beautifully within the rest of the story and support the author's style and tone.	

Knowledge Demands

Comments	Rating
The text brings with it the entire context that most readers will need to understand it. However, broader context knowledge will be helpful for readers as the structure of this text is very complex. For example, experience with varying literary formats from diary to informational texts will be helpful. If readers understand how these forms use and convey information, they will be able to better navigate the variety of formats in this text. Also, a strong background with the genre of fantasy will be helpful. Genre experience will provide readers with the ability to fully imagine setting and to keep people and events straight in their minds, two things that are complex enough in this book to be points of confusion for some readers. The author's use of a wide vocabulary could also prove a challenge for some readers; preparation with strategies for deciphering unknown words will be helpful for this text.	4

Reader Dimensions of Text Complexity

Envisioning Independent Readers

Comments	Rating
This novel is in a unique format, and most readers will not have encountered such a construction before. Encountering text outside of one's experience such as this provides strong opportunities to help readers evaluate and select reading based on their own personal tastes. This text will also allow them to expand their experience with unfamiliar genres; it uses important genre conventions and formats, which provides a fine platform for readers to explore how genre and format make meaning and also how authors use these to convey information. Also, as the setting and number of characters can be challenging, this is a good platform to apply comprehension strategies. The wide vocabulary will also allow students to apply recognition strategies. Using all these strategies will help them learn how to monitor their understanding and make adjustments.	4

The Adolescent Reader

	Comments	Rating
Adolescent Development	All fairy-tale types address some basic universal expectations. Those based on the hero journey especially touch on the steps that are necessary to progress though life. These are diluted, but this	2

 From *Integrating Young Adult Literature through the Common Core Standards* by Rachel L. Wadham and Jonathan W. Ostenson. Santa Barbara, CA: Libraries Unlimited. Copyright © 2013.

	Comments	Rating
	novel has them, so it also is constructed along these developmental lines. The story also connects to developing one's identity and standing up for moral decisions in the face of evil.	
Individual Makeup and Experience	The majority of the characters in the text are female. As such, gender plays an important part in the text, so it is most likely to appeal to girls over boys. This text is also very complex on many levels, so a reader's cognitive skills will play a strong role in their ability to understand. For those who love the genres of fantasy and romance, this text will be very appealing. The complexity level is high, so it will challenge a wide variety of readers.	3

The Reader's Aptitude

	Comments	Rating
Interest	This text will be of great interest to readers. The format is unique, but the action and pace of the story will keep readers engaged.	3
Experience	Readers who bring outside experience with fantasy will find this text less complex. As the book extends well beyond the standard fantasy conventions, however, it will be complex even for those with this experience. Professionals can build on readers' experience and interest in fantasy to create strong connections and develop independent reading behaviors as well as expand their vocabulary.	3
Motivation	The connections to traditional fantasy will be motivating for readers who love that genre. The interesting story and format of the novel will also motivate many readers who are drawn to these unique aspects.	3

Task Dimensions of Text Complexity

Comments	Rating
This text has many classroom applications. Units centered on traditional fantasy could use it. It will also allow readers to study how authors construct narratives to create meaning (R3). The author's use of various points of view will provide a variety of connections (R6). The text could be used for activities that delve into how point of view changes the meaning of a narrative. In addition, assessments that work with how the passage of time also changes the point of view are a fine match for this text. The novel could also be used for a study of style (R4). As the different narrators have varying styles, activities that discuss how style and tone enhance character development are also a good match here. Lastly, the study of how varying formats create and share information could also be foundational for this text. Different formats use varying conventions of style and language, many of which the forms in this novel bring to light. This study could be extended into writing activities where students write in different formats (diary, letter, memoir, encyclopedia entry, etc.) (W4, W9).	4

Overall Assessment

Comments
The Lexile puts this text at a 10th–11th-grade complexity. The audience level, while varying, also puts the text at this same level. Each of the structural elements and language conventions also put this text at a very high complexity level. While the reader dimensions are varied, it has strong task connections and could be used in a variety of contexts. Overall this text fits well into the Lexile band as all its dimensions fit very well at the 10th- and 11th-grade band.

Part II

Planning Instruction Using Young Adult Literature and the Common Core Standards

Introduction

In the first half of this book, we have shown how we analyze texts to determine their complexity, and we made the argument that young adult literature is complex enough to meet the considerations of the common core standards. The question now is, How do we make these books a part of a vital and engaging curriculum?

In this half of the book, we will provide concrete, well-elaborated ideas for designing learning environments that incorporate young adult literature into the ELA curriculum. We want to take you through a step-by-step process to show you that in a very practical context, the common core and young adult literature are a dynamic combination for teaching and learning. To accomplish this, in chapter seven we will first explain our choice for a pedagogical theory. Our classroom experience and a growing body of research show that constructivist-oriented approaches to teaching, embodied most effectively in inquiry approaches to learning, can best facilitate learning for the students in secondary classrooms. We'll explain our rationale for choosing inquiry-based approaches. We will also outline a heuristic for planning inquiry units that incorporate young adult literature and the common core standards. We will describe the process that we've found successful when planning a unit like this—a process that's informed both by our experience as classroom teachers and by our work with pre-service and in-service ELA teachers. Then in chapter eight we'll invite you into a "think-aloud" that demonstrates this process by describing how we think through the planning of an inquiry unit using Karen Hesse's wonderful young adult novel *Out of the Dust*. An entire unit will thus be outlined for you, including meaningful learning activities and strong connections to the common core standards.

Finally, in chapters nine and ten we'll present the "raw materials" for developing units using a variety of young adult novels. While we want to be specific and concrete in this section, we don't intend to be overly prescriptive in describing how to incorporate young adult literature in your classroom. As the classroom teacher, you know best the context in which you work, the needs and interests of your students, and the resources you have available to you. So our goal in providing these materials is to give a starting point for your own development of instructional units that have young adult literature at their heart and meet the demands of the common core in satisfactory ways.

We have worked to make this part of the book useful for teachers of all experience levels, since no matter your experience level, one of the most challenging parts of a teacher's job is planning. Teachers who really care about their students and their learning realize that planning is about so much more than simply filling time. We don't want the learning that happens in our classrooms to be random—the result of mere coincidences in our interactions with students. Such an approach does not allow for what we call maximal learning: the most learning happening for the largest number of students. To achieve maximal learning, we have to be methodical and purposeful about how we plan. The choices we make, from our learning objectives to the texts we read and write to the daily activities we plan, must be connected in meaningful ways. This methodical approach to planning is what we will outline in this section. We also believe that this methodical approach is of significance when we consider the CCSS. Since much of its implementation is left to professionals, how well we plan will not only color the results of how competently we implement the CCSS, but it will also play a big part in how articulately we can communicate to others that we are achieving what the CCSS requires of us.

But what are we planning for? What is our ultimate goal for the students in our charge? The common core standards suggest a worthy answer. An ultimate goal of the standards, and of classroom instruction consistent with the standards, is to create students who are independent, self-directed learners. This is a noble goal that fits with the reasons why many of us probably entered this profession: to create literate, independent learners.

As we plan, we must remember that in articulating our goals, the CCSS documents imply no direction on how these goals are to be met. The purpose of these documents is to identify the levels of achievements that students should meet at each grade level, but not to define how teachers should help students meet these standards. Pedagogical questions such as these are to be determined by individual teachers or schools. We are encouraged, instead, to develop full, content-rich curricula that meet these standards in proven and effective ways. The gap between the outline that the CCSS gives us and the implementation of daily practice is the one we seek to fill in this part of the book. By discussing strong pedagogical theory and outlining the ways we personally plan instruction, we hope to provide you with the strongest model for everyday practice that will maximize student learning and meet the demands of the common core standards.

Chapter 7

Inquiry Learning

We see ourselves standing at a crossroads right now, at the juncture of important forces: research into teaching and learning is yielding important insights into how we teach, and the work of the common core authors has laid out an influential definition of what we should be teaching. This crossroads presents us with important choices about how we will implement new expectations for performance, and we must make these choices wisely. As we've argued so far in this book, we see young adult literature as an effective medium for meeting the common core standards, and we now want to make the case for an approach to teaching students what they need to know to meet those standards. That approach takes what we know about how to best facilitate learning and brings it together in inquiry learning.

Defining Inquiry Learning

Constructivist methods of teaching, embodied best in what has come to be known as an inquiry approach, are a solid fit for the charge of the common core standards to create independent, actively engaged learners. Inquiry is, at its heart, teaching and learning that is centered around the authentic exploration of meaningful questions or themes. These questions and themes can generate an authentic purpose for what we teach our students (Wilhelm, 2007). Rather than simply covering material and parceling out knowledge to students from our expert teacher perches, when we embrace inquiry teaching we put students at the center of the learning; the onus for negotiating material and making meaning rests with the student.

When inquiry is used in ELA classrooms, its application often features the following elements:

- *A strong anchor text (or texts).* As ELA teachers, many of us are used to teaching literary units with instruction centered on the study of a single text. With inquiry learning, we don't have to change much about this; we can still have a primary text that we use as a vehicle for exploring our central question or theme. We also include supplementary texts that add depth to our study by providing additional perspectives and views—other novels, newspaper or magazine articles, short fiction pieces, video clips, poetry. These can provide opportunities for effective practice of literacy strategies in more accessible or less complex environments. And the common core standards emphasize this use of multiple texts and points of view in reading instruction.
- *A relevant, meaningful guiding question or overarching theme.* This question or theme should explore something that matters—to students, to us as teachers, to people who practice in our discipline. Many of the choices we make in planning the unit

are geared around this question or theme; texts and activities and assessments we choose for students will often be connected back to the question or theme. Threading the question or theme throughout the unit helps students make important connections, encouraging deeper understandings of the topics explored in the unit.

- *An assessment that allows students to create new knowledge from what they've explored in the unit.* This assessment ties to the essential question or central theme in a meaningful way by providing students a vehicle through which they can answer the question or share conclusions about the theme. Good assessments also provide a learning experience for students: they should stretch students to develop new skills or refine existing skills while providing an opportunity for feedback on their efforts.

Inquiry learning designed around these foundational features provides an effective structure for all teaching and learning for three main reasons that we now outline more fully: it is consistent with what we know about how learning happens, it places students' needs and interests at the center of instruction, and it taps into natural motivations of teenagers.

Inquiry Learning Embraces How Learning Happens

Where would we be today if our most noted inventors, scientists, and thinkers had not wondered about possibilities? Edison's light bulb, Watt's steam engine, and the creation of the Internet all resulted from their inventors asking questions about the world around them and the possibilities for change. Without the questions and challenges posed by these individuals, we would not have the amazing technological advances we benefit from today. Clearly, questions and wonderings have driven much of what we've learned and developed as a species, and it makes sense that channeling learning in the direction of questions and wonderings would be a good fit for the way people naturally think and learn.

In the field of cognitive sciences, researchers in the area of constructivism have argued that knowledge is constructed within the mind of the learner. They show that learning is an active process in which the student must engage his or her faculties to make sense of experiences. For constructivists, students are not empty vessels, passively waiting while teachers "fill" them with knowledge, but rather active meaning-seekers who want (and need) to be engaged in the learning process (Driscoll, 2000). Learning happens as the result of learners' experiences, as they are actively engaged in analyzing and questioning and exploring these experiences (Applefield, Huber, & Moallem, 2001). Researchers in this field argue that we learn a lot from asking questions, experimenting, evaluating the results, and trying new approaches when things don't initially yield the results we expect. The confusion or uncertainty that spawns these questions or experiments is at the heart of learning, as Kuhlthau, Maniotes, and Caspari argue (2007). But in schools, students often feel that questions or confusions are "wrong"—that they reflect a lack of mastery or skill, when the opposite is actually the case.

Questioning forms the foundation of critical thinking and leads to deeper learning for students, and looking to this as a foundation for our pedagogy is a natural choice (Langer, 1995; Marzano, Pickering, & Pollock, 2001; Nystrand, 1997). If our goal is truly to create independent college and workplace-ready learners as the CCSS asks, framing instruction with questions and teaching students to ask their own questions play a vital role in meeting these standards. Embracing an inquiry approach to teaching will help us better align our practices with what we know about how people learn, making it a better way to facilitate learning in the classroom.

Inquiry Learning Places Students at the Center

If, as constructivists argue, learning is more about creating our own knowledge through having our own experiences with content, then we need a model of teaching that emphasizes the student's role in learning. And if the learner's role is different, then the teacher's role also changes: teachers should be designing learning experiences that allow the students space to examine and question, to investigate and try out new ideas or procedures, and to reflect on their experiences. In inquiry classrooms, teachers model for students how to examine and question, helping them become metacognitive and aware of their own learning styles, processes, and strategies. Some may feel that teachers take on a lesser or reduced role in such an environment, but this is not true. A teacher's expertise is even more essential in this environment, as they are required to break down complex concepts and processes into more concrete, accessible pieces for novice learners. And skilled teachers are needed to properly scaffold learning experiences for students that will lead them purposefully toward skill development. The teacher, as an expert in his or her discipline, also gives feedback and coaching as students develop skills and approximate expert performance.

If the learner's personal construction of knowledge is at the center of instruction, we must also place students' needs and interests at the center of many of our instructional choices. Perhaps more than with past generations, this generation of young people has many different forces vying for their attention and time. While designing instruction that meets individual needs has always been a critical component of good learning, it is certainly more so today given the appeal of TV and other popular media like the Internet, social networking, and communications technologies. This is not to suggest that we pander to students' interests or embrace fleeting social fads simply to dazzle and tickle our students' fancies. Rather, we should ask ourselves how the instruction we want to deliver has meaning in students' lives today. We do this by tapping into students' interests, connecting to real-world events and problems, and connecting to relevant aspects of students' worlds and lived experiences.

By incorporating into our instruction questions and overarching themes that relate to students' lives, we can tap into their natural interest and motivation to learn. In an inquiry learning model we can also connect to learner interests by using a variety of texts to explore essential question in depth. The more variety we incorporate, the more likely it will be that we find at least one text that interests each of the students in our class. Such variety can also provide ways for us to legitimize what students value outside of the classroom, helping us tap into students' multiple interests and out-of-school talents that otherwise might be overlooked.

Inquiry Learning Taps into Natural Motivation

The role that motivation plays in learning has been long appreciated by teachers, but not really studied seriously until recently. Psychologists like Mihaly Csikszentmihalyi (1990) and investigative journalists like Daniel Pink (2009) have looked at motivation in contexts from schools to the workplace and identified similar characteristics of experiences that motivate us to achievement. These writers suggest that the traditional notion that we are motivated by extrinsic rewards such as grades or money does not accurately describe the phenomenon of motivation. They instead show that we are most motivated when we feel in control, when we feel we have some skill or competence, when we have an appropriate challenge (with support if needed), and when we have clear goals and feedback.

Sadly, we can easily see how schools may not foster these conditions very well. When students have little choice in the books they'll read or the kinds of assignments they must complete, they lose a sense of control. It shouldn't come as a surprise that students confronting graded essays heavily marked with red pen or assigned books that are thematically and syntactically too complex might feel a lack of confidence about their abilities. In addition, students facing fill-in-the blank worksheets or dull questions will also find little to give them confidence in their abilities. School, for too many of our students, seems a place without a meaningful purpose, disconnected from the reality they live in or hope to live in in the future.

While some of these issues are outside our control and result from teenagers' own perceptions about school, we can control many important motivating factors; an inquiry approach to teaching maximizes student motivation and leads to better learning and engagement. Inquiry learning can allow students to control their learning by providing complex questions that afford multiple branches of exploration. Young adult texts, when used as part of this inquiry, provide a built-in sense of real meaning and purpose for teens who can relate to the characters, conflicts, and themes of these books. Inquiry learning also places a premium on scaffolded learning experiences that present students with an appropriate level of challenge under the right support that encourages successful experiences that build students' confidence.

Inquiry learning—because it addresses natural processes of learning, puts students at the center, and taps into natural motivations—is one of the strongest instructional pedagogies out there. With the transition to the common core, the time is ripe to embrace this approach in our classrooms and create environments that will nurture independent, actively engaged learners. When coupled with young adult texts, we have a powerful one-two punch that gives us a way to help students learn what they need to in order to be ready for a future of college study, rewarding careers, and active participation in society.

This is an admittedly surface-level discussion of what inquiry learning is and how it can provide meaningful learning for our students. Many resources exist that can provide a deeper understanding of what inquiry learning can do for your students; we provide you with a few of our favorite resources in box 7.1.

Box 7.1   Professional Resources for Inquiry Design

Understanding by Design by Grant Wiggins and Jay McTighe	From the two men who started us thinking about essential questions, this book has loads of advice on crafting questions and a wide variety of examples of effective questions.
What's the Big Idea? by Jim Burke	Burke gives a spirited defense of using questions in the classroom and provides many real examples of how to work questions into teaching units.
Engaging Readers and Writers with Inquiry by Jeffrey D. Wilhelm	Wilhelm emphasizes writing and reading strategies within the context of inquiry units; his opening chapters provide good advice on crafting solid questions.
Orchestrating Inquiry Learning by Karen Littleton, Eileen Scanlon, and Mike Sharples	The authors of this text speak to how inquiry learning can lead to higher-order thinking skills, especially when supported by technology.
Exemplary Classroom Questioning: Practices to Promote Thinking and Learning by Marie Pagliaro	Pagliaro describes how classrooms can be structured around questions. She offers advice on how teachers can use questions and also on helping students construct their own questions.

Planning for Inquiry Learning

So how do we design inquiry-based instruction? Through our experience, both in the classroom and in preparing future teachers at the university, we have developed a process for planning these units that we share in the rest of the chapter. We describe this process as a set of steps but want to stress that this does not imply a step-by-step, rigid process; this outline actually represents a more organic, recursive process. What we do in one stage of the planning often influences what we do in other stages, and a decision we make about something in a later phase could cause us to revisit earlier decisions and revise them.

Step One: Choosing an Anchor Text and Devising an Essential Question/Theme

Our planning usually begins in one of two places, with either ideas about the essential question or unifying theme we'd like to explore with our students or ideas about the text (or set of texts) we'd like to study with them. Without a doubt these two decisions should be closely married, as not every text will allow for exploration of every essential question or theme. In addition, we may not have a wide array of options for the texts, since available resources can only be stretched so far, after all. So in these cases we may not have a good deal of latitude in terms of choosing an essential question or theme. Since the question of texts is often the most limiting factor, we'll proceed first to talk about factors that influence our choice of texts and then discuss how we devise a good essential question or unifying theme.

Choosing an Anchor Text

Choosing an anchor text to use as the center of a unit is an important choice, as almost everything else in the unit will depend on that choice. Since this is a book about using young adult literature with the common core standards, you shouldn't be surprised that we'll advocate here for choosing young adult titles. We made the case for this in the first half of the book, but it bears repeating here that we feel strongly that young adult titles can be sufficiently sophisticated to meet the exacting demands of the common core. There is sufficient quality out there now in the genre that young adult literature need not even be coupled with classic texts to justify its study in the classroom. And if we couple young adult literature with the demanding environment of inquiry learning, we've got a combination that can't be beat.

When choosing texts, many of us who have relied on book lists or tradition or even "what's in the bookroom" as criteria to guide our choices may find the decision to be particularly challenging. However, applying the three-tiered model of complexity in the common core allows us to advocate strongly for almost any text we wish to use as part of an inquiry-based unit. Sifting through all the possible choices is an exciting process, but it can seem daunting given the wide-open nature of the task. To guide your decision making, we offer a few criteria that we have found helpful in making text selections.

- A primary concern should be our students' developmental needs as well as their interests, experiences, and motivation. When considering this criterion, we ask questions about what kinds of topics or issues our students are developmentally ready for, what they might be interested in, and also what kinds of reading skills they need to develop. Of course, young adult literature is a natural fit for students' needs and interests, but it also provides accessible texts in which students can practice and hone their reading skills.
- We need to also be concerned with the complexity of the text, as students need to be reading increasingly complex texts so they can develop independence as readers. It is up to teachers to challenge students with appropriately complex texts. Fortunately, as we demonstrated in the first part of the book, young adult texts provide a wide

range of levels of complexity. By using the quantitative, qualitative, and reader and tasks dimensions we outlined in previous chapters, we can easily identify appropriately complex texts for our students.

- Lastly, of central importance to text selection is an understanding of our instructional purposes: we need to consider what we're planning to do with the text. Clearly, each text provides an opportunity to teach and refine reading skills, but some texts require unique skills. For example, a text like Hesse's *The Witness*, about the rise of the Ku Klux Klan in a small town, is told in free verse poetry, a form that will require unique skills in interpreting figurative language and inferences. Some books will be better suited to a certain skill set we hope to develop with students, and our choices should reflect that.

Young adult literature offers us a vast array of texts to which we can apply the above criteria to find the right titles for our classrooms. But one of the biggest challenges, especially for those with little experience with the field, is navigating the vast number of texts in this growing area. With hundreds of titles published each year, it is challenging for teachers to keep up so they can find the books that would be appropriate for their classroom. We have found this challenge easier to address if we look to others to provide support and suggest relying on fellow teachers or librarians, and even the recommendations of students to help you focus on the best titles. In box 7.2 we have included some of our favorite resources for staying abreast of the field.

In addition to sifting through a wide selection of books, one of the other challenges we face in choosing texts is limited resources; this is especially true since, for many of us, embracing young adult literature in our classroom means procuring new sets of books. Most book rooms are likely populated with copies of classic texts, and while young adult literature might appear on the shelves of classroom or school libraries, a teacher may need more than the one or two copies these sources provide. In addition, if your school or district has spent money on an expensive anthology series, there might be precious little left for young adult books. Even when resources are tight, there is no need to despair. There are a variety of ways that you can face this challenge and expand the number of resources you have to draw upon. The following ideas are ones that we have had success with.

- Many of the schools that we've worked and observed in rely on classroom sets of books, and teachers don't have kids take the books home. This approach allows us to stretch classroom sets further, since we only need to have a number of copies equal to our largest class. This does mean that class time has to be devoted to reading the book, and while this is challenging, it also provides meaningful opportunities for careful reading and group instruction.
- Using literature circles or book clubs in your classroom (Daniels, 2002) is one of the best ways to stretch limited copies of titles. Since students read a book in small groups, fewer copies of each book are required. Literature circles emphasize the social nature of reading, and since these groups are designed to eventually run without too much guidance, they also encourage independent reading and meaning-making.
- While we are inclined to select one novel for whole-class study, this need not be the case for all of our teaching; we might consider using multiple anchor texts or teaching units where students each select their own text. This allows teachers to draw on existing classroom or school libraries that may only have one or two copies of a given book. Again, structures like literature circles or book clubs can be a great

Box 7.2   Resources for Discovering YA Books

Assembly on Literature for Adolescents (ALAN)
Part of the National Council of Teachers of English, ALAN (http://community.alan-ya.org/Home/) advocates for young adult literature. They produce a journal, the *ALAN Review* (http://scholar.lib.vt.edu/ejournals/ALAN/alan-review.html), and have a yearly workshop devoted to young adult authors and their books.

Bloggers
Individuals who blog about young adult books abound and can provide great insights into the world of young adult books and their readers. A list of YA Bloggers can be found at: http://yabookblog directory.blogspot.com/p/ya-book-blogger-list.html
However, some of our favorite YA book bloggers are:
Kiss the Book: http://www.kissthebook.blogspot.com/
Persnickety Snark http://www.persnicketysnark.com/
The Story Siren: http://www.thestorysiren.com/
YA Book Nerd: http://yabooknerd.blogspot.com/
Young Adult Book Reviews: http://youngadultbookreviews.com/

Goodreads.com (http://www.goodreads.com)
A social media site for people who love books, this website is a great way to connect with others who love young adult books and to find out what they are reading. Many young adult authors are on Goodreads and provide connections to their blog and other media through the site. User-compiled lists in the "listopia" section and their giveaways are also helpful.

EarlyWord: The Publisher/Librarian Connection (http://www.earlyword.com/)
Designed for librarians to help them keep an eye on the publishing industry, this website offers a great deal of information about adult, children's, and young adult books. Of particular interest are their links to publishers' catalogs (http://www.earlyword.com/catalog-links/) and their newsletter, which provides a summary of information every Friday (http://www.earlyword.com/newsletters/sign-up/).

Review Sources
Many professional review sources provide reviews of young adult books and information about what's new and what is coming out.
Children's Book and Play Review (http://lib.byu.edu/sites/cbpr/)
The Horn Book (http://www.hbook.com/)
Kirkus Reviews (http://www.kirkusreviews.com/)
Publishers Weekly (http://www.publishersweekly.com)
VOYA (http://www.voya.com/)

TeenReads (http://www.teenreads.com/)
Produced by the Book Report Network, this website offers reviews of young adult books, lists of new books coming out, and contests.

Voice of Youth Advocates (VOYA)
A magazine for young adult librarians that provides book reviews, book lists, articles, and news. Arguably the best journal out there that covers young adult literature, you can subscribe to it in print, and free content is provided online (http://www.voya.com/).

Young Adult Library Services Association (YALSA)
A division of the American Library Association, YALSA gives yearly awards for young adult books and creates numerous best books lists. All of the awards and lists can be found at http://www.ala.org/yalsa/booklistsawards/booklistsbook. Access is free after providing a little demographic information.

way to implement this approach. There are many professionals who advocate for these types of approaches, including Donalyn Miller (2009). Miller's method, while designed for a sixth-grade class, can be easily adapted into any grade, a fact that we have seen teachers use with success.

- Purchasing used or remaindered books is a fine way to get a number of books at a reasonable cost. Online resellers, such as Amazon.com, half.com, and abebooks.com, often offer a reasonable price on these books. And with some larger used sellers doing business through these sites, you may be able to combine shipping costs.

- Look for other inexpensive alternatives such as book clubs. We all remember those Scholastic book club flyers that we brought home in elementary school. While we tend to disregard these in the upper grades, they still are a great way to not only obtain inexpensive books for our upper-grade classrooms, but also allow students to get books into their homes at a reasonable price. The Arrow and Tab Scholastic Book Clubs (https://clubs.scholastic.com/) offer a wide variety of classic and young adult titles at low prices. They also offer incentives for teachers that can help stretch limited funds.

- Some of the teachers we've worked with have found funding by writing small grants or asking local businesses to help with classroom costs. A good source for some of these opportunities is through the National Council of Teachers of English at http://www.ncte.org/grants/sec. Your school or district may have other resources.

- You can join with other teachers to share sets of books, giving you more options and purchasing power. We also encourage you to talk with your school librarian and/or district media specialist. These professionals can either help you find ways to purchase books that you can check out when your students need them, or they may be able to provide resources that you had not already thought of. We often tell our students that besides the janitor, the librarian in their schools is going to be one of their best collaborative resources.

- Lastly, a promising area to consider are books published in the public domain. Some reputable authors, including Cory Doctorow, have published their books for free and made them available in a number of electronic forms. Amazon.com often cuts the price on books for their Kindle device (or the Kindle reader application for Windows and Mac), sometimes offering titles for free. The selection in this direction is usually slim, but may be worth the effort.

Devising an Essential Question or Unifying Theme

The essential question or unifying theme forms the heart of the entire instructional unit, so it's important that we devise a strong one to support students' learning and exploration of the texts. In addition, a good essential question or theme will also motivate students as they explore, and it provides a basis for our unit assessments and learning objectives.

It may seem at first that we're talking about two different ways to structure instructional units, but we actually think that essential questions and themes have a lot in common. Both seek to unify instruction around a central idea, and both seek to help students make meaningful connections among texts, concepts, and activities. The use of essential questions as a way to frame instruction dates to the work of Wiggins and McTighe (1998), and thematic units can trace their history to the calls in the 1950s for English teachers to "integrate" their instruction. Both approaches have been around for a while, and we recognize that some teachers may feel more familiar with one than the other. We want to embrace both of them in our approach here by briefly discussing each.

Thematic approaches to teaching literature arose out of a reaction to organizing literature in English courses chronologically, a practice that has dominated the field for a long time. Thematic units arrange the study of literature around themes or overarching concepts, rather than studying them in chronological order. For example, in such a unit a teacher might have students read and examine *Stargirl* by Jerry Spinelli as part of a unit about identity. Students study other novels, poems, short stories, or even dramatic works at the same time to allow for further exploration of the theme; study of writing and language are integrated in such a way that they help support students' exploration of the theme. Thematic units have many benefits over traditional, chronological schemes for organizing content. When we read literature focused on a topic, students can more naturally make connections between the works and to their own lives (Peck, 1989). The single focus of a thematic unit also allows for deeper exploration of a topic, providing students multiple perspectives and giving them a variety of opportunities to revise and expand their thinking about the topic. Thematic units allow teachers to use materials that appeal to students while still attending to other demands of the curriculum (Maxwell, Meiser, & McKnight, 2011).

The approach of using essential questions to frame a unit of study is similar to the thematic approach in that it also taps into a central theme or idea. The difference here is that we take the idea and phrase it in the form of a question that then forms the keystone of our unit. By placing a question at the center of our instruction, we tap into students' curiosity and the benefits of inquiry learning that we outlined earlier in this chapter. However, identifying and articulating a good essential question can be challenging for those who have never approached instruction in this way; fortunately, there are plenty of resources available today that can help. For instance, in their groundbreaking work on using essential questions, Grant Wiggins and Jay McTighe (1998) described good essential questions in this way:

- *Essential questions get at what really matters in a discipline and in life.* A good essential question will strike at something that matters to people in a content area. Those of us in the field of literature, for instance, might really care about narrative construction, so a question that would matter to us would be, *What makes a powerful story?* Thematic and philosophical questions matter to us, such as, *How can we maintain our humanity in the face of cruelty?* or *What can challenges teach us about our character?* These questions matter to humanity as a whole, and we read and study literature because it offers potential answers to these questions.

- *Essential questions arise time and time again in our learning and in the history of a discipline.* Good essential questions tap into issues that have long been a part of our quest for understanding. These are questions that we, as humans, have been grappling with for centuries or longer. Even as individuals, we may have found ourselves asking these questions multiple times in our lives or our careers.

- *Essential questions raise additional important questions.* Part of why these questions have been around for a long time is because they are connected with other, equally important questions. If we're asking how we maintain our humanity in the face of cruelty, we're also likely to ask about the roots of cruelty and why some feel they have a right or need to act cruelly to others. A good essential question is part of a larger set of issues that sparks many questions such that even as we approach an answer for the original question, we're already thinking of new questions to explore.

- *Essential questions can be answered in different ways.* In order to generate sustained interest and exploration, a good essential question can't be easily answered or can't have one "correct" answer. There must be multiple explanations or answers possible after a sincere exploration of the issues the question raises. Different people are likely to answer these questions differently, based on their own values and life experiences and interpretations of those experiences.

- *Essential questions are connected to individuals' interests and lives.* If essential questions meet the above criteria, they'll almost certainly provoke sustained interest and hold up to lengthy exploration by a wide variety of individuals. In teaching literature to secondary students, however, we find that it is just as critical that our essential questions be connected to their lives. High school students are likely to find a question like *What makes a good relationship?* appealing because it connects to their lives and experiences. While finding questions that connect with students' lives can be a challenge, doing so is critical to establishing questions that will not only frame instruction but motivate students to learn in depth.

Following these guidelines will give us a solid start in developing essential questions. Additionally, there are many solid resources you can refer to for help in devising essential questions and unifying themes; the books we referred to earlier in our discussion of inquiry learning can provide more substantial exploration of this issue. It can take some time to become good at devising strong questions, but it's well worth the effort. We find that framing instruction this way taps into students' natural interests and curiosity, providing a powerful structure for learning.

As we consider possible essential questions or themes, we need to simultaneously consider our choice of anchor text(s); we want the two decisions to be as tightly connected as possible. Clearly, the more a novel explores the ideas at the heart of our unit, the more effective students' reading and learning will be. For instance, John Green's funny and warm-hearted novel *An Abundance of Katherines* deals with a teenage boy's failed relationships and his frustration with romance in general. While on a road trip, he encounters yet another romantic possibility, and he has to decide whether to take a risk and try again. This novel allows for the exploration of a number of essential questions, such as *What is worth risking everything for?* or *What makes a strong, healthy relationship?* The novel explores issues related to this question in quite a bit of depth and could foster meaningful classroom discussion of either question. On the other hand, Wendelin Van Draanen's book *The Running Dream* addresses a different set of essential questions. In this novel the protagonist, a track star, loses both legs in an accident and has to adjust to life with prosthetic legs; as she struggles to recapture the joy of running, she also learns what life is like for those with disabilities and handicaps. This book lends itself nicely to questions like *How do we overcome challenges?* or *What does our reaction to life-altering changes say about who we are?* Again, the sophisticated treatment of these issues in this book would provide many opportunities to explore these questions in depth.

The decisions about anchor texts and essential questions or themes will often be a symbiotic sort of choice—with one feeding the other. A key consideration when crafting essential questions for an inquiry unit, then, is whether or not the anchor text we use allows for substantial exploration of that question; the anchor text itself must allow for deep exploration so we can use it to teach students important literacy skills as part of our unit.

Step Two: Developing a Unit Assessment

After choosing texts and developing questions or themes, we next turn to assessments. When Einstein set out to explore questions about the nature of time and the universe, he didn't do so simply to pass the time. He had a purpose in mind, and he planned to find a way to share with others what he had learned as a result of his questioning. In the same way, we don't want to set up questions and themes for our students to explore without providing them the means, both formal and informal, to share what they learn as a result. In designing units around young adult literature and essential questions or themes, it's important that we also give significant thought to how we assess students' learning, especially at the end of the unit.

Peter Smagorinsky (2007) suggests that in planning for how we assess learning at the end of a unit, we should design an assessment that gives students a chance to construct their own understandings and to synthesize what they've explored in the texts and activities of the unit. This same objective is implied in many of the common core anchor standards for reading and writing. So the culminating assessment we design for a unit should allow students a chance to share the conclusions they've reached as part of exploring the question or theme of the unit, and it should push students to develop new skills and grasp unfamiliar concepts. We want students to engage deeply in the content of the essential question or theme, and in so doing we want them to develop thinking skills that will serve them in the future. Lastly, as we create a final assessment we must also consider the standards and learning goals inherent in the CCSS we want students to meet.

As ELA teachers, the first thoughts that might come to mind about assessments like this would be something along the lines of a written essay; that's the way many of us were assessed by our teachers. The written essay is still an important genre for students to write in, but other genres and even new media play an increasingly important role in how we interact with others and engage with ideas in the larger society outside of school. While we mustn't abandon the written essay, we ought to be pushing ourselves beyond it to find different and equally mean-ingful ways for students to show their learning. As forms of communication in society evolve, it is vital that we help students understand how to navigate and communicate ideas using other media (Kajder, 2010).

At the same time, we have to be careful that these different forms of assessment don't become gimmicky or superficial. Part of the reason why formal writing assessments have staked such a place in ELA classrooms is because they can provide rigorous assessment. As we bring in alternative projects and assessments to the classroom, we must take care that these assessments hold similar rigor. We should attend to elements of process and illuminate standards of quality in expression in these different forms just as we would with traditional writing assessments.

Deciding on the form of a final assessment can be tricky, especially for inexperienced teachers or for teachers who want to move beyond the comfort of the traditional written essay. To provide a foundation to help envision some alternatives to traditional assessments, we suggest keeping the following questions in mind while thinking about final assessments.

- *What modes are my students expected to master?* Our students will be expected to meet the writing, speaking, and listening standards in the CCSS, so these will serve as the basis for much of our assessment work. The common core does not dictate specific *forms* that students should write in (e.g., personal essay, research paper, newspaper op-ed piece) but rather the *modes* in which they should write (i.e., the purpose for which they should be writing: to inform, to argue, or to tell a story). These modes of writing can take on different forms. We can argue, for instance, in an essay or in a speech or even in an op-ed newspaper piece. We can tell a story through creative nonfiction, through a short story or one-act play, or even through a live-action video. Finding forms that match the mode we are targeting is a good first step in identifying assessments.

- *What genres do professionals write in?* As the common core expects us to create career-ready students, looking to the forms that professionals in the workforce write in can serve as a great starting point for developing assessments. Many professionals may not write formal essays, but they write in lots of different genres: letters, reports, brochures, advertisements, instructions, even PowerPoint presentations or other visual forms. By considering the genres in use in the world around us, we can come up with ideas for our assessments that would not only be authentic but would also teach students important strategies for analyzing forms of communication that will allow them to write in ways that will prepare them for the work they will be doing one day.

- *How might digital media and technologies enhance a traditional assessment?* Connecting assessments to new technology not only taps into students' lives outside the classroom, but it can also address the 21st-century writing and literacy demands of the CCSS. Adding in a multimedia or technological component can enhance many traditional assignments. For example, the traditional research paper can be informed by primary research (interviews, polls, etc.) conducted via Facebook pages or e-mail or even videoconferencing. Technology or multimedia can also be used to replace a traditional form with a newer form. The traditional personal narrative essay could become a visual slideshow of images with students' narration recorded as voice-over audio. A character analysis essay could be presented as a mini-documentary instead, complete with "talking heads" presenting, in a visual form, the same information and analysis we might find in a traditional written piece.
- *Are there forms that aren't written that might meet our needs?* Speaking and listening are valuable communication skills, and the common core places emphasis on these nonwritten forms. While oral speaking may not currently have the stature it once had in English classes, oral forms of communication remain important today. An oral speech or presentation might be an appropriate form for an end-of-unit assessment; this form will allow students to build essential skills while it provides them an opportunity to present their learning in a different way. To capitalize on oral forms, we might also ask our students to prepare for a formal debate or panel-type presentation as a way of offering interpretations of a text's themes or analysis of characters.

Regardless of its form, our final assessment for an inquiry unit should provide for connections among the anchor text, the essential question, and the meaningful skills and knowledge that students need to develop. This can seem like a tall task. We'll describe the thinking that goes into this process in more detail in chapter eight, but to give you the basics of how this works, let's return to one of the examples we used earlier. If we were teaching Green's *An Abundance of Katherines* with the question of *What is worth risking everything for?*, we could use a few assessments to measure students' learning and understanding developed during the unit; each of these would connect the text, the question, and our students' skills. For example, we could have students write a personal narrative in which they connect the text and question by reflecting on a time when they took a risk and explore why they did so and what they learned as a result. Or students could use research skills to explore the life of a historical figure who took great risks and connect this to the book's themes. Or students can use analytic thinking to explore the text's themes, creating a video slideshow detailing the risks taken by the protagonist, the inherent values at work in the risks, and a judgment about the worthiness of those risks. Any of these assessments, if given the proper rigor, would provide students a means for exploring the text and the essential question as well as provide an opportunity to develop or refine skills in writing and critical thinking.

In addition to how our assessment connects our text, question, and skill set, we also want to consider student motivation as a factor in designing the final assessment. Recent research into motivation in a school setting indicates how we can construct assessments to be more motivational for students. Smith and Wilhelm (2002) apply Mihaly Csikszentmihalyi's (1990) theory of flow to the literacy behaviors (in and out of school) of teen boys. As they observed a large group of boys engage in plenty of literate activities outside of the classroom, they wondered about their lack of motivation for literacy within the schools. Smith and Wilhelm then reasoned that the in-school literacy experiences were not motivating in the same way as the boys' out-of-school experiences. They describe in their work the conditions that need to be in place for optimal motivation and, thus, maximal learning. Some of these conditions that are appropriate to consider when we plan an assessment include:

- *A sense of control and competence.* Most of us gravitate toward activities where we feel in control and where we have developed skills that make us feel competent. This is not to suggest that we should only ask students to engage in assessments that they like or can do well; such assessments would be useless, given that the point of school is to add new skills and understandings to our repertoire. This does suggest, however, that we ought to offer students a sense of control whenever possible and help them develop the knowledge they'll need to successfully complete the assessment. The issue of student control can be tricky, within the limitations of our classrooms and curricula, but one of the best ways to give students a sense of control is to offer them choice in their assessments. Offering students a choice of topics on which they can write or allowing them to choose the genre or form that their writing will take are examples of the kinds of choice we've found motivating to our students. For our students to feel competent, we need to help them develop the knowledge they'll need to successfully complete the assessment. This need can be addressed by carefully considering the knowledge demands of an assessment and how to help students acquire that knowledge, as explained in the next two parts of this chapter. By delivering effective instruction to help them gain the required skills and knowledge, we help students develop this all-important sense of competency.

- *An appropriate level of challenge.* Although this may seem counterintuitive at first, we are motivated by experiences that challenge us. Personally, we know this to be true since we find teaching to be a motivating experience in large part because of the challenge it provides us. In addition, journalist Daniel Pink (2009) notes, in his research on motivation in the business world, that inherent challenges in tasks often provide more motivation than even monetary rewards. Smith and Wilhelm (2002) cite numerous boys from their studies who talk at length about the rewarding challenges of video games that gradually ramp up the difficulty as the player becomes more and more competent. These boys didn't want to engage in tasks that only required skills they had already mastered. We must keep in mind that this is not just any challenge but an "appropriate" level of challenge. Tasks that are too far out of our reach will not motivate but frustrate us; for optimal learning, we want to develop assessments for students that will help them grow and develop new skills without frustrating them. These findings echo the idea of Vygotsky's (1962) zone of proximal development, that place where a learner can develop new understandings if coached by a more capable peer. Assessments should provide a level of challenge that causes students to stretch, supported by our expert modeling and feedback, but not overwhelm or frustrate them.

- *Clear goals and feedback.* As we design assessments, we must also keep in mind that students are motivated by a clear goal and feedback about progress toward that goal. Many of the boys that Smith and Wilhelm (2002) observed were motivated to play video games, in large part because the goals in these games are always quite clear

(clear the level of enemies, defeat the end-of-level boss, collect all the gold coins, etc.), and the feedback is built into the experience (sound effects accompany successes or failures, counts of coins or points rise as the player succeeds, a "death" clearly signals a failure to achieve the goals). Sports also provide clear goals and feedback: the "clunk" of the basketball bouncing off the rim is all a player needs to know that the shot didn't go in. Students, however, don't always get these same clear goals and feedback in their school experiences. One of the things we've heard teenagers complain about quite a bit is when teachers give unclear instructions or grade papers and projects in unexpected ways. If we want to boost our students' motivation to complete assignments, we should work hard to make our goals for assignments as clear as possible. This may entail completing the assignment ourselves, as sort of a "dry run" to see just what is required; this can also help us anticipate trouble spots students may have in the process of completing the assessment. Giving clear feedback may be trickier than developing goals and expectations, since as teachers we cannot provide the immediate feedback that video games or sports do. However, we can still be clear and up front about how we will grade students' work. All of us appreciate knowing how we will be evaluated on a task before we complete it, and such knowledge helps us direct our efforts toward success. To make this happen, Maxwell, Meiser, and McKnight (2011) suggest that we should design our evaluation procedures at the same time as we design our assessments. This is only fair, they suggest, given that knowing how we are going to evaluate the final product will help us be explicit with students about our expectations. Students deserve, just as we all do, to know how they'll be evaluated before they begin working on a task. And having clear expectations and a sense of how they will be evaluated helps motivate them as they complete tasks in the classroom.

This section has outlined a variety of considerations that we should keep in mind as we develop final assessments for instructional units. Balancing these issues gives us the structure we need to develop assessments that provide our students with a chance to construct their own understandings and to synthesize what they've explored in the texts and activities of the unit. These assessments will then be a keystone for the rest of our unit that locks all its pieces into place.

Step Three: Developing Learning Outcomes and Processes for Daily Instruction

With the text and essential questions selected and a vision of a final assessment in mind, the next step in planning is to outline the process that will lead us to that final outcome. This process leads to defined learning outcomes and plans for daily instruction. We know some may argue that learning outcomes should be determined first in the process, or at least before we determine the form of assessment. We don't necessarily disagree with this idea, and would mention again that this process is fluid; of course, we may begin our unit planning with some idea of objectives in place.

Our decision to discuss this issue here rests on our feeling that it is necessary to begin planning with an end in mind, so we suggest (as do writers like Wiggins and McTighe (1998)) that we establish the assessment before we do detailed planning. Having a vision of the end assessment will help us ensure that the planning to get there is consistent and meaningful. We have often encountered teachers who assign research papers, and as they're grading the papers they bemoan the lack of quality in students' work. All too often, we find this due in part to the fact that the instructors did not plan ways to help students master the component skills and behaviors that produce a strong piece of research writing. It's less effective to just assign a paper and expect great results; instead, we need to take the students though the steps of defining a topic, finding sources, evaluating sources, and synthesizing them into a product.

A second reason for placing this discussion last is that we find that the selection of text, questions, and assessment plays a significant role in the determination of outcomes and processes for learning. How we match a text with a task will impact our judgment of its complexity; the same holds true for the outcomes we expect. If we choose a text that needs high levels of intervention to help students meet the text's knowledge demands, part of our outcome will have to be aimed at delivering that intervention. As we plan, we must consider the new skills and understandings students will need to acquire in order to successfully engage in the unit. These considerations naturally lead us to develop the overall objectives or learning targets for our unit and inform the daily planning.

How do we determine the specific nature of the knowledge that our students will need to develop as part of an instructional unit? There are a number of sources we can look for to help with this, including the core standards, the text we've chosen to anchor our unit, the essential question or theme we're using to frame the unit, and the nature of the final assessment we'll ask students to complete in order to demonstrate their learning. We'll take each of these in turn and talk about their implications for identifying the knowledge demands of a unit.

The Core Standards

The common core standards play an important role in our determination of what knowledge and outcomes are expected of our students. After all, these standards outline for us the literacy skills and understandings that will be required of them in college and the workplace. Important assessments will be linked to these standards, and schools and teachers will be held accountable for students' performance on these standards. We see the standards playing a role throughout this process of determining what kinds and the specific nature of knowledge developed as part of an instructional unit.

As we identify learning targets for students through our analysis of the anchor texts, final assessments, and essential questions, we should seek to connect those to the common core standards. For example, in teaching a unit anchored by *Whirligig* by Paul Fleischman, we can identify through our analysis of the text's complexity that this novel will require some understanding of unconventional story structures and the pattern of the hero's journey. These structural concerns lead to strong connections to the common core reading anchor standards R.1 (read closely to determine explicit and inferential meanings), R.3 (analyze how and why individuals, events, and ideas interact), and R.5 (analyze the structure of texts). In addition, as with most units, we'll want to help students refine their ability to distill thematic understandings from the text, so reading anchor standard R.2 (determine central ideas or themes) will certainly apply to this unit as well. Having identified these standards, we can use them to shape our daily instruction toward meeting these objectives.

The Text

The text or set of texts we choose as an anchor for the unit will typically make knowledge demands of our students. Sometimes these demands will be in the form of background knowledge that students need in order to make sense of the story. With Geraldine McCaughrean's *The White Darkness*, for instance, some understanding of Antarctica or even of Robert Scott's trip to the Antarctic and Titus Oates's role in that trip provides important background for students. Other times, the structure of the text might require some strategic reading, such as when a story is told by more than one narrator or when the novel contains multiple plot lines that need to be kept track of. In the graphic novel *American Born Chinese* by Gene Luen Yang, the multiple story lines will be challenging to many students, and they will need help keeping track of and connecting the story lines as the story progresses. Texts rich in symbolism or metaphor will also demand more of students than those that are told more literally. Those that play with traditional prose structures or that use unique structures will likewise require more skill. With *Out of the Dust* by Karen Hesse, told in free verse poetry, students will need to familiarize themselves with poetic conventions and interpret Hesse's figurative language to make good sense of the story and its themes.

Part of our task in planning, then, is to analyze the text to determine what kinds of knowledge we need students to develop as part of the unit. By anticipating the challenges students might have with texts, we can prepare instruction that will equip them with background knowledge and reading strategies they'll need to make meaning from the text.

The Essential Question

We must also consider the knowledge demands of the essential question itself; rich and complex essential questions may demand new skills and attitudes from students. Our essential questions explore multilayered concepts that students may not be immediately familiar with. Identifying the requisite knowledge needed to sufficiently explore the essential question will help us establish appropriate learning goals. In addition, our essential question may require cognitive skills from our students, not the least of which may be a capacity for sustained attention to a topic, as described by Sheridan Blau (2003). As we develop our objectives we must consider demands that the essential question will place on our students if we hope to have them fully explore the question or theme at the heart of the unit.

Let's explore this with the example of Walter Dean Myers's book *Monster* and the essential question, *How do we determine the truth when stories conflict?* To be able to examine this question in depth, using this text, students will need to be able to summarize and recall details of a story. Without this ability they won't be able to see when stories conflict. Likewise, they'll need to be able to make comparisons and notice places where the stories conflict. At this point, the thinking demanded of students becomes more challenging because we need to explore implied motivations and subtleties about characters in order to try to understand why some characters in this book might lie or distort the facts. Students will also need to be able to tolerate some ambiguity and uncertainty about the stories, since black-and-white answers aren't easy to come by in this book. While tolerating uncertainty is not necessarily a strategy, being able to formulate a conclusion and defend that conclusion with details from the text is one that may need to be explicitly taught. Understanding these varied implications of the essential question and the demands exploring this question can place on students will, once again, help us to develop strong learning objectives for our units.

The Final Assessment

Whatever form the final assessment takes, we want to use it as an opportunity to help students demonstrate the knowledge they've gained. At the same time, we can take advantage of this opportunity to teach students new things about writing, composing, and communication. Information about the writing process itself, about composing in different forms, about using language in creative and appropriate ways, and communicating in various ways will be important to convey to students. If we use the final assessment as a learning activity in this manner, then we need to identify the knowledge demands of this task.

Reflecting on the process students should undertake to complete the project or task can help to identify these demands. We have found that it can help to actually complete the assignments we give students ourselves, so as to more concretely understand the processes inherent in completing the task and to spot potential problems. The first couple of times one author assigned his students a multimedia slideshow, for instance, he completed one himself first. Going through this process allowed him to better create instructions for the tasks students needed to complete with the computer software. It also allowed him insights into spots in the process that could be troublesome, and he could later devise instructions or warnings to students about those spots.

Let's look more closely at an example of this. If students, for instance, were to complete a comparison-contrast essay as their final assessment, a teacher might recognize a few knowledge demands of this task. First, students would need to understand how we make meaningful comparisons and contrasts; second, they would need to know some different organizational structures that this kind of writing suggests; third, the teacher might also decide that knowing how to effectively use transitions would be beneficial to students writing in this mode. These demands suggest important learning objectives that the teacher will need to address as part of the larger instructional unit to ensure that all students are prepared to meet the demands of the final assessment.

We now have in mind some outcomes we need to include as part of our instruction processes, the demands of which will inform the day-to-day plans that make up the meat of our instructional units. Daily planning used to be the bane of our existence as novice teachers; each day we'd drive home, asking ourselves, "What will I do in class tomorrow?" In that view, the end goal of planning seemed to be finding a way to fill class time rather than using class time to build toward meaningful learning. Since we've started planning the way we outline in this chapter, our attitudes have changed. When we start with a clear understanding of the text, essential question, and the final assessment, daily planning becomes an exercise in identifying the steps that will lead us there. We feel better able to connect concepts that students must master to explore the unit content. We also can easily identify discrete skills they need to gain in order to meet the demands of the final assessment and of reading the text, and so forth. This is not to say that daily planning is not a lengthy or complicated process, especially if an instructional unit spans four to six weeks or more (as they often do). But selecting the activities and experiences that will lead students to those objectives we have identified becomes less onerous when we have clearly identified goals in mind.

Principles That Guide Planning

Daily planning requires a lot of teachers, and we want to end this discussion by sharing some general principles that should guide it. These emerge from our own experience and from the literature of the past few decades that has examined best practices. Following these principles has helped us maximize our instructional efforts, allowing us to reach more of our students and help them gain new skills; the principles have become paramount for us in planning instruction. They include using a gradual release of responsibility, scaffolding learning experiences, capitalizing on the power of social interaction, and considering variety and transfer. We will discuss them in general here and then showcase them in chapter eight as we show you how we incorporate them into our own planning.

Gradual Release of Responsibility

When we teach important procedures or processes, we want to structure those experiences around principles of the gradual release of responsibility; we have also heard this approach referred to as mentoring students or as apprenticing them into complicated behaviors. As first described by Pearson and Gallagher (1983) and elaborated on later by Duke and Pearson (2002), in this approach, teachers should first model strategies or behaviors for students using direct descriptions and explicit demonstrations. They should then allow for guided practice in which the students begin to engage in the strategy or behavior and the teacher provides feedback of a holistic or suggestive nature (rather than a right-or-wrong nature). The process should then gradually remove support and help as students become more competent at implementing the strategy or behavior on their own. Research has shown that this approach works well in reading comprehension instruction (Lloyd, 2004) as well as in writing instruction (Fisher & Frey, 2003). With the ultimate goal of the common core standards being to develop independent readers and writers, this model makes strong pedagogical sense as it supports our efforts to help students move away from reliance on the teacher.

How does this model inform our planning? Once we have identified important strategies or behaviors that our students will need to develop as part of our instructional unit, we plan learning opportunities that will help them, and we plan these based around this idea of the gradual release of responsibility. If our students need to know how to write an introductory paragraph as part of the unit, we will plan instruction where we first talk with students about what makes for a strong introductory paragraph (perhaps by analyzing a number of professional models). We will then plan to model for students how we would write an introductory paragraph for the kind of writing we've assigned. This would involve, ideally, composing an example at a computer or overhead projector while our students observe. This process may be messy, and we may make mistakes or stumble, but doing so can actually teach them important things about the process of writing (Bomer, 1998). Once we've modeled for students, we will then plan to write an introductory paragraph with them, working together on composing and providing feedback as we work together; during this time of guided practice, we would gradually remove ourselves as appropriate so that by the end of our collaborative writing, students are doing most of the work. Finally, students would be ready to write the introductory paragraphs for their own writing pieces.

It is this last phase of guided practice, in which we shift performance responsibility for a task from our shoulders to those of our students, that Pearson and Gallagher (1983) identified as most critical to students' learning. It is also the phase that in our experience is most challenging as a teacher. We must learn to give suggestive feedback to students, prompting them about directions they should go rather than giving them the "right" answer or telling them what to do. The questions we ask and the feedback we give during this phase are critical to helping students take ownership of the task rather than relying on us to complete it.

Scaffolding

Most teachers in the ELA discipline today are likely familiar with the notion of scaffolding. In many of the textbooks for teaching English and literature, we see frequent analogies drawn between this construction and its parallels for student learning (Langer, 1995; Smagorinsky, 2008; Wilhelm, Baker, & Dube, 2001). Just as scaffolds in the construction world help builders reach places that they couldn't reach without it, instructional scaffolds can help our students reach places cognitively that they otherwise wouldn't be able to.

What do instructional scaffolds look like in the ELA classroom? First, they rely heavily on an expert who understands the processes at work; teachers who are experts in the discipline can model processes for less experienced learners. Teachers can also provide the feedback learners need and can gradually remove these instructional supports as learners demonstrate increased competency. A good instructional scaffold will also provide enough support to allow the learner to do something new without making the task overly simple. Lastly, a good scaffold will effectively limit the complexity of the task, allowing the learner to focus more attention on the most important element of the task.

As an example, let's suppose we want to teach ninth-grade students how to make strong inferences while reading, a critical skill for comprehension. As a first step, we might identify the things we do as expert readers when we make inferences. These would include steps such as identifying important details, looking for patterns, comparing these to our own experience, coming up with an educated guess. Second, as we design instructional activities to help students develop expertise in these skills, we must select accessible texts with appropriate vocabulary or syntax. These texts minimize the irrelevant demands placed on the reader by a complicated text and allow students to focus exclusively on the skills of making inferences. Lastly, as we develop individual activities, we would begin by modeling for students how we use the skills involved in making inferences and ask students to notice and comment on our modeling. We will then move to guided practice as a whole class or in small groups, giving feedback to students as we work together to practice these skills. Once we see students getting the hang of it, we shift to having them practice independently. As we see students grasping the concepts and skills, we will gradually increase the difficulty of both the tasks and the texts to build our students' expertise.

Social Interaction

The popularity of such socially mediated technologies as Facebook, Twitter, and even text messaging reveals a critical need for us as people: social interaction. Teenagers are no different and, in fact, may be even more invested in sociality, as any teacher can testify who has watched students flood school hallways during passing periods with chatter and laughter. That social interaction would matter to teens is no surprise, but recent research in motivation and learning underscores this in significant ways.

In connecting adolescents' literary habits with motivation, Smith and Wilhelm (2002) found that social interaction played a significant role in these teenagers' lives in and out of school. These youths' friendships mediated many of their experiences with music and television and even video games—one boy in the study admitted playing video games even though he wasn't good at them because of the sociality it provided. For teachers, this idea goes beyond mere friendships or socializing in the school cafeteria; it can be a vital component of learning. As Vygotsky (1962) argues, learning occurs in social situations and is mediated through our use of language, a decidedly social tool; many other constructivist thinkers have likewise argued that social negotiation is a critical condition for effective learning (Driscoll, 2000).

To honor teens' desires to be social and the benefits of sociality in learning, there are a number of things we can do. Engaging students in discussion about literature is a start, of course, and we can do so as whole classes or, even better, in small groups. Teachers who rely on structured small-group discussions are permitting students to engage in a purposeful kind of socializing in the classroom. The use of more involved techniques such as literature circles or book clubs in classrooms is another way to allow for such socializing. Students can also benefit by working together on collaborative projects. Tackling complex tasks together allows for social interaction at the same time as it encourages students to rely on and learn from each other, thus providing another level of scaffolds for students who need them.

Variety and Transfer

On its face, having some variety in our classroom activities and assessments would make sense just as a way of preventing boredom or complacency with learning in the classroom. Even teachers appreciate some variety in presenting concepts or in the texts we study with students—it helps keep the job more interesting. In addition, since students learn in a variety of ways, our use of multiple kinds of learning activities helps to ensure that we are maximizing learning opportunities for as many students as possible. However, variety provides another important element of daily planning, one related to a key component of learning: transfer.

Transfer seems quite often to be the Holy Grail of teaching and learning. Few things are as rewarding to teachers as when we see a student take skills learned in one context (how to write an introductory paragraph, for example) and apply those skills in a different or unique situation (how to create a compelling introduction for a multimedia slideshow). Transfer of learning from one context to another is true evidence of a student's internalizing concepts or procedures, and transfer is often behind many of our larger learning objectives with students. In fact, the ultimate goal of the common core standards to create independent readers and writers suggests strongly that students would be able to transfer skills from context to context.

In the educational literature, we read about two different kinds of transfer: near transfer and far transfer (Macaulay, 2000); both are important to our work as teachers. In near transfer, students are transferring knowledge (concepts, skills, or behaviors) between situations that have much in common. For instance, when a student takes what she learned about writing a thesis statement for an argumentative essay and applies that to writing a thesis statement for a research paper, she has engaged in near transfer. This may be the kind of transfer we most often ask of our students—taking what they've learned from one writing or reading situation and applying it to additional, familiar situations. In far transfer, students are taking skills learned in one context and applying them to a situation that has little, if anything, in common with the original context. An example of far transfer would be the student who takes what she has learned about writing introductory paragraphs for traditional essays and transfers those into composing in a digital media and crafting an introduction to a photo slideshow. While her purposes may be the same in both contexts, the tools she uses (words and sentences versus images and music) are very different. It is far transfer, Macaulay (2000) argues, that is more significant in discussions of learning.

An underlying assumption of this idea of far transfer is that we will provide variety for students in the forms we use to assess students' learning and in the contexts in which we practice the skills we hope they develop as part of our units. As we plan assessments, identify objectives, create activities, and plan ways to model and practice strategies with students, we should seek to do so by using a variety of contexts and approaches. Not only does this help to keep the learning interesting for students, but it also helps aid in the near and far transfer of important literacy skills. Ultimately, it helps us prepare students who are good at adapting to unfamiliar situations, a disposition that we think will become all the more important in the rapidly evolving communications environment of our world.

Conclusion

Our purpose in outlining the process of planning for inquiry has been to show that this approach can meet the primary objective of the common core standards: creating independent readers and writers out of the students we have in our care. We applaud this goal and embrace it wholeheartedly, knowing that inquiry learning is the process that can take us there. This process allows us to place the needs and interests of each of our students in a central role in our planning and teaching. Inquiry learning is the way we can best equip our students with the concepts, skills, and behaviors they need to fulfill this important goal of the CCSS. The whole process of carefully choosing young adult titles that match students' interests and challenge their skills, framing those texts in a meaningful essential question or theme, and identifying appropriate learning targets, creates instruction that will not only appeal to students but meet the demands of the common core and the ever-evolving world.

To put the principles we have outlined in this chapter into more concrete form, we will offer a full explanation of our own thinking in developing a specific unit in the next chapter; we hope that chapter will allow you to see our own planning processes in depth. We provide more general outlines in chapter nine to give you materials to help in this process of planning.

Bibliography

Applefield, J. M., Huber, H., & Moallem, M. (2001). Constructivism in theory and practice: Toward a better understanding. *The High School Journal, 84*(2), 35–53.

Blau, S. (2003). Performative literacy: The habits of mind of highly literate readers. *Voices from the Middle, 10*(3), 18–22.

Bomer, R. (1998) "Transactional heat and light: On making learning more explicit." *Language Arts, 76*(1), 11–18.

Burke, J. (2010). *What's the big idea: Question-driven units to motivate reading, writing, and thinking.* Portsmouth, NH: Heinemann.

Csikszentmihalyi, M. (1990). *Flow: The psychology of optimal experience.* New York, NY: HarperCollins.

Daniels, H. (2002). *Literature circles: Voice and choice in book clubs and reading groups.* Portland, ME: Stenhouse Publishers.

Driscoll, M. (2000). *Psychology of learning for instruction.* (2nd ed.). Needham Heights, MA: Allyn & Bacon.

Duke, N. K., & Pearson, P. D. (2002). Effective practices for developing reading comprehension. In *What research has to say about reading instruction.* A. E. Farstup & S. J. Samuels, 205–242. Newark, DE: International Reading Association.

Fisher, D., & Frey, N. (2003). Writing instruction for struggling adolescent readers: A gradual release model. *Journal of Adolescent and Adult Literacy, 46*, 396–407.

Kajder, S. (2010). *Adolescents and digital literacies: Learning alongside our students.* Urbana, IL: NCTE.

Kuhlthau, C. C., Maniotes, L. K., & Caspari, A. K. (2007). *Guided inquiry: Learning in the 21st century.* Westport, CT: Libraries Unlimited.

Langer, J. A. (1995). *Envisioning literature: Literary understanding and literature instruction.* New York, NY: Teachers College Press.

Littleton, K., Scanlon, E., & Sharples, M. (2012). *Orchestrating inquiry learning.* New York, NY: Routledge.

Lloyd, S. L. (2004). Using comprehension strategies as a springboard for student talk. *Journal of Adolescent and Adult Literacy, 48*, 114–124.

Macaulay, C. (2000). Transfer of learning. In *Transfer of Learning in Professional and Vocational Education*, V. Cree & C. Macaulay (Eds.), 1–26. New York, NY: Routledge.

Marzano, R. J., Pickering, D. J., & Pollock, J. E. (2001). *Classroom instruction that works: Research-based strategies for increasing student achievement.* Alexandria, VA: Association for Supervision and Curriculum Development.

Maxwell, R. J., Meiser, M. J., & McKnight, K. S. (2011). *Teaching English in middle and secondary schools.* (5th ed.). Boston, MA: Pearson.

Miller, D. (2009). *The book whisperer: Awakening the inner reader in every child.* Hoboken, NJ: Jossey-Bass.

Nystrand, M. (1997). *Opening dialogue: Understanding the dynamics of language and learning in the classroom.* New York, NY: Teachers College Press.

Pagliaro, M. (2011). *Exemplary classroom questioning: Practices to promote thinking and learning.* Lanham, MD: Rowman & Littlefield Education.

Pearson, P. D., & Gallagher, M. C. (1983). The instruction of reading comprehension. *Contemporary Educational Psychology, 8*, 317–344.

Peck, D. (1989). *Novels of initiation: A guidebook for teaching literature to adolescents.* New York, NY: Teachers College Press.

Pink, D. (2009). *Drive: The surprising truth about what motivates us.* New York, NY: Riverhead Books.

Smagorinsky, P. (2008). *Teaching English by design: How to create and carry out instructional units.* Portsmouth, NH: Heinemann.

Smith, M. W., & Wilhelm, J. D. (2002). *Reading don't fix no Chevys: Literacy in the lives of young men.* Portsmouth, NH: Heinemann.

Vygotsky, L. S. (1962). *Thought and language.* Edited and translated by E. Hanfmann and G. Vakar. Cambridge, MA: MIT Press.

Wilhelm, J. D. (2007). *Engaging readers and writers with inquiry.* Jefferson City, MO: Scholastic Teaching Resources.

Wilhelm, J., Baker, T., & Dube, J. (2001). *Strategic reading: Guiding students to lifelong literacy 6-12.* Portsmouth, NH: Heinemann.

Wiggins, G., & McTighe, J. (1998). *Understanding by design.* Alexandria, VA: Association for Supervision and Curriculum Development.

Chapter 8

Model Unit Plan

As teachers, we all recognize the value of modeling for our students and how such a practice can provide concrete examples of complex processes that help learners better comprehend. That's our goal here: to help you see how we put into action the principles we shared in the last chapter. We'll take you through most of the process of planning a complete instructional unit that embraces a young adult novel as its anchor text and meets the demands of the common core. Our hope is that by "thinking aloud" through this process, we can reveal important understandings about how we plan more effectively.

Our primary goal in creating this unit, in line with the objectives of the common core, is to give students the learning experiences they need to develop the skills and behaviors that will shape them into proficient, independent readers. The choices we make in the unit will all be made with this goal as a guide, and we hope the explanations here will show you how we can accomplish this.

We first share our vision for the hypothetical classroom in which we would deliver this unit of instruction. We envision teaching this novel in a middle grades classroom and have settled on grade 8 as where the book we've chosen is commonly taught. We expect that our classroom would represent the typical diversity of race, gender, and socioeconomic status of almost any metropolitan area in the United States. We also expect that our classroom would be filled with students reading at different levels—some below grade level and some above, but this book should be manageable for most of our students. Additional texts that we bring in can help support struggling readers or challenge those who are reading at higher levels.

Step One: Choosing an Anchor Text and Devising an Essential Question/Theme

Choosing an Anchor Text

The choice of an anchor text is critical, as a good anchor text will interest students and allow for significant exploration of a thematic concept. For our unit we've chosen Karen Hesse's *Out of the Dust*. This book, a collection of free verse poems, tells the story of Billie Jo, a young girl living during the Great Depression who must come to terms not only with the physical harshness of that time but with much inner turmoil. The harsh and debilitating conditions of the dust bowl are mirrored in her home as she watches her pregnant mother die as the result of an accident that Billie Jo has a hand in; she struggles to come to terms with these events as she watches her father deal with grief for the loss, compounded by failure after failure on the farm. We've analyzed *Out of the Dust* in order to ascertain better how we might use the text in a classroom and to determine its appropriateness for our students; this analysis, along with all the other materials referred to in this chapter, can be found in appendix C.

As historical fiction, *Out of the Dust* is well suited to making connections with other texts (many of them informational texts, an area emphasized by the common core). Historical fiction also provides a number of topics on which students can conduct authentic research and inquiry activities. This book also provides ample cross-curricular activity if you're fortunate to find yourself in a position where you could work with other content teachers in studying this book and related issues. Additionally, as a work of free verse, the book allows us to explore significant elements of our own discipline such as figurative language and the conventions of poetry. In our experience, free verse actually strips away some of the complexity of other forms of poetry, allowing us to focus on imagery and the writer's craft in meaningful ways. Students who might feel intimidated by a poetic text can find free verse to be more accessible, allowing us to help students experience the emotional and artistic power of this kind of writing.

Devising an Essential Question or Unifying Theme

A good place to start thinking about essential questions is by considering the themes of a work, and there are a number of themes that emerge from *Out of the Dust* that could provide a seed for our inquiry. Billie Jo must learn to forgive herself, perhaps more than anyone in the book, as she seeks to make sense of her role in her mother's accidental death. She learns to forgive her father for the way he distances himself from her in his grief, and even for how he seeks out the companionship and love of another woman. In a sense, she also comes to forgive the land for its harsh cruelties and to see it (and love it) the way her father does. Billie Jo must also face her challenges, coming to understand that seeking escape from problems doesn't really solve anything. Only when she embraces her challenges, reaching deep inside for the resolve to endure and overcome them, can she truly learn and grow. Finally, Billie Jo recognizes the comfort and inspiration that can come from art, embodied in her own piano playing and the way she comes to terms with her burned hands, hands that for a time preclude her from playing. As with her mother before her, this appreciation of art can inspire and maintain Billie Jo in the harsh conditions of the dust bowl.

These themes are significant, and they are treated in so much of literature and art. Their depth in this text ensures that we can find many other texts that can support our study. The themes' universality will encourage exploration, be connected to students' lives and experiences, and engage with issues that are relevant to our discipline. A few possible essential questions are evident from the book's themes:

- **What does it mean to forgive, and why can forgiving be so difficult?** Forgiveness is a word that we toss around lightly sometimes, but it is truly a complex concept offering opportunity for significant exploration. Many works of literature and art explore the difficulties of forgiveness in many contexts and in many ways, suggesting that this is a question that we have yet to (if we ever truly will) find a full answer to. Forgiveness is also something that teenagers are dealing with in their own lives, ranging from the social slights common at this age to heavier topics like divorce and abuse. Studying the book from this perspective not only can provide these students with recognizable themes and conflicts, but can help them explore issues that are relevant to their lives.

- **How do different people react to and deal with grief or loss?** Loss and grief are significant themes worthy of study and offer a wealth of possible intertextual connections. There is plenty of loss to go around in *Out of the Dust*: Billie Jo and her father lose their mother and wife and the unborn child she's carrying, Billie Jo loses her ability to play the piano given the scarring from the accident, her father loses his crops over and over again. Each of these characters reacts differently to these events, but, ultimately, they both deal with their grief by learning to embrace and strengthen each other. This book, with its strong examples of loss and recovery, provides opportunity for exploring this topic in some depth. It's also a theme that many middle and high school students have experience with, from the loss of pets to the loss of friends or siblings or even to the loss of a parent due to death or divorce. In addition, there are other kinds of losses teenage students are familiar with, including the loss of innocence that is an inevitable part of growing up.

- **How can challenges help us grow?** Many of us may acknowledge the idea that we grow from challenges, but that doesn't make it any easier when we're faced with them. Billie Jo's challenges, emphasized by her inability to play the piano and the scarring from the fire, are a critical part of her character development and provide rich material for exploration. The changes that Billie and her father undergo can reveal important understandings about how challenges help us grow and learn. Our students are constantly facing their own challenges, and exploring the nature of challenges and our reactions to them can be a meaningful course of inquiry for teenagers to help them not only connect with literature but to find strength in facing their own problems.

- **How can we stay positive and hopeful in the face of hardships and setbacks?** Psychologists have shown that a positive outlook is one of the most important factors in being able to deal with life's challenges. The question of how we stay optimistic in the face of problems offers us an opportunity to study, in the context of this book, literary and psychological concepts simultaneously. Billie Jo and her parents react to the trials and failures of farming during the Great Depression in different ways, but their reactions tie to common threads of focusing on what's good, reaching out to others for help, and facing rather than running away from what wants to bring us down. The characters in this book provide a wealth of opportunities to explore this question with students. Anyone who has worked with teens knows that their lives can seem hopeless at times, whether it be due to problems at school, with friends, or at home. Seeing how characters deal with challenges can be empowering for teens by helping them to see authentic examples of psychological development.

- **How does the structure of a text allow the author options for developing a theme?** For those looking for an essential question that might interest a specific group of students or be more explicitly tied with our discipline, we suggest this question about the free verse form of the novel. The question may not have the broad appeal of the others here, but it would interest students in writing courses, and the unique form of the novel allows for plenty of exploration of this idea. Hesse is able to create images and evoke feelings through the shortened lines and careful phrasing of her free verse that owe much to that form. When studied in comparison to other texts with different forms, this question could inform student writing and their appreciation for others' writing in significant ways.

- **How do historical events shape the story told in a piece of historical fiction?** Again, this question may not have the broad appeal of other questions, but it's well suited to a writing class or a group of students who enjoy the study of the writer's craft. This question is also inspired by the common core standards that encourage teachers to help students make connections between a historical period and the setting of a novel. *Out of the Dust* would be a very different story were it not for the tragedies of the dust bowl and the privations of the Great Depression. However, Hesse's goal in writing the book was probably not so much to present a factual, complete picture of the time period as it was to treat universal themes in an authentic context. The study of how Hesse used selective details and events of the time period can shed light on the author's craft and help students see important connections between the historical record and fiction that seeks to capture a time period.

Each of these themes or questions has great potential for grounding a unit of study. Choosing an essential question is not an exact science, and personal preferences and the needs of our students often play the most important role in the decision. While we could have selected any one of these themes or questions for our unit, we choose to focus on the theme of hardship and hope by exploring the essential question, *How can we stay positive and hopeful in the face of hardships and setbacks?* We chose this question because we know that exploring it with our students will provide them with important insights about human nature that may inspire something in their own lives. In addition, since this is a question that's explored at length in the book, but not in explicit ways, we will also be able to help students develop critical thinking and interpretive skills as we study *Out of the Dust*.

Step Two: Developing a Unit Assessment

Having chosen an essential question to shape our study of *Out of the Dust*, we now need to consider how students can demonstrate that they've gained new knowledge from studying this book and exploring the question. These considerations will inform the learning objectives we establish for the instructional unit as well as the final assessment we design to measure student learning from the unit. We first need to consider what new knowledge we hope students will gain before we can contemplate a final assessment or product that would fit these needs.

When we consider what new knowledge we hope students will develop as part of our unit, we're using the word "knowledge" in the broadest sense of the word: we include declarative knowledge (facts, figures, formulas), procedural knowledge (how to use certain strategies or perform certain functions), conditional knowledge (when to use certain skills and strategies), and even affective knowledge (attitudes and emotional responses). To embrace all these types of knowledge, we first consider the skills or understandings students will need to make sense of the text we've chosen, and then what they'll need to be able to adequately explore our question, Each of these knowledge demands fits within the aspects of complexity and rigor the common core asks us to consider. However, we ought not to limit ourselves solely to what is represented in the common core standards, as these are designed as only minimal performance standards, and wherever we can enrich students' experiences, we should do so.

Knowledge Demands of the Text

- Since *Out of the Dust* is written in free verse, students are likely to be put off or unsure of their abilities when first encountering the book, so there is much we can do to help them negotiate this text. We'll want students to be familiar with figurative language and certain conventions of poetry in order to better decode and interpret the free verse in this novel. Given the sparseness of the free verse text, we think that students will need to read between the lines quite a bit and make inferences about events and characters as Hesse presents them. Along those same lines, we think students would benefit from learning to ask substantive questions of the text while reading this form. Questions help us make sense of the text and connect it to our own lives, to the world around us, and to other significant texts. (These demands connect to anchor standards R1, R4, R5, and L5)

- Students will benefit from building some background knowledge about the Great Depression and life in the dust bowl; this knowledge will help them as they make inferences and analyze characters during our reading of the text. This information can come from written texts, from videos and documentaries, and from images showcasing life during these time periods. Visual texts especially can also help students visualize the unfamiliar places and events (like dust storms) of the historical era. The process of finding and gathering this information can teach students some important inquiry skills, and the information they find can help them learn to use background knowledge to make sense of a text. (These demands connect to anchor standard R7.)

Knowledge Demands of the Essential Question

- The essential question and the challenges of the text will require significant discussion in class, as we work with students to explore the ideas and meanings of these. The sharing of ideas, perspectives, and opinions that occurs in class discussion will provide students with meaningful exploration of these ideas. This unit should provide opportunities for students to learn how to share ideas and respond to others' points of view. But we ought not rely on students to know how to maintain a strong discussion or listen actively to others or synthesize multiple viewpoints; we need to teach these skills explicitly and reinforce them with multiple opportunities for speaking and listening. (SL1)
- The essential question we've chosen will most likely be answered by looking at the characters in the novel, so a focus on characterization makes sense in our thinking. Students will need to understand how an author creates and shares information about characters, but they will also need to know how to make meaning from this information—how to make inferences and ask questions about characters that lead us to better understandings of their inner struggles, emotional dispositions, and motivations. Students will also need to define some terms and concepts such as hope, optimism, hardship, and failure. We expect that students would have a basic understanding of these ideas, but this essential question requires them to gain a more nuanced understanding of these ideas, and our study of the novel coupled with other texts should help accomplish this. (R1, R2, R3)

Knowing what knowledge will be demanded of our students from the text and essential question we can now consider what type of final assessment or product would fit these needs. When it comes to designing a final assessment that would serve as a vehicle for students to share the knowledge they've gained, we like to explore multiple possibilities before deciding on a particular product. We believe in using a variety of forms to assess student learning, and we define "writing" in the broadest sense of the word, to indicate composition in just about any medium. Doing so allows students to practice skills in a variety of contexts, thus leading to better transfer of skills. It also allows students to tap into different skill sets and talents or intrinsic abilities as well as allows them to see examples of authentic communication that better mirror what they see in the world around them. Our final choice, of course, will be based on contextual factors related to our students, the rest of the instructional year, and our own interests. We consider the following options based on our essential question, the text we've chosen, and the expectations of the common core for writing.

- **Narrative Writing**. We could challenge our students to write in a narrative form about the theme of hardship and hope, showcasing what it takes to be positive in difficult times. This could take the form of a personal narrative where students share an experience (or set of experiences) when they were tempted to lose hope given the struggles they were experiencing and how they stayed hopeful in spite of those struggles. Or we might ask them to find someone they know—a parent, older sibling, relative, neighbor—who has overcome great hardship and interview that person about how he or she was able to maintain hope for the future. In their writing, students would share the story of this person and the ways in which they kept their optimism in the face of failure and hardship; they would also connect what they learn from this "real life" person and what they've learned from the characters in *Out of the Dust*. Alternatively, we could challenge students to write a fictional piece in which they address some of these same issues through a tight narrative with a clearly defined problem and characterization that showcases what they've learned from the unit about how to maintain hope.

- **Informational Writing**. We could ask students to consider writing in informational forms that could offer how-to or self-help advice to those facing hardships. Students could investigate, for instance, factors contributing to teen suicide (a very real consequence of losing hope for teenagers) or issues around bullying. The students could then craft brochures or other informational genres with advice and counsel for struggling teens. Instead of a brochure, students could even take the same research and use it to inform the creation of a 30-second Public Service Announcement that might air on TV or the Internet (the series sponsored by Google called "It Gets Better" could be an inspiration for these kinds of products, although the content of these videos might be too sensitive for large classroom study). Students could also research historical figures who struggled through the Great Depression or other difficult times in history and present biographical pieces on these people and how they maintained hope and persevered; these could be written pieces or multimedia presentations.

- **Other Modes**. Students could also be asked to create extended definitions of a concept like hope or optimism and support their definition by connecting to the characters in *Out of the Dust* in addition to their own experiences. This extended definition could be in traditional written form or could take advantage of visual media and take the form of a collage or a multimedia presentation. Students could also create a character analysis piece—perhaps even in the "body biography" vein where a visual outline of a person is used to explore external and internal aspects of a fictional character (there are many websites out there that discuss this activity in more detail). In this piece, they could choose one or more characters from *Out of the Dust* and, using textual evidence, analyze how the character maintained hope in the face of hardships. Other topics for similar analytical pieces could include analyzing the symbols of the book and how they work to express the themes of hardship and hope, or looking at how the free verse form helps to enhance these themes.

The possibilities for assessments may seem limitless, a fact that makes choosing the form and nature of the final assessment difficult. In making our choice, we look first at what can best help capture the learning that students will do as part of the unit, knowing that a good assessment will not only measure our objectives but will also allow students to develop new skills and understandings (Smagorinsky, 2008). And we also consider what we're passionate about teaching our students—what forms and genres we feel strongly about.

With these considerations in mind, we've chosen to have students create a photo-essay, a digital version of a more traditional character analysis essay. In this piece, students will analyze a character through use of significant passages from the book, accompanying those passages and their analysis with Depression-era photos and other images. The passages our students select for inclusion in their presentation will show their understanding of how the essential question is addressed in the book through this character. Since Hesse organizes her long poem into individual single poems that act much like chapters, we are able to easily use individual selections for study in this unit. Students will choose a single poem or a small selection of poems that show how characters in the book experience failure and despair yet stay resilient and hopeful. The chosen images will help to establish tone and mood for their text selections, and they will meet established conventions of photo slideshows.

We choose a digital form of representation for this final assessment for a number of reasons. First, we know that students will engage in similar kinds of thinking as they analyze characters whether the end product is traditional writing or a digital genre. Secondly, we believe in a variety of assessment types; asking students to write only in traditional forms limits their exposure to the broad possibilities in today's world, a world that we need to prepare them for. This is especially important in this new century as the evolving demands of the workplace require students to be literate in different media (Leu, et al., 2007; Kajder, 2010; New London Group, 1996). Finally, we also appreciate that adolescents are motivated by the opportunity to create texts that look similar to those they see in the real world (and photo-essays are increasingly popular, especially in news journalism); as well, they appreciate having skills that they've developed outside the classroom legitimized by their use in the classroom.

We now need to consider what additional knowledge, skills, or strategies students will need in order to successfully complete this photo-essay project. In addition, we should consider what concrete or experiential knowledge they'll need to handle the thinking required for this project. We consider the following skills to be essential for our students.

- Students will be creating explanatory texts that address the essential question, but they will need to be purposeful in their selection of text passages, audio, and images so that their presentation conveys a coherent, unified message. So students will need plenty of coaching and help to explore the question, see how characters in the text address the issues of despair and optimism, and to identify important, meaningful passages in the text. They will also need some coaching on how we put these separate elements together effectively to communicate a message (in this case, their interpretation of how characters in the text face failure or despair while maintaining hope). (These demands connect to anchor standards W2 and W9.)

- Students will need to learn how multimedia authors use images and audio to help enhance a message. We'll use digital mentor texts and walk students through the process of analyzing the mentor text to help uncover the strategies behind the author's choices in selecting images, transitions between images, and selecting audio to accompany the images and text. As students compose their own multimedia projects, we'll help them use these strategies in their own work (connecting to anchor standards SL2, SL5).

- While this project will look different from a traditional essay, there is still a process students will go through to compose it; this process will share some features with traditional writing but also have unique aspects. We will want to shepherd students through the writing process for a digital composition, showing them how we handle planning, drafting, and revising for this kind of writing. Since we'll be using some powerful software to compose our multimedia products, we can also help students learn a lot about the revision process by encouraging them to try different sequences of images and different transitions. We will have the opportunity to help students see how their audience's reaction helps inform these choices (connecting to anchor standards W5, W6).

Step Three: Developing Learning Outcomes and Processes for Daily Instruction

At this point in the planning, we have chosen an anchor text, established an essential question, identified a culminating assessment, and considered the new skills and understandings students will need to acquire in order to successfully engage in the unit. With this in hand we can now plan a more detailed pathway to help our students achieve these ends—our learning outcomes and daily activities, in other words. Our goal as we plan for specifics is to tightly integrate the anchor text (and related texts), the essential question, and the preparation for the final assessment, so our daily instruction will need to help students explore the essential question, understand and interpret the anchor text, and give students opportunities to develop the skills and knowledge they will need to successfully complete the final assessment.

Detailing our vision of daily instruction can be a bit challenging; we want to model for you how we plan and give you a unit that's usable in your own classroom. In order to create something useful, we recognize that a wide variety of teaching schedules and assignments exist, and because of this we have chosen not to give detailed lessons for each day of this multi-week unit. Given that each of you teach in such unique and varied situations, those detailed lessons would likely not be as helpful as more general suggestions that can readily be adapted to fit your situation. Consequently, we've chosen to break out the instruction in weeklong sections, outlining the activities and goals we'd hope to accomplish in a week's worth of time. We hope this will help you to visualize how this instruction might fit into your teaching and provide a structure that is readily adaptable so you can easily pull this unit out of this book to use it in your classroom. We give reading blocks for each week, where appropriate, based on our sense of how much text we could explore with average middle school students in a week's time.

Week 1

In this week, we first want to introduce students to the essential question at the heart of our unit as well as the central text, *Out of the Dust*. We'll do this primarily by bringing in some informational and nonfiction texts that describe situations similar to those faced by the characters in *Out of the Dust*. We also want to start preparing students to develop the skills they will need throughout the unit, so in this week we also front-load things for them so they are prepared to read and comprehend the text.

Introducing the Question

We have chosen four activities designed to get our students thinking critically about our essential question and to give them the background knowledge needed to engage in the text and complete the final assessment. Not all classrooms will need to make use of all four activities, and we may choose to use one over another based on the makeup and needs of our classes.

Our first activity integrates nonfiction texts in an effort to spark discussion and debate about our question of remaining hopeful in the face of challenges. We want to study texts that tell about real people and how they rose above failure or setbacks, maintaining hope for the future. Texts about Thomas Edison and his many failed attempts at a light bulb, Abraham Lincoln and the many times he lost elections before winning the presidential election, and even Hank Aaron and his efforts (often failing) to break into Major League Baseball as an African American would be nice fits for this unit. The books in box 8.1 provide some examples of biographies that we might use, either in whole or in part.

We'll use our reading of these texts as a way to model how to analyze a character or historical figure in order to identify how he/she stayed hopeful and how to record our conclusions in a graphic organizer. This organizer (see the "Keepin' the Faith"

Box 8.1 Biographies That Show People Rising above Challenges

The Big Book of Dummies, Rebels, and Other Geniuses by Jean-Bernard Pouy
Bill W.: A Different Kind of Hero: The Story of Alcoholics Anonymous by Tom White
Charles Dickens and the Street Children of London by Andrea Warren
Ghosts in the Fog: The Untold Story of Alaska's WWII Invasion by Samantha Seiple
Hank Aaron: Brave in Every Way by Peter Golenbock
Jim Thorpe: Original All-American by Joseph Bruchac
Lincoln: A Photobiography by Russell Freedman
The Longitude Prize by Joan Dash
Steve Jobs: American Genius by Amanda Ziller
Thomas Edison by Charles E. Pederson

organizer in appendix C) will allow our students to keep track of the lessons we learn while reading about how people maintain hope in the face of challenges and setbacks. We could ask students to read and study alone, or we could have them form literature circles, assign each group a biographical story or excerpts, and have them fill in details in the organizer for the historical figure in their book. Students could share their findings with other groups by giving a short presentation in which they share the basics of their reading and the lessons they learned about the historical figure.

As we introduce informational texts as supplements to our explorations, we also start helping students recognize and engage in comprehension and analysis strategies for nonfiction texts. By showing them the role that external text features (headings, illustrations and captions, charts, etc.) play in structuring an informational text, we can help our students gain essential reading skills. We will also want to introduce them to the idea of reading these pieces in critical ways, asking questions about what's represented and what's left out of informational texts. To do this, we like Gallagher's (2004) idea of using a graphic organizer, a t-chart with one column summarizing what a text says and the other exploring what it doesn't say (e.g., what information is left out, what questions are unanswered, which voices are not recognized or valued). Modeling and practicing this behavior with students will help them become more critical readers of informational texts, an important step to exploring our essential question and to students becoming independent readers.

To explore additional dimensions of our essential question, for our second activity we have devised some scenarios related to the idea of facing challenges and maintaining hope. We've used scenarios like this often in the past (inspired by Wilhelm, Baker, and Dube, 2001), and they are thought-provoking ways to have students start exploring issues related to our essential question and anchor text. In this activity, students respond in writing to prompts associated with the scenarios and then discuss their reactions in small groups or with the whole class. This activity is designed to help students begin to see how these issues can play out in real lives. The materials for this unit in appendix C contain an example of scenarios and questions that could be used for this activity.

Our next activity, designed to help students connect the essential question and our anchor text to their own lives and situations, will be to do some in-class writing that helps them consider the challenges modern teenagers face and the ways they might face failure or setbacks. We start by making a list of some of these challenges and posting them somewhere in the room; we'll reference these lists as we go through the book discussing the ways that Billie Jo and her

Box 8.2 Articles on Resilience

Loss, Trauma, and Human Resilience by George A. Bonanno (http://www.dhhs.nh.gov/esu/dbhlibrary.htm)

Psychological Resilience on Wikipedia (http://en.wikipedia.org/wiki/Psychological_resilience)

Psychological Resilience and Positive Emotional Granularity: Examining the Benefits of Positive Emotions on Coping and Health by Michele Tugade, Barbara Fredrickson, and Lisa Barrett (http://www.ncbi.nlm.nih.gov/pmc/articles/PMC1201429/)

The Relationship between Personality Traits and Psychological Resilience among the Caribbean Adolescents by Grace Adebisi Fayombo (http://www.ccsenet.org/journal/index.php/ijps/article/view/7450)

The Road to Resilience from the American Psychological Association (http://www.apa.org/helpcenter/road-resilience.aspx)

family face failure and stay hopeful. This visual display can lead students' discussions to their own challenges and the parallels between the book and their own lives.

Lastly, to help students build a connection to the essential question, we will help them define terms that will relate to our question. In this week we focus on a term that is popular today and that describes the kind of hope or optimism we see in the characters in *Out of the Dust*: resilience. As a psychological term, this word describes an individual's ability to "bounce back" from failure and to continue trying in the face of defeat or seemingly overwhelming challenges. To help define the term, we can read excerpts from articles about resilience, some of which are presented in box 8.2. Study of this word, and other vocabulary throughout the unit, can be integrated into the methods of word study you already use in your classroom.

Taking Note and Keeping Track

One of the challenges in an extended inquiry unit is keeping track of all the ideas we explore and the conclusions we reach about our essential question and the text we're studying; this can be particularly difficult for younger students who aren't used to taking notes or keeping track of ideas like this. As teachers, we need to help support students' learning in these units by giving them tools to help keep track of our ideas and conclusions. The graphic organizer described in the previous section helps serve this purpose, and it's an example of the kind of thing that we find ourselves doing on a continual basis throughout the unit. Our chart on "Keepin' the Faith," for example, would be added to throughout our reading and discussion in this unit.

Another way we suggest helping students juggle all these ideas is through a journal or learning log. Throughout the unit, we will ask students to respond to short writing prompts, usually as a way to explore specific ideas, ask questions, or connect to the material. These writing assignments would not be graded in the traditional sense, but rather collected and reviewed as we move through the unit. Points can always be assigned for completion or effort, but we prefer students to feel less self-conscious as they complete these writings in order to best capture their thinking, so we don't evaluate this writing in the traditional sense. (For more on our attitude toward this kind of writing, you can look to sources that talk about writing to learn on the Internet; a host of published professional resources, including Toby Fulwiler's (1986) book *Teaching with Writing*, would also provide more information.) As we introduce students to these concepts through readings and discussions, we can model for them how to use their journals to track conclusions about how people and characters find or cling to hope in the face of terrible failures. The graphic organizers we use throughout the unit can be kept safely in these journals, and each student will be asked to refer to his or her journal frequently during the unit.

Front-loading the Reading

We have a number of activities to introduce our anchor text and lay a foundation for reading it. To begin, we will have our students do one of our favorite activities, an anticipation guide. This is a technique we learned from Vacca and Vacca (1993) that introduces students to important themes, conflicts, or issues before they begin reading a text. In the anticipation guide, students respond to a number of statements (inspired by the book's themes and phrased in such a way as to generate discussion) individually and then discuss their responses in small groups or as a whole class (or both). We can take advantage here and work in ideas that have developed as we introduced our question in our previous activities that relate to the real people they studied and their own personal connections they made. We've included an example anticipation guide in appendix C.

Since this text is poetic, to introduce it we also want to have some discussions here about how we read poetry. We would begin this discussion by asking students what they know about poetry. Most of them will be familiar with some poetry and can probably even share some examples of poetry that they've read in the past (often from poets like Shel Silverstein or Jack Prelutsky). Music lyrics from popular songs can also be relevant examples of poetry. As we discuss what students know and their experiences with poetry, we're likely to face some resistant attitudes. We're also likely to hear students say things like "poems must rhyme" when talking about the characteristics of poetry. This is the time to tell students that *Out of the Dust* is likely quite different from the poetry they're familiar with. As part of this discussion of poetry, we want them to recognize a few things:

- Free verse is different from the poetry students may be used to; the most significant difference is that free verse has no rhyme scheme. We can show students some samples of free verse and ask them to infer what's different about these poems from those they may be familiar with.
- When we read poetry, we pay more careful attention to the way lines break, but we still read through punctuation. In other words, there may be line breaks between the capital letter and punctuation mark, and we don't typically stop reading or decoding at a line break; instead, we pay careful attention to punctuation. We will also point out how many punctuation marks (commas, semicolons, colons, and dashes especially) mark boundaries between phrases or clauses but not the termination of an idea. We want to pay careful attention to punctuation and use it to help us keep ideas together; modeling and practicing this with short excerpts of poetry will help students understand how to do this (resources for this are presented in box 8.3).
- In poetry, we often see more uses of figurative language,

Box 8.3   Accessible Examples of Poetry

The Arrow Finds Its Mark: A Book of Found Poems edited by Georgia Heard, illustrated by Antoine Guilloppe

Borrowed Names: Poems about Laura Ingalls Wilder, Madam C. J. Walker, Marie Curie, and Their Daughters by Jeannine Atkins

Dizzy in Your Eyes: Poems about Love by Pat Mora

Forget-Me-Nots: Poems to Learn by Heart compiled by Mary Ann Hoberman, illustrated by Michael Emberley

Forgive Me, I Meant to Do It: False Apology Poems by Gail Carson Levine, illustrated by Matthew Cordell

Poem Runs: Baseball Poems and Paintings by Douglas Florian

Skywriting: Poems to Fly by J. Patrick Lewis

Time You Let Me In: 25 Poets under 25 selected by Naomi Shihab Nye

You Don't Even Know Me: Stories and Poems about Boys by Sharon Flake

such as similes, metaphors, and symbols. This is important vocabulary that we'll want students to be familiar with as part of our unit. These terms may already be familiar to our students from previous study, but there are many excellent ideas out there already for teaching these concepts; a favorite location for us is readwritethink.org, a database of wonderful lesson ideas cosponsored by the NCTE and IRA.

Week 2 (Assigned Reading: Winter 1934 and Spring 1934)

In this week, we'll start our reading of *Out of the Dust*. To do so, we'll first want to build some background knowledge with students about the Great Depression and the dust bowl. Students may already know something about this period, and we'll want to rely on that knowledge; we'll also want to build specific background knowledge about the challenges and trials faced by people at this time period to more fully open up the text to students. This week will also continue our instruction on reading poetry as well as identifying and interpreting figurative language. Lastly, since we'll be spending some significant time in the text, this is also when we want to introduce students to characterization and how we read to focus on characters.

Building Background Knowledge

To begin this week, we decide to first build background knowledge about the era of the Great Depression and the dust bowl. We'll do this by having students explore the many images from the NWP's photo archives of the time period. Dorothea Lange and others shot hundreds and thousands of images of the time, documenting the people and the hardships they faced. These images are often in the public domain today and are readily accessible to those with an Internet connection (see box 8.4).

We suggest having students spend some time browsing these images and having them select two images that strike them—one that prominently features people and one that features the land. We will assign brief written paragraphs in their journals about each image they choose, asking students to explore what it is about the images that strikes them and how these images portray the challenges of the time. In exploring the images of people, students should also speculate as to how people survived in these difficult times. Exploring these images will help prepare students for the text (allowing them to better use strategies of visualizing as they read) but also establish a frame for considering failure and optimism as a major theme of the book. This activity will also start preparing students to choose their own images as part of their final assessment, as we could ask students to bookmark all the images that stand out to them; later, they could revisit these bookmarks to find appropriate images for their photo-essay.

Box 8.4 Depression-Era Photographs (those with* indicate a searchable database)

About.com's collection of Great Depression Pictures (http://history1900s.about.com/od/photographs/tp/greatdepressionpictures.htm)

*America from the Great Depression to World War II: Photographs from the FSA-OWI, 1935-1945 (http://memory.loc.gov/ammem/fsowhome.html)

A Photo Essay on the Great Depression (http://www.english.illinois.edu/maps/depression/photoessay.htm)

Photos of the Great Depression and the New Deal (http://docs.fdrlibrary.marist.edu/gdphotos.html)

*Picturing the Century: One Hundred Years of Photography from the National Archives—The Great Depression and the New Deal (http://www.archives.gov/exhibits/picturing_the_century/galleries/greatdep.html)

In addition to these visual elements, we will also explore a wealth of nonfiction texts about the Depression. Some excellent examples of books written for young adults include Russell Freedman's *Children of the Great Depression*, which chronicles life for children and teens during this time period; Albert Marrin's *Years of Dust*, which details the dust bowl phenomenon from a historical and scientific view and includes amazing photographs; or Jerry Stanley's *Children of the Dust Bowl*, which focuses mostly on the Oakies who traveled to California but describes conditions in the dust bowl and tells the inspiring story of these transplants who, against frightening odds, built a school for their children in California. These books (or excerpts of them) can give students greater understanding of the historical events against which *Out of the Dust* is set.

Our students can take notes or write in their journals about the information they find from these books; time permitting, they can also prepare and give short multimedia presentations on specific topics (e.g., the dust bowl, prices in the Great Depression, the government's role in providing jobs, music of the time, etc.). These presentations and notes would be useful to review as we read, to encourage students to compare the historical events to their portrayal in the novel (as suggested by the common core standards). For instance, familiarity with these historical events will assist students later in analyzing the way Hesse uses historical details (such as the rain and its effect in the dust bowl, the ever-present dust, and the families who leave for better opportunity in California) in the telling of her story and the explication of her themes. Having students prepare a visual presentation could also introduce them to the software we will be using later for their final project, helping us prime them to present things visually.

We present these activities as possibilities and, again, stress that choosing one or more to complete in class should be heavily influenced by our students and the makeup of our classes. In our own experience, we and teachers we've observed have sometimes spent so long in building background knowledge that students are weary of the book and its setting before we even begin reading. We should work to strike a careful balance here, building enough background to get students off on the right foot for the reading, but not overwhelming them; background can also be built later, as needed, in our reading (as we do with the video documentaries of the dust storms later in the reading).

Supporting Poetry Reading

For this week we will study the Winter 1934 and Spring 1934 sections of the text. This section of the text offers a good point to reinforce the terms of figurative language and literary analysis, especially the concepts of simile, metaphor, personification, and symbol we touched on in week one. The poems "Apple Blossoms" and "Apples" are very fitting for discussions about symbolism and how Ma's dedication to the apples is similar to Pa's commitment to the farm; we can begin to talk here about how these things symbolize hope for these two characters. The poems "On Stage" and "Fields of Flashing Light" are also well suited to practice in identifying figurative language and interpreting its meaning.

There are also a number of poems here that bear closer reading to analyze Hesse's artistic use of language and the conventions of poetry to convey important meanings. In the poem "On Stage," for instance, Hesse attempts to recreate the keys of a piano with the structure of the lines of the poem; students will almost certainly notice this, and we should ask them why they think Hesse chose to do this, how this decisions heightens the imagery created by the words of the poem. The very short but powerful "Breaking Drought" offers a similar opportunity to explore how repetition (in the lines "of wind and sun,/of wind and clouds,/of wind and sand") creates more vivid images and how Hesse often uses short, staccato lines (as in "a little/rain/came.") to draw emphasis to certain facts and images. The book is filled with poems like this that deserve closer attention, and each reader/teacher is likely to have some favorites. Fortunately, given the brevity of these, students are likely to tolerate repeated readings as we help them examine some of these details about craft and meaning.

We can also begin to make connections back to the background knowledge we've built before reading and show how those help us interpret the content of individual poems. In the poem "Losing Livie," for instance, we can connect to our understanding of migration at this time, since the state of California is used throughout the book as a symbol of hope and better times. Or this might be a good time to introduce readings about the Oakies and other migrant groups during the Great Depression if we didn't take the time to do so before we began the reading. The poem "Debts" could be connected in a similar way to readings about the government's efforts to stave off financial ruin for so many families in the dust bowl.

Introducing Characterization

Given the essential question at the heart of our unit, this is also the time to begin focusing attention on the characters in the novel. The first few poems in the book introduce the characters we'll be reading about for the rest of the book, and it's a good time to begin our analysis of them. To help students keep track of the major characters and to help them analyze issues of failure and optimism through the lens of characterization, we will use a simple graphic organizer, a chart to track the characters (see the Character Tracking Chart in appendix C). This chart helps students track the challenges and failures experienced by each of the three main characters as well as the ways they face those; also, the chart asks students to explain these reactions, so that we can begin to understand the connection between optimism and other character traits these three exhibit. Finally, the chart provides space for students to note down significant lines from the text related to these things as a way of keeping them focused in the text itself; these lines can be discussed in class, looking for examples of strong writing, figurative language, and evocative imagery. They can also provide raw materials for the product students create as part of their final assessment. We will use this chart as we read the entire book, continually adding to it as we read and discuss each section and explore the characters and their reactions to failure and setbacks.

To begin analyzing characters, we will read the early poems and then model for students how we want them to use their chart. In one of the strongest early poems, "Fields of Flashing Light," we see the first description of the terrifying and destructive dust storms. As we read the poem together, we can ask students to notice how the three characters react to the dust storm: Billie Jo goes outside and passively watches the destruction; Pa runs out, half-dressed, to do something, even though Billie Jo tells him, "You can't stop the dust!"; and Ma recruits Billie Jo to help her seal up the cracks in the house to prevent dust from coming in. We can make notes on the chart about how Ma and Pa try to take some action while Billie Jo doesn't—and debate which action shows more hope or a refusal to give up hope. The poem ends with a compelling image—Pa seemingly beaten, having failed to stop something as unstoppable as a dust storm, but refusing to cry. This, too, could be added to notes about Pa and how his refusal to cry reveals his refusal to give up hope and surrender.

As we progress from these first poems into the remainder of the text, we will ask students to purposefully select poems that highlight the setbacks and challenges and characters' reactions to them. Students can mark these poems with small post-it notes or can take note of them in their journals; while these highlights will form excellent discussions in class, once we come to the final assessment, students can review their marked poems for use in their final project. As we move through the text, we would also provide time each week for students to meet in small groups and share the poems that they've marked and their reasoning as a way to encourage more students to join the discussion.

Week 3 (Assigned Reading: Summer 1934, Autumn 1934, Winter 1935)

This week our emphasis will focus on the characters in this section, looking at how Hesse's characterization helps to explore issues related to our essential question by reading and analyzing specific poems that provide insight into characters and themes. There is a lot of reading in this week, a choice we've made in an effort to keep moving through the text at a decent rate that will help students stay focused. Fortunately, with the short poetic texts, this is less quantity of text than it might initially seem; the flip side of this, of course, is that we might spend longer on certain poems given their power or connection to the themes and essential question we want to explore in the unit. A number of poems stand out to us and would be worth the extra time spent in analyzing them to deepen our understanding of the characters and themes. We will continue to use our graphic organizers and journals here to help students keep track of important ways these characters show their attitudes toward failure and setbacks; we also want to move into deeper analysis of characters' motives and emotional states. Notes for the organizers can come from discussions held in class as we talk about these poems or from individual reading.

Poems for Character Analysis

To study the characters in depth we will begin by focusing on the poems that explore each character individually.

- Ma: To focus on Ma's character, we will look at the first three poems in this section. In these, we see Ma's desperate hope for rain, her fears about the future (as witnessed by her crying over the birth of a neighbor's quintuplets), and her willingness to reach out and care for the boy traveling through town on his way to the West. While the accident takes Ma away early in this section, we can still examine her reactions to challenges and how reaching out to help others seems to bring some hope and comfort to her. Ma is perhaps most characterized by her absence and how Billie Jo sees frequent reminders of her; the most poignant of these is in "Scrubbing Up Dust," where we read of Ma's intolerance for a mess and her unending quest to keep the house clean. Billie Jo's feelings about this seem ambivalent, but this poem shows something about Ma and her response to failure and setbacks that should be noted.
- Pa: The loss of his wife is a blow to Pa, and his otherwise optimistic nature is shaken in this section of the book. Digging a hole for the pond, a suggestion Ma made early in the book, seems to give him some purpose, but later when he considers going back to school, he expresses some of the same doubts Ma had earlier about the farm's chances of success. Digging the pond and getting hired on at the power company both represent an effort to exert some control and make the situation better, just as when he plants the fields. These should be noted in the organizers as ways that Pa maintains hope in the face of real challenges. Much of what we see of Pa in this section, though, is filtered through Billie Jo's eyes; her mention of his drinking and his role in the accident and her view of his digging (in poems such as "Drinking" and "The Hole") show her feelings toward him, and we must help students view these poems critically, understanding how Billie Jo's perspective may not be completely

objective. His distancing himself from Billie Jo, seen in poems like "The Empty Spaces" and "Birthday," is also worth discussing, as this shows part of Pa's reaction to the challenges he's facing. As with Billie Jo later in the book, he seems to be seeking escape, and only starts to heal once he seeks to build a stronger relationship with Billie Jo. The poem "Outlined in Dust" is particularly significant here as an example of their growing distance but also Billie Jo's first inclination that she and her dad are more alike than not, a factor that will eventually bring her some comfort and help her forgive and heal.

- Billie Jo: We see throughout these poems Billie Jo's developing sense that leaving her home will lead her to a hopeful place, concretely represented in the text by California. Both the family that temporarily lives in the school house and the ragged boy her family helps as he travels west reveal a growing motivation for Billie Jo to find hope elsewhere, anywhere that isn't where she is now. The poems with the family in the schoolhouse also reinforce earlier themes about reaching out and helping others as a way to deal with struggles and setbacks; we can highlight these poems and the lessons learned on our "Keepin' the Faith" organizer. The up-and-down cycle of hope and failure and the struggle to hold on to hope is also shown in her attempts to play piano, although it eventually becomes too much for her scarred hands. There are moments where she thinks she can still play (as in "Dreams" and "The Competition") and, in so doing, recapture some of the carefree lightness of the dance hall where the problems of the dust bowl could fade away. But those moments are brief, and they leave Billie Jo even more desperate than before, especially as Mad Dog seems to be finding escape and hope in his work for the radio. By noting these things in the character organizer, students can begin to see how failure and hope are something of a cycle, where we can expects lots of ups and downs. How the characters in the book respond to this pattern seems important to whether or not they can maintain hope. We can help students see that for Billie Joe, the piano playing mirrors her father's digging a pond by giving her a sense of purpose; this understanding is a meaningful connection to our essential question. To further explore this idea at this point, we will listen to a few songs from the Great Depression, as music plays an important role especially in the Winter 1935 set of poems. These can include "Brother, Can You Spare a Dime?" (with its historical references to men proudly building skyscrapers and valiantly fighting in the war who can now no longer care for themselves or a family), "Happy Days Are Here Again" (with its hopeful tone), and "Whistle While You Work" (which suggests trying to forget about the seeming futility of work in a time when everything you plant could be blown away or covered in dust). (Additional resources for Depression-era songs are given in box 8.5.) By analyzing the lyrics of these songs, we can open up a discussion to the way music can help us keep hope during difficult times—either through the tone of the music or through the lyrics of songs. Students could share examples of songs that make them feel better when they're down, helping to make connections between their own lives and the book.

Box 8.5 Depression-Era Songs

A Depression-Era Anthem for Our Times (http://www.npr.org/2008/11/15/96654742/a-depression-era-anthem-for-our-times)

A Depression-Era Playlist (http://www.smithsonianmag.com/arts-culture/A-Depression-Era-Playlist.html)

Manufacturing Memory: American Popular Music in the 1930s (http://xroads.virginia.edu/~ug03/jukebox/front.html)

Songs of the Great Depression (http://www.library.csi.cuny.edu/dept/history/lavender/cherries.html)

Poems for Thematic Analysis

We can also explore specific poems in this section that connect to our essential question. Again we will explore these poems in whole-class or small-group discussions, and students will add the information they gain to their graphic organizer and journals.

- "Wild Boy of the Road": In this poem we see Billie Jo's family helping out others who are less fortunate. In discussing the poem, we would connect back to our essential question and ask why, when things were so difficult for their own family, would they help this boy? The discussion could lead to conclusions about how reaching out to others and giving of ourselves in difficult times can help keep hope and optimism alive. This motif is repeated elsewhere in the book, as with the family that moves into the schoolhouse and benefits from collective efforts of the children. This poem also reminds us of Billie Jo's sense of hope associated with California, a motif that's repeated throughout these sections and is connected to our essential question.
- "The Accident": The poems around the accident that takes the lives of Ma and the unborn baby boy are, of course, worthy of critical study. This poem in particular uses figurative language to the fullest in conveying the horror of the accident; it's also a good study in how Hesse breaks down words and phrases to emphasize fragments of the experience.
- "Devoured": Billie Jo's injuries and the insult of the devastating grasshoppers in this poem provides a good chance to revisit our character chart and add some of the devastating events and characters' reactions to them; the class can begin to speculate about how these characters will react now that hope seems totally lost.
- "The Hole" and "Night Bloomer" and "First Rain": Pa's behavior in digging the hole is perhaps a way for him to recapture something of his dead wife, and it seems to bring a sense of purpose and hope to him. The flower that blooms at night but wilts in the harsh heat of the sun could be a metaphor for the way that nature has beaten down and destroyed the hopes and happiness of this small family. The downpour that comes in the third of these poems offers a small glimpse of hope, and students can discuss how glimpses of good things like this can restore hope in the midst of seeming futility.
- "Dust Storm": This poem reminds us of the perilous conditions and the fact that, in spite of some of the minor glimpses of hope, things are still bleak for Billie Jo and her father. With this poem, we would bring in excerpts from video documentaries of the dust bowl to give students a more vivid sense of what these storms were like. A particularly good one is "Surviving the Dust Bowl" from the *American Experience* PBS series since it collects actual film footage of dust storms and interviews with people who remember them (and it can be viewed for free from the PBS website). Making use of excerpts of this documentary can be especially powerful here, as the photos and film used can help students visualize what's happening in the poem; the comments from interviewees will also echo much of what is written in the poem. We can also analyze how Hesse's syntax and word choice help to create these vivid images. Students can explicitly compare these images to Hesse's words to see how the historical reality informs the literary text, an important requirement of the common core standards.

Week 4 (Assigned Reading: Spring 1935, Summer 1935, Autumn 1935)

We reach the end of the book in this week, and there are significant things that happen for Billie Jo and her father. Things reach their lowest point for Billie Jo, and she finally decides to leave the farm, only to realize what she's lost and return after a few days on the rails. Hope reenters both of their lives as they take steps to care for themselves and as a new woman enters their lives. In this week we will focus our discussion on specific poems that help us go into greater depth with hope, a fundamental issue in our essential question. To that end we will focus on three issues in these final sections: how hope is built by interactions with others, how wanting to escape can generate a false sense of hope, and how taking concrete action can strengthen hope.

The Role of Community or Companionship in Hope

A significant poem in this section of the book is "Blankets of Black," describing perhaps the worst dust storm of the book. As Billie Jo and her father travel to the funeral, they (and the entire procession) are overwhelmed by a dust storm and find shelter in a local house with other members of the funeral possession. As Billie Jo says, if it weren't for the hospitality of this family and the company of the people taking shelter, she thinks the storm may have broken them. After reading this poem, we can ask students to write about someone who has helped them through a difficult time and have them share how other people can provide strength during setbacks and how they help keep us focused on the future. While sharing this writing, we can also direct the conversation to wonder how we can help others stay positive who are enduring difficult challenges. Students can look at other places in the book where a sense of community helps people bear with the difficult times (e.g., when the committee comes asking for donations and Ma gives some food and a baby outfit sewn from a feed sack or when the students help the family that moves into the schoolhouse). We will also add these conclusions to our notes in the "Keepin' the Faith" organizer.

Escape Often Brings a False Sense of Hope

In this section, starting with the poem "Out of the Dust," Billie Jo finally decides to leave her home. To introduce this poem, we will review the historical texts we read earlier and the images we have studied, especially relating to the Oakies and other migrants; this will help students draw connections between the materials presented in these historical documents with the fictional elements Hesse portrays. While reading the poem itself, we will ask students to pay attention to the reasons they see Billie Jo express for leaving. To start, we will use some in-class, informal writing about when students have wanted to escape some situation (reminiscent of the "Want to Get Away?" commercials from Southwest airlines—some of which are viewable on YouTube if a little humor might be appropriate at this point). In the writing, they should explore why escape seemed so tantalizing and why it may or may not have been a good idea. Students can share their own experiences and connect the discussion to how escape may not always be the answer to difficult situations. We will ask them to compare Billie Jo's experience with the historical information they have discovered. For instance, they can compare her experiences with the Oakies who often came to California and found little opportunity and even more hostility rather than the green fields and plentiful work they had imagined. Students can then make predictions about whether they think escape would be a good thing for Billie Jo right now and what might happen to her.

Billie Jo's decision to come home and what prompts that decision (in the poem "Something Lost, Something Gained") are, of course, worth exploring. To help students track her reasoning in this poem, we would use a graphic organizer like an "open mind" organizer where the outline of a brain or head is pictured and students record within the outline what they see going on inside the head of the character—writing down questions, thoughts, or memories that they think are running through the character's mind while students read. It's important for students to try to see what Billie Jo is thinking so they can trace the source of her decision to go home, to see how her family and her home are such an important part of who she is. Again, this connects nicely to conclusions we've already been reaching about how people cling to hope in desperate times, but to see them realized now in Billie Jo shows us important things about how she is growing.

Taking Action Can Build Hope

Significant poems in the section include "Hope" and "Hope Smothered," which document the rise and fall of hope through the actions of rain and growing crops. "Hope" provides an excellent study in the rhythm that Hesse is able to create with her clipped lines and broken phrases. Students can chart the length of lines in the poem (using graph paper or inputting them into an Excel spreadsheet that could create a bar graph) to help visualize the flow of phrases and words. We can then contrast this with a similar graph from "Hope Smothered," so we can discuss the differences in these two poems from a structural perspective; students should speculate about why the lines in "Hope Smothered" are noticeably longer than in "Hope." This should help them see how Hesse conveys strong emotions in the latter poem with fragments and draws emphasis to single words and ideas that convey that hope (such as in the series "into the/hard-pan/earth/until/it rained/steady as a good friend/who walks beside you"). We can also point out the return of the dust in the former poem—how Billie Jo had taken off the gummed-up tape from the windows (in a hopeful gesture) but that now the dishes are all covered in dust.

The final section of poems (Autumn 1935) brings a closing sense of hope to Billie Jo and her father. The first poem, "Cut it Deep," shows the steps that she and Pa take by going to the doctor—he to look at the cancerous spots on his skin and she to seek help for her hands. Further hope comes in "The Other Woman" as Pa and Billie Jo allow another person into their lives. With these instances, we need to ask students to consider what it is about these events that helps to inspire hope—the taking of action, the doing of something (mirrored in Pa's seemingly pointless efforts to dig the pond)—versus the attempt to escape that brings few positive outcomes. Also in the poem "Music," Billie Jo's efforts to work the skin in her hands to be more flexible and to eventually clean the dust out of the piano also represent steps she takes toward restoring her former self. Students can reflect on these poems and how both Pa's and Billie Jo's action develop hope and record conclusions in their notes.

A Final Discussion

We don't like to leave reading a book without some kind of final, culminating discussion with students. There are many forms this discussion can take, but for this book and this unit we choose to have a fishbowl discussion with our students. In a fishbowl discussion, three or four students sit in the middle of a larger circle containing the rest of the class; the students in the middle are the only ones who can talk, and the students on the perimeter must "tap in" and replace a student in the middle before sharing. The teacher avoids talking at all in an effort to have this be a student-led discussion. We have sometimes provided the prompts for this discussion or, at other times, had students devise questions or prompts for the discussion. In helping students devise their own questions for the discussion, we have traditionally taught them a questioning hierarchy (such as Raphael's (1982) Question-Answer-Relationship framework or Christenbury and Kelly's (1983) Questioning Circles) to help them learn valuable skills about leading discussions.

In this case, we want students (either through our prompts or their own devised questions) to explore significant issues related to the book and to our essential question; we'll provide students with these questions as prompts or encourage them to devise similar questions on their own:

- Consider the title of the book—what does it mean?
- How do the characters in this book find hope in the middle of all these terrible events?

- How do you think you would have survived in this time period? What would have strengthened and encouraged you?
- Why do you think Hesse chose to use free verse poems for this book? What does this poetic form do that works well? How are they perhaps not the most effective way to tell the story?
- What are your thoughts about Billie Jo? Do you like her by the end of the book or not? Why or why not? How has she changed during the book?
- What are your thoughts about Pa? Has he changed over the book? Do you like him by the end?
- How do you think things will go with a new woman in the house? How do you think Pa feels about this? Why do you think he would like another woman around? What about Billie Jo's reaction? What do you see going well, and what do you see being a challenge for this new family?

The best thing about a fishbowl discussion is that the teacher is on the sideline. Too often, in our own experience and in observations we've made in other classrooms, the teacher can dominate a discussion, and students don't have the chance to learn something from it. We see this final discussion as a place to have what Smagorinsky (2008) calls "rough draft" or exploratory speech—to explore ideas, posit possibilities, and see things from other people's perspective rather than show off what we are already certain of. The exploratory nature of this discussion at the end of the reading is important, as it will help students synthesize ideas from across the book and connect them to our essential question. This should result in a good foundation for our final project.

Weeks 5–6

After finishing the book, we turn our attention to how to formally assess students' learning from the unit. We want to give them a chance to share what they have learned about the essential question and the issues of hope we've explored. We also want them to show what they've learned as a result of the poetic analysis we've been able to do. And, finally, we hope to give them a chance to show what they've learned about analyzing characters by allowing them to engage in some analysis of their own. The photo-essay will allow our students to communicate their experience with the text while at the same time supporting it with textual evidence; it also allows us to help students develop understandings about composing in different media. We recognize that this will seem unfamiliar ground to some readers, and suggest other pieces written by one of the authors that may shed additional light on this process (Ostenson, 2012; Ostenson & Gleason-Sutton, 2011).

While much of the writing process in a digital genre like this is similar to the process for traditional writing, there are some significant differences between the two. Our goal here is to scaffold instruction in such a way that students can succeed at the final assessment, even if it seems to be a bit of a stretch for them. We'll do this primarily by breaking down the task into separate steps and tackling each step at a time. This task involves giving models, exploring ideas, selecting poems and images, storyboarding and compiling these elements, and revising and publishing the piece. Afterwards, by asking students to reflect on their process, we help them clarify what they've learned both about the writing process and about digital writing.

Giving Models

Most students benefit in writing by examining models, both of a finished product and of the process that gets us to the finished product; we see evidence of the former in many classrooms, but not so much the latter. As Bomer (1998) reminds us, it can be difficult for some students to see the underlying steps that go into creating a finished product without a more explicit modeling of the process itself. If we compose alongside students, they get to see how we make decisions and how we work through challenges in the writing process. This can be valuable mentoring for our students, and so we suggest doing so in this case.

It's still helpful to see a model of the product early in the process so students have a clear sense of our expectation; we have such a model that can be viewed online (https://vimeo.com/40972225). We created this model not only to show you what our expectations for the final product would be but also so we can be more clear ourselves about the process our students will be going through in completing the task. We chose to focus our essay on Ma, thinking that she might be the most difficult since she's not as physically present in the book; fortunately, we found more than enough material for our essay, which implies good things for students who chose Billie Jo or Pa. (There are also many existing examples of photo-essays that you could use if you don't have time to create your own—the online versions of news magazines like *Time* and *Newsweek* or of newspapers like the *New York Times* have plenty, and a general Google search will yield results, too.)

In using a model to help our students understand the expectations for the product, we find that they benefit from multiple "readings" of the model. In this case, we will watch this photo-essay two or three times; in the first viewing we simply want students to observe and take in the effect of the photo-essay. In subsequent viewings, we want to lead a discussion about what students notice, with the idea being that they should tell us what works in the photo-essay and how it's working. We would use questions such as these:

- How would you define a photo-essay? What features or characteristics do you notice in this piece?
- What do you notice about the images that I've chosen to use? Which images do you like the best? Why?
- What do you notice about the poem selections I've chosen? How are they connected with the images? Do the two work well together?
- What am I trying to communicate in this photo-essay? What impression do you get by the end? How do you think I accomplished this?

While we want most responses to these questions to come from the students, we should feel comfortable here sharing our choices, trying to give students a glimpse into the thinking behind our model. It's helpful for students to start taking notes during this discussion since it often results in good pointers for them about how to make a successful photo-essay; posting these notes in a public place or having students keep them in their journals will help facilitate their future use of them. The important thing here is to have students define the genre—especially since it's likely to be unfamiliar to many of them—and to start talking about how we put a photo-essay together.

Exploring Ideas

The next step is for students to gather ideas and make a decision about the character they will choose for their photo-essay. To begin the assessment, we will ask students to create body biographies for Billie Jo, Pa, and Ma (see Smagorinsky, 2008, for description). Using the notes on the character graphic organizer to complete this can help tie together the characterization in the book and emphasize the ways that these characters have found hope in the midst of despair. On the outside of the body biographies, students will list the challenges and failures that have plagued these characters; on the inside, they will create images or icons that symbolize the things that have brought them hope and given them courage to face these challenges. This will prepare students to begin thinking about how they'll portray some of these same issues in their essay, and it should help most students choose which character they find appealing to focus on for the assessment.

Nevertheless, some students may need more assistance. One strategy to help students select a character to focus on is to have them get into small groups and share the notes from their journals, character organizers, and body biographies. If students feel pretty certain about the character they'd like to choose, then they can get into a group with other students who have chosen that character and discuss some ideas they have; for students who are less certain, this discussion should help them solidify their ideas. We suggest using questions like these to spark discussion and keep students focused on exploring the right ideas:

- What are some of the challenges this character faces? When does he/she fail or face setbacks? How does he/she respond to those setbacks or failures? (What does he/she do and how does he/she feel?) Which poems show these?
- What gives the character hope? How does he/she stay optimistic? How do other people help, how does hard work help, or what other things make a difference? Which poems help point this out?
- What kinds of things did we conclude help people hold on to hope? Does this character make use of any of these things?

Alternatively, we're also fans of an idea that Gallagher (2004) describes called the positive-negative chart. In this activity, students take a single character and chart something about that character using a line graph, plotting negatives and positives along the line. We can focus on a number of things in plotting this line, such as a character's behaviors or attitudes or even other characters' perceptions of the focus character. In the case of our work with *Out of the Dust*, we would ask students to choose one of the major characters (Ma, Pa, or Billie Jo) and plot the major attitude shifts of each of these characters throughout the novel. (See appendix C for an example.) Completing this chart alone and then sharing with other students who chose the same character would be a valuable way of gathering possible ideas for the photo-essay.

By the end of this phase, students should have a character chosen and a pretty good idea of what they want to say about that character. We would have students write a half page on who they've chosen and what they want to say about how this character held on to hope in the midst of despair or failure. This task will help them clarify their ideas and can also give us a sense of whether or not students are ready to move on.

Selecting Poems and Images

Since students marked poems they particularly liked or that moved them while we read, the task of choosing poems should be straightfoward. The task now is to select a handful of poems that deal with the challenges or setbacks experienced by a character and the ways that he or she held on to hope. The key is to choose the most powerful, evocative poems (or excerpts) for the photo-essay. We want to model this for students, most logically by explaining some of the choices we made in our model essay. Again, this is why completing the project ourselves can give us important insights into this process that we can then share with students. We can share why we chose the poems we did, what criteria went into those choices, and encourage students to consider similar things as they review the possibilities.

At the same time as we're considering poems, students can start selecting images to accompany these poems. We previously looked with them at the archives of Great Depression–era photos, so students should already be familiar with these. We'll require students to stick to those images because they're readily available, they've been shot by professionals, and they capture the spirit of the book quite nicely. As they revisit these databases, it will be especially helpful to use those that feature keyword searches, so they can find images related to the text they've chosen more quickly. We'll suggest to students that they choose two or three (or more) images as possibilities, and then experiment in the storyboarding (later) until they find the images that are the best matches.

Students will need some time in the computer lab to revisit these pictures. The important thing here is to help them choose appropriate images that reinforce the text of their text selections. For many students, it will be helpful to have text choices made before they start looking at images; others may benefit from finding a striking image that evokes something from their reading of the book and then trying to figure out why the image is so meaningful. The sequence of choices may be a bit back-and-forth here, with students finding pictures that match perfectly with a piece of text or finding a picture first that inspires a choice from the text. Again, we need to model both sequences here, and can do so by talking about the choices that we made with the choices in our model photo-essay. In the piece we put together for the book, for instance, we knew we wanted to use excerpts from poems showing Ma at her piano, but one picture we came across of a woman and her multiple children inspired us to also include parts of the poem on the quintuplets born to neighbors.

Storyboarding

With decisions made about the pictures and the poems or excerpts that will communicate their message, students are ready to start drafting. To start, we'll ask them to do what the professionals do: use a storyboard. A storyboard is an excellent way to have students start organizing their material, an important step as the sequence of images and text can enhance or detract from the message. Students can choose to present things chronologically, as they happened or appeared in the book; this might be the most logical choice, and it should be considered, but it may not be the most effective choice. Or they may want to organize pieces from least to most important, starting with more minor challenges and leading into the more significant challenges, for instance. Students could also choose to group together text and images that deal with the challenges faced into one segment of the essay and into another segment group those pieces dealing with how the character found hope. Or they may want to choose a different organizational pattern that makes more sense given their materials.

Again, to help students with this process we need to talk about the decisions we made with our own photo-essay and try to uncover the reasoning behind our organizational choices. This can give students a sense for how we make these decisions. We think a key move here is to explore possibilities, so we encourage students to put images and text into the appropriate boxes on the storyboard template (see the Hope Photo-Essay Storyboard in appendix C for an example) and then cut them out so that they are independent and can be easily moved around and reordered. Students should explore at least two or three different ways of organizing their materials before they make a decision. Once they've settled, they can tape or glue the squares back onto a blank piece of paper in the order they've chosen.

This is also the time to think about transitions between images. Most software packages that we'd use to compose the photo-essay will allow for transitions—and some may give a lot of choices. We can talk to students about the transitions they've seen in movies—from the ubiquitous jump cut (where one images cuts right into the next) to the dissolve (where one image dissolves into the next) to the wipe (where the new image moves across the screen, covering the old image) to the fade (to black or white). In our experience, students can often tell us what effects these transitions provide, and this allows us to talk about which would make good choices for their own photo-essays. Again, talking about our model essay and the choices we made for transitions is important here, as is cautioning students about using a wide variety of transitions or really unusual transitions. If they think about the movies they've seen, they'll realize that directors use a small set of transitions (most often just jump cuts and fades or dissolves); few even dare to use wipes (except George Lucas in his *Star Wars* films). Less is more in this case, and we don't want our transitions to take attention away from the images and text we've so carefully chosen and arranged. We will provide students with a list (and even demonstrations) of the different transitions available to them and have them make notes on the storyboard as to which transitions they plan to use between images.

Again, sharing with students how we thought through these decisions in our own composing is important. In our model essay, we chose to organize around a few central ideas that seemed to bring hope to Ma: her pregnancy, playing the piano, helping others, combating the dust of the prairie, and the apple trees. We sorted poems into these categories and organized them so they would communicate something important about each idea. Then we added some pictures—usually more than one for each poem or excerpt. We save the idea of apples for last because we found that one most poignant—Ma's hopes for the apples are mirrored by Billie Jo's desire for them, and the storm that nearly wipes them out represents the ever-present specter of failure.

Compiling Materials

With a completed storyboard, it's time now to get down to the work that students most often enjoy: putting this all together in the software. Although compositing images and text into frames can be done completely in video-editing software, students might find that overwhelming or too complex. So we suggest the first step be to create still "slides" that contain text and/or images, depending on how students wish to present their materials. We have found it easier to compose these stills in separate image-editing software; free or inexpensive applications are available for Windows and Macintosh platforms (a program called GIMP is one of the most powerful and popular free image-editing applications). Creating a blank slide with the proper dimensions (1024×768 pixels in our case) allowed us to create a template on which we could place images and text. Different still slides can be saved as separate files, thus ensuring that each slide matches the others in the set.

Once the stills are designed, there are a number of software packages available for compiling them into a photo-essay, from simple packages like Microsoft's PhotoStudio to more complex applications like Microsoft's Movie Maker or Apple's iMovie. We would suggest using one of the latter two as they are more full-featured and are usually already available (or can be downloaded for free, in the case of Movie Maker) on school computers. If these are not an option, software liked Microsoft's PowerPoint, Apple's Keynote, or even the free Google Presentation application (part of the Google Docs package) would be suitable alternatives.

Some of our students will be familiar with these tools, but many of them will need help learning how to make the software do what they want. While we won't go into details here due to the variety of applications you might choose from, we can identify the skills we need to teach students:

- How to import images into the software
- How to crop images to allow for focus on what's most important
- How to add text to an image
- How to arrange them in order in the software's timeline
- How to insert text onto a slide or as a caption for each image
- How to insert and edit transitions

- How to save the file while we're working on it
- How to export the final version into a movie file

If you're unfamiliar with how to do these things, numerous tutorials exist on the web that can guide you; it's also likely that you have students in your classes who are skilled in using these applications, and you could rely on their expertise to teach the class and help other students as they work.

The most effective way to teach these is through short mini-lessons where we demonstrate the basic steps of each of these processes while students observe. Handouts with step-by-step instructions and screen shots of important steps can be time-consuming to create but invaluable in preventing the inevitable "How do I . . . ?" type of questions that can eat up all our time in the computer lab. (An example of one of the handouts we've used is included in appendix C.) If we have some students in our classes who are familiar with the software and can get their work done fairly quickly, we might recruit them to help students who are less adroit with the software.

This is the most time-consuming but exciting part of the process, as many students are learning new skills and also having fun experimenting with different transitions, texts fonts, and even colors for fonts. We encourage this kind of experimentation as this is how we sometimes discover really effective ways of using images and text to communicate. The software available today allows for and even encourages this—when we do something we don't like, our previous version is a simple "Undo" command away.

Revising

For writing teachers who have struggled with having their students engage in meaningful revision, working in multimedia can seem like a dream. In our experience, students often engage in spontaneous revision activities as they ask for a classmate's opinion on what they've put together so far or as they play with different transitions, engrossed in making their product just right. The experimentation that today's software tools encourage plays a big part here, but so does our students' natural inclination to share these essays with others.

We still need to have some concrete, structured revisions here to make sure that all students benefit from feedback. It's clear that these photo-essays are meant to be viewed by others, so that's where we take revision. We will put students into small groups (we suggest that partners work best, but if that's not practical, groups should have no more than three individuals) and have them share their "finished" products with each other. We ask students to look at specific elements of the piece to comment on, including questions such as these:

- Consider your emotional response to the piece: What feelings does it evoke? Do the author's choices (images, transitions, poems, etc.) reinforce this emotion? Can you think of ways to make the emotional impact stronger?
- Consider the message of the piece: Can you see clearly what the author wants to say about this character and his/her challenges and how he/she finds hope? Which images/transitions work well in supporting this message? Which don't work so well?
- Consider the sequencing of images: Can you see a clear organizational pattern in the work? How appropriate is that pattern for the message? Would an alternative pattern work better? Do the transitions work well, or do they distract from the piece?

We can model this feedback process for students by looking at our own piece or at another photo-essay from another source and asking these questions, thinking aloud about our responses. Students should take notes about what others say regarding their essay; once they've had feedback from at least two sources, they can take some time to consider any final changes.

Reflecting

As we seek to teach students about the writing process through this project, it's critical that we have them reflect on what they did and what they've learned about writing as a result of this project. Dean (2006) argues that without this important step, we don't allow students the chance to internalize the lessons they've learned and help them see ways to transfer this knowledge to different contexts. This is especially important given that we've asked students to compose in an unusual genre with this project, and not all of them will see the relevance of what they've learned here to other writing situations. In addition, we've found that having a written reflection helps us understand students' choices in multimedia composition and facilitates our own feedback and grading.

Once students are finished with their photo-essays, we will ask them to write a written response in which they talk about the images and poems they chose, why they chose and arranged them in the way they did, and what they were trying to communicate with some of their choices. We can also ask them to write about what they've learned about writing, thinking in terms of how they gathered ideas, how they organized ideas, and how they relied on others to help them perfect their final product. This will help students think more globally about the lessons they've learned with this project and how they might apply to other writing contexts.

Publishing

Creating in multimedia gives us an opportunity to make texts like these photo-essays more visible to other students in the class or even to parents at home. Exported photo-essays could be uploaded to video sharing sites like YouTube or Vimeo or TeacherTube. Making these videos public, however, needs to be done with caution; student work, if made public like this, needs to be anonymous to help deal with privacy concerns. If students use their personal accounts to post to these sites, they might leave connections to other videos they've posted or to personal information; the teacher might want to create an account for the class to use to circumvent this problem. The most preferable option might be to host these videos on school servers where privacy could be strictly protected, but that may not be possible in many districts.

We think publishing should be a celebration—of what students have learned by making the photo-essay and of what they've learned from studying the book and our essential question. To properly celebrate, we'd host our own "film festival" and watch the students' finished pieces; we might even take nominations for awards: "Best Depiction of Hope" or "Best Use of Images" or "Best Essay on Billie Jo" or the like. If your experience is anything like ours with these digital compositions, students are usually quite proud of what they've produced and appreciate the opportunity to have others view their work.

Conclusion

In the unit plan we've presented in this chapter, we have created a rigorous course of study that challenges students to explore a text that we think holds plenty of complexity and meaning. In fact, it was difficult to limit the kinds of activities we could do with this text to a scope appropriate for this chapter; Hesse's book is truly a piece of quality literature, and it deserves a place in the classroom as much as anything from the classical canon. We began this book by making the argument that young adult literature could take the place of the canon and meet the demands of the common core standards while claiming the benefit of being more relevant and interesting to teenage readers. We have supported this argument at length throughout the pages of the book, but find that the best proof is "in the pudding," as they say. In the instructional unit we've developed here, we hope you too can see the potential these texts have for creating proficient, independent readers.

Bibliography

Bomer, R. (1998). "Transactional heat and light: On making learning more explicit." *Language Arts, 76*(1), 11–18.

Christenbury, L., & Kelly, P. (1983). *Questioning: A path to critical thinking.* Urbana, IL: NCTE.

Dean, D. (2006). *Strategic writing.* Urbana, IL: NCTE.

Fulwiler, T. (1986). *Teaching with writing.* Portsmouth, NH: Boynton/Cook.

Gallagher, K. (2004). *Deeper reading.* Portland, ME: Stenhouse Publishers.

Gazit, C. (Producer), & Steward, D. (Co-Producer). (2007). *American experience: Surviving the dust bowl* [Motion picture]. USA: WGBH Boston.

Kajder, S. (2010). *Adolescents and digital literacies: Learning alongside our students.* Urbana, IL: NCTE.

Leu, D. J., Zawilinski, L., Castek, J., Banerjee, M., Housand, B.C., Liu, Y., & O'Neil, M. (2007). What is new about the new literacies of online reading comprehension? In Leslie S. Rush, A. Jonathan Eakle, & Allen Berger (Eds.), *Secondary School Literacy: What Research Reveals for Classroom Practice* (37–68). Urbana, IL: NCTE.

New London Group. (1996). A pedagogy of multiliteracies: Designing social futures. *Harvard Educational Review, 66*(1), 60–92.

Ostenson, J. (2012). Reflections on the writing process in digital media. *Statement, 48*(2), 16–21.

Ostenson, J., & Gleason-Sutton, E. (2011). Making the classics matter through essential questions and digital literacies. *English Journal, 101*(2), 37–43.

Raphael, T. (1982). Question answering strategies for children. *Reading Teacher, 36*(2), 186–190.

Smagorinsky, P. (2007). *Teaching English by design: How to create and carry out instructional units.* Portsmouth, NH: Heinemann.

Smith, M. W., & Wilhelm, J. D. (2002). *Reading don't fix no Chevys: Literacy in the lives of young men.* Portsmouth, NH: Heinemann.

Vaca, R. T., & Vaca, J. L. (1993). *Content area reading* (4th ed.). New York: HarperCollins Publishers.

Wilhelm, J., Baker, T., & Dube, J. (2001). *Strategic reading: Guiding students to lifelong literacy 6-12.* Portsmouth, NH: Heinemann.

Chapter 9

Raw Materials for Unit Planning

Introduction

One of the biggest challenges of unit planning for us is getting all the right materials in one place to come up with a strong unit. We may have the idea of a deep essential question that deserves study, but that's only the first step; we also need to gather texts to support exploring the question. On the other hand, we might have an idea for an assessment or activity that is tied to a common core state standard, but we don't have an idea of an essential question to tie it to. Or we may face an even bigger challenge when we are at a complete loss of what essential questions, texts, and activities could all go together. In chapter eight we presented our full heuristic of how to plan a unit; however, we realize that not everyone is going to need this step-by-step information. Once we've grown comfortable with planning, what we need is to just get all the right materials in place. In this chapter we offer you those raw materials. You can take these and use whatever process you feel comfortable with to craft this foundation into exciting units that will enhance and support your students' learning.

Raw Materials Form

We begin by offering you a form we've designed that helps articulate and combine all the essential elements that build an inquiry-learning unit. These elements can be divided into three categories: essential questions, texts, and assessments. To articulate the essential questions, we offer two boxes on the form. At the top is a box to indicate theme; this most likely will be the brief overarching theme that your unit will be based on and can also serve as a title for the unit. The Potential Essential Questions box on the top left is where we articulate the important essential question(s) covered by the unit.

Secondly, we offer boxes for texts to be used in the unit. We feel that there are three types of texts that will be important, and we offer boxes for each. On the top right we offer a box for anchor texts. These texts will be those that are foundational to the unit by providing the anchor(s) needed to study the essential questions and themes in depth. In addition, supporting texts are also important to any unit; these can add variety, help build background knowledge, further the exploration, or connect to the anchor text. We suggest that support texts are a fine way to include nonfiction, multimodal texts, poetry, and other supporting forms in our ELA classrooms. We especially like using multimodal texts that address our themes, so we have also included a place on the form to record any multimodal connections our unit may have.

Lastly, we offer a box to outline possible assessments and activities that would connect the anchor text and essential question with the common core standards. While we are not likely to use all the assessments we might list here, we think it's important to brainstorm multiple possibilities for consideration. Once we have articulated the elements in this form, the next step would be to use the heuristic we outlined in chapter eight (or your own planning pattern) to make daily lesson plans, assignments sheets, and activity guides in order to implement the plan in a classroom.

These forms can serve as a basis for individual planning, but they can also be good ways to collaborate in planning. Sharing this information with other teachers can help them to build their own units without them having to gather their raw materials on their own. Collaboration can also assist us by getting other teachers' views of possible texts or assessments that we may not have considered. Our experience has shown collaboration to be an invaluable way to build stronger units than we normally would have if we planned in isolation.

Raw Materials Models

In this spirit of collaboration and sharing, we offer you 12 sets of raw materials that we would use to create our own units. We have selected a variety of essential questions, texts, and assessments to give you a ready-to-use set of ideas. We hope that some will take these materials and create engaging units for their students; for others these may serve only as a jumping-off point to add your own texts or ideas, as our questions, assessments, and texts could most certainly be mixed and matched. We also encourage you to change or build on our ideas to suit your teaching style and your students' learning needs. You can find a blank form in appendix B if you would like to utilize this format to record your own ideas.

As we offer our assessment ideas, we indicate the anchor standard that we think most logically applies to that activity. While the grade-level standards can be more specific, as we have done before we have chosen to only represent the anchor standards in an effort to remain flexible about grade levels to which these could apply. Following our previous pattern we express the standards as a code. The letter indicates the type of anchor standard (R=Reading; W=Writing; S=Speaking; L=Listening). The number after the letter indicates the number 1–10 of the anchor standard. So, again, an R1 indicates reading anchor standard one, which revolves around making inferences and addressing areas of uncertainty.

For all texts, because editions, availability, and access vary, we have chosen only to indicate the most basic bibliographic information, including title and author for books or creator/director and title for music and movies. Catalogs for libraries and booksellers or social media (http://www.goodreads.com) and Internet search engines can provide you with the full information for these titles. While we realize that not all these books will be suitable for everyone in every situation, we have sought to include a wide range of titles that cover a variety of interests and subject matter. These text recommendations are personal ones given by the authors, and no other endorsement beyond this is given or implied. We encourage each professional to read, and read about, the books that we offer to find the ones that are best for their teaching situations. Issues such as availability, funding, personal tastes, students' reading ability, students' maturity level, and other individual circumstances will govern what books will be best for any one situation. These recommendations embrace a variety of reading and interest levels and cover many different types of literature, including relevant, contemporary social issues for all ages of children. Professionals are encouraged to select materials most suited to the readers and situations they are working with.

Theme: Changing the World

Potential Essential Questions	Potential Anchor Texts
• When should we stand up against authority or the status quo? • Why is it so difficult to stand up for what we know is right? • What do people who change the world have in common? • What things can teenagers have influence on in the world to make positive change?	• *Charles Dickens and the Street Children of London* by Andrea Warren • *Claudette Colvin: Twice toward Justice* by Phillip Hoose • *Fight On! Mary Church Terrell's Battle for Integration* by Dennis and Judith Fradin • *My Family Shall Be Free! The Life of Peter Still* by Dennis Fradin • *Temple Grandin: How the Girl Who Loved Cows Embraced Autism and Changed the World* by Sy Montgomery • *Hitler Youth: Growing Up in Hitler's Shadow* by Susan Bartoletti

Potential Assessments (Unit Projects)

- Students could identify a problem in their school or local community (W7, W8) and could do a number of projects related to taking some action about that issue. One form might be a brief video documentary in which they interview concerned citizens and compile background research to present in a traditional documentary form (R7, R9). Another form might be an op-ed piece in a local newspaper or magazine. Students could also create an action plan with concrete steps, take those steps (as appropriate and reasonable), and report (either in writing or through an oral presentation) on the results. This report could be made more authentic by making/presenting it to a body like a local city council, school board, or other civic group (W1, W4, SL3).
- Students could research a historical figure (R9, W7) who made changes in the community around him or her. The research reports could take on multigenre forms, where genres varying from letters and newspaper articles to interview transcripts or journal entries could tell the story of the changes enacted by the person (W2, W3). These forms would allow students to explore essential questions in more depth, as they might write fictionalized accounts (W3) that meet these purposes but still stay true to the historical events.
- Teachers could introduce students to literary theories that examine class structure or social justice issues in interpreting literary texts (R2, R9) (see Appleman's book in the resources listed below for more on this). The teacher could model and practice with students how to identify elements of these frameworks and how to interpret texts using these frameworks (R5); this practice would be appropriate as a way to discuss and explore the selected anchor text for the unit. Students could then write an analytic piece in which they argue for an interpretation of a reading (young adult novel or classic) through these theoretical lenses (W1).

Connected/Supporting Texts	Multimodal Connections
Sources for Readings: • *Readings for Diversity and Social Justice: An Anthology on Racism, Antisemitism, Sexism, Heterosexism, Ableism, and Classism* edited by Maurianne Adams, et al. • *Society Sisters: Stories of Women Who Fought for Social Justice in America* by Catherine Gourley • *Charles Dickens and the Street Children of London* by Andrea Warren	*Websites:* • *DoSomething.org*: a website that encourages young people to make a difference in their communities • *takeactiongames.com/TAG/HOME.html*: a website that uses media to raise awareness about social issues • *thedocumentaryproject.org*: a website devoted to using media to bring together youth to build a creative community

(continued)

From *Integrating Young Adult Literature through the Common Core Standards* by Rachel L. Wadham and Jonathan W. Ostenson. Santa Barbara, CA: Libraries Unlimited. Copyright © 2013.

Novels:
- *Ask Me No Questions* by Marina Budhos
- *Flush* by Carl Hiaasen
- *Geography Club* by Brent Hartinger
- *Sold* by Patricia McCormick

Professional Resources:
- *Actions Speak Louder Than Words: Community Activism as Curriculum* by Celia Oyler
- *Critical Encounters in High School English: Teaching Literary Theory to Adolescents* by Deborah Appleman
- *Critical Theory Today: A User-Friendly Guide* by Lois Tyson
- *Documentary Storytelling, Third Edition: Creative Nonfiction on Screen* by Sheila Curran Bernard
- *Literary Theory: A Very Short Introduction* by Jonathan Culler
- *Practice What You Teach: Social Justice Education in the Classroom and the Streets* by Bree Picower
- *The Shut Up and Shoot Documentary Guide: A Down & Dirty DV Production* by Anthony Q. Artis
- *Teaching for Diversity and Social Justice* edited by Maurianne Adams, Lee Anne Bell, and Pat Griffin
- http://www.tolerance.org/activities (plenty of activity ideas for social action/change)

Documentaries:
- *Arctic Tale* (2007) made by Paramount, directed by Adam Ravetch and Sarah Robertson
- *Girls Rock!* (2008) made by Liberation Entertainment, directed by Arne Johnson and Shane King
- *March of the Penguins* (2007) made by Warner Brothers, directed by Luc Jacquet
- *Quantum Hoops* (2007) made by Green Forest Films, directed by Rick Greenwald
- *Waiting for "Superman"* (2011) made by Paramount, directed by Davis Guggenheim

Theme: Genre and Meaning

Potential Essential Questions	Potential Anchor Texts
• How does the form of a text influence its meaning? • How do genres arise, and what needs do they fill? • How do authors use multiple genres in effective ways? • What new genres are emerging, and how are they being used?	• *Countdown* by Deborah Wiles • <u>Emily the Strange</u> series by Jessica Gruner, Rob Reger, and Buzz Parker (illus) • *Give a Boy a Gun* by Todd Strasser • *Locomotion* by Jacqueline Woodson • *Monster* by Walter Dean Myers • *Nothing but the Truth* by Avi

Potential Assessments (Unit Projects)

- Students could take a preexisting story (short story or even novel that they've studied/read recently) and retell it through different genres (R9; W3), following the models given in the anchor text(s); these genres might include letters, interviews, web pages, blogs, newspaper articles, etc. A written reflection in which students explore how the different genres facilitated telling the story different ways would be important to assign as well (R5, R6, R9).
- Any research topic (W7, W8) could be presented in a multigenre format, with different genres conveying different pieces of knowledge students gained as part of the research. Allowing students to choose topics for research and genres will give them a wide variety of experiences (R7, R8, R9).
- Students could analyze (W8) the genres used in one of the anchor texts (or another novel presented in multigenre form) and explain how the genre choices made by the author help make meaning (R3). For instance, in Myers's book *Monster*, the choice to use a screenplay has important implications for how information is presented in the novel and how readers interpret it as well as how the protagonist sees his life and circumstances (R5). Such choices are purposeful and can provide the source for meaningful analysis.
- Students can write an analysis of an unfamiliar genre and then create a written piece that meets the expectations of that genre (R5, R6). These could range from traditional genres (newspaper article, interview transcript, radio news report) to more recent genres (blog entry, photo essay, IM chat transcript) (W2). The analysis should thoroughly explore the unfamiliar genre, its audience, expectations, and conventions (W4); the piece students create should match that analysis and show solid understanding of the unfamiliar genre.
- Students could analyze a story told in different genres—taking a novel and comparing it to its film or stage play version (R7), or looking at an ancient myth (R9) that's been retold in a modern film or TV version. The analysis should focus on the different genres and what those genres allow for in terms of communication and making meaning (R5, R6).

Connected/Supporting Texts	Multimodal Connections
Writing Guides: • *Big Fat Paycheck: A Young Person's Guide to Writing for the Movies* by Colton Lawrence • *Essay Writing for High School Students* by Alexander L. Terego • *Extraordinary Short Story Writing* by Steven Otfinoski • *How to Write Poetry* by Paul B. Janeczko • *Writing about Nature: A Creative Guide* by John A. Murray • *Writing Fiction: A Hands-On Guide for Teens* by Heather Wright	• Kinetic typography models (an example of a very modern genre, numerous examples on the Internet and YouTube by searching the above phrase) • Photo essays from Time.com, nytimes.com, or other news magazine sites • Audio/film/dramatic versions of popular novels (*Hunger Games*, Percy Jackson and the <u>Olympians</u> series, <u>Harry Potter</u> series, *Diary of Anne Frank, Journey to the Center of the Earth, Speak, Beastly, The Sisterhood of the Traveling Pants*)

(continued)

From *Integrating Young Adult Literature through the Common Core Standards* by Rachel L. Wadham and Jonathan W. Ostenson. Santa Barbara, CA: Libraries Unlimited. Copyright © 2013.

| *Professional Texts:*
 • *Genre: An Introduction to History, Theory, Research and Pedagogy* by Anis S. Bawarshi and Mary Jo Reiff
 • *Genre Theory: Teaching Writing and Being* by Deborah Dean
 • *Thinking through Genre: Units of Study in Reading and Writing Workshops Grades 4-12* by Heather Lattimer | |

Theme: Exploration and Frontiers

Potential Essential Questions	Potential Anchor Texts
• Why do human beings push to explore and cross frontiers? • What are the benefits of exploration? What are the costs? • What will be the next great frontier we explore as human beings? • How does exploration make us better human beings? • Why do we willingly accept the risks of exploration?	• *Amelia Lost: The Life and Disappearance of Amelia Earhart* by Candace Fleming • *Emperors of the Ice: A True Story of Disaster and Survival in the Antarctic, 1910-13* by Richard Farr • *New Found Land: Lewis and Clark's Voyage of Discovery* by Allan Wolf • *Shipwreck at the Bottom of the World* by Jennifer Armstrong • *Team Moon: How 400,000 People Landed Apollo 11 on the Moon* by Catherine Thimmesh

Potential Assessments (Unit Projects)

- Using the anchor text in addition to other sources, students could choose an historical explorer or a modern pioneer—any figure who has broken frontiers literal or figurative. After some research (W7, W8), they could present a summary of the person's life and how he or she explored new frontiers or broke new ground. This presentation could be oral (a speech or slideshow presentation) (SL3) or written (an informative biographical piece) (W2) or take on another form (photo essay, wiki/encyclopedia entry, documentary, etc.) (W1). Deeper meaning would be explored if students connect what they learn about this figure to the essential question for the unit.

- Students could look into someone in their family history who is a pioneer or frontier-pusher; perhaps the first member of their family to immigrate to the United States or the first member to attend college or something similar. If that person is still alive, students could interview him or her and find out about the boundaries this person pushed (W2); if the person is no longer living, students could interview family members about that person. The interview could be presented in an oral report (SL4) or written up in a traditional published interview format or even presented in a radio interview or TV documentary format (W2).

- As the students read about different explorers, have them record in a graphic organizer the qualities that the people they are reading about have (R6). Students will use word walls or notebooks to record their findings. Have students use dictionaries to define the terms they come up with from this work; they can expand on these definitions by writing their own definitions (R4). Have them further expand on these definitions by writing short informative essays (W2) about what those words mean; they can also connect the texts to their own lives by including in the essays ways they can develop these qualities in themselves.

- Compare different forms of information by having students read news articles, nonfiction texts, and documentary films (R9). Have students determine how information is presented in each form and compare differences and similarities by studying the forms and what types of information they convey and at what depth it is conveyed (R6). Students should determine why the different forms convey information in different ways by targeting certain audiences (W4). Have students take information from one form and add information as needed to transfer the information into another form by writing their own news article, short informational essay, or movie script (W1, W2).

- Have students use the informational sources to write a piece of historical fiction that focuses on one person or event (W3); this assignment would combine research strategy learning and writing (W7, W8). This writing assignment would allow them to develop some skills in creative expression, including some of the language standards (R4, L1, L3) from the common core. It could also, if a reflective component were added, allow students to explore how the historical facts influence fiction writing.

(continued)

Connected/Supporting Texts	Multimodal Connections
Articles:	*Documentary Films:*
• News articles about movie director James Cameron's deep-sea dives in March 2012	• *The Greely Expedition* (2011), from *The American Experience* PBS series: http://www.pbs.org/wgbh/americanexperience/films/greely/
Other Novels:	• *From the Earth to the Moon* (1998), from the HBO series directed by Michael Grossman
• *Born for Adventure* by Kathleen Karr	• *In the Shadow of the Moon* (2007) directed by David Sington, starring Buzz Aldrin, Neal Armstrong and Stephen Armstrong
Biographies:	*Web Resources:*
• *Almost Astronauts: 13 Women Who Dared to Dream* by Tanya Lee Stone	*Federal Resources for Educational Excellence: U.S. History Topics, Famous People, Explorers*: http://free.ed.gov/subjects.cfm?subject_id=150&toplvl=172
• *Antarctica: Journeys to the South Pole* by Walter Dean Myers	*NASA*: http://www.nasa.gov/home/index.html
• *Extraordinary Explorers and Adventurers* by Judy Alter	
• *Race to the End: Amundsen, Scott, and the Attainment of the South Pole* by Ross McPhee	
• *Westward Ho! Eleven Explorers of the West* by Charlotte Jones	

Theme: Future Societies

Potential Essential Questions	Potential Anchor Texts
• How can we improve our current society? • What concerns that we have today will become worse in the future? • How do authors use futuristic societies to warn us about potential problems today?	• *The Declaration* by Gemma Malley • *Feed* by M. T. Anderson • *Little Brother* by Cory Doctorow • *Matched* by Ally Condie • *Unwind* by Neal Shusterman

Potential Assessments (Unit Projects)

- Have students study what futurologists are predicting using websites and videos (R9). Have students (individually or in small groups) create their own futuristic society that resolves problems in today's society; this could be a broad society or it could be more focused, at the level of schools, for instance. Students would create informational texts (W2) that describe aspects of the society. They could also create a persuasive brochure that advertises for their community (W1).
- Have students identify a problem in today's society and suggest a solution; this could take the form of a traditional argumentative or persuasive essay or a documentary or photo-essay format (W1, W2). Research could be done in a variety of databases and with print resources; check with your librarian to see what resources are available in your area. Sources such as Opposing Viewpoints, CQ Researcher, or Academic Search are good sources that may be available in your area (W7, W8). Students might be encouraged to draft an action plan (W5), in which they settle on something they themselves can do to help solve the problem. They could report on these efforts through a variety of genres including a newspaper article or public speech/presentation (W2, SL4).
- Given the popularity of this genre, a number of books could be read by students in literature circles. At the end of their reading, each literature circle group would create a presentation that analyzes the society depicted in their book (R9), how it connects to issues or concerns of today (R9, W9), and the weaknesses they see in the society depicted in the book. To connect to the larger essential questions, this presentation could also explore what warnings or cautions the author of their book is trying to give present-day readers.
- Students could be assigned to read a dystopian novel independently and then write in the book review genre an analysis of the book that summarizes important plot points, analyzes characters and their changes over the book (R3, R4, W9), identifies themes of the book (R2), and connects all of this to the essential question for the unit. Students could also do a sophisticated analysis by comparing and contrasting the dystopias presented in the two books or the way the author told the story in the two books (R9).
- Create a book trailer (search "Making Book Trailers" on the web for more information on how to do this for free) that emphasizes theme when the focus is on the story's secrets and the consequences or revelation of the secret (R2). Have the students do a rereading of the text to identify the most important plot points, then have them find visuals that explain the important elements and talk about why they do. Students could also find music that fits the tone and style of the work and explain why. Have them create and publish their work (after addressing appropriate copyright concerns) on a website (W4, W6, W9); they can find a free tool at http://education .weebly.com/.

Connected/Supporting Texts	Multimodal Connections
Young Adult Novels: • *After the Snow* by S. D. Crockett • *All These Things I've Done* by Gabrielle Zevin • *Article 5* by Kristen Simmons • *Divergent* and *Insurgent* by Veronica Roth	*Online Videos:* • TED: Ideas Worth Spreading (http://www .ted.com/): Offers a variety of talks on modern problems • World Future Society (http://www.wfs.org/):

(continued)

From *Integrating Young Adult Literature through the Common Core Standards* by Rachel L. Wadham and Jonathan W. Ostenson. Santa Barbara, CA: Libraries Unlimited. Copyright © 2013.

• *Fever* by Lauren DeStefano • *The Pledge* by Kimberly Derting *Other Novels:* • *1984* by George Orwell • *Brave New World* by Aldous Huxley • *A Clockwork Orange* by Anthony Burgess • *Fahrenheit 451* by Ray Bradbury • *The Handmaid's Tale* by Margaret Atwood	An organization of people dedicated to exploring the future • YouTube (http://www.youtube.com): Search "future" or "future societies" for a variety of videos depicting many perspectives on the future direction society may take.

From *Integrating Young Adult Literature through the Common Core Standards* by Rachel L. Wadham and Jonathan W. Ostenson. Santa Barbara, CA: Libraries Unlimited. Copyright © 2013.

Theme: Forgiveness

Potential Essential Questions	Potential Anchor Texts
• What does it mean to truly forgive? • Why is it so difficult to forgive? • Is it important to forgive? • Can we seek justice and forgiveness at the same time? • Is it harder to forgive ourselves or other people?	• *Breaking Night* by Liz Murray • *Hate List* by Jennifer Brown • *If I Stay* by Gayle Forman • *Once Was Lost* by Sara Zarr • *Out of the Dust* by Karen Hesse

Potential Assessments (Unit Projects)

- Students could write a personal essay in which they describe a time (or times) when they had to forgive or when they were forgiven (W2). The narrative would describe the situation in vivid detail and highlight lessons learned by the author through his or her experiences (W3, L3).
- Students could write a comparison-contrast essay in which they look at cases where victims of crimes have talked about forgiveness and/or about seeking justice (W1, W2). They would explore the implications of either attitude and evaluate those attitudes in terms of which may be healthier or more productive. In the essay, students might also wrestle with the idea of whether justice and forgiveness are mutually exclusive.
- Students could create a photo-essay in which they explore significant cases of forgiveness, researching stories of victims of crimes or war or other injustices (R7, W2). Captions for the photos would describe the case, giving details of the crimes and details of the victims' forgiving attitudes. Musical accompaniment would enhance the tone or mood of the piece.
- Students could write an analytic essay examining poetry or song lyrics that discuss forgiveness (R2, R9). Students would need to conduct meaningful textual analysis of the words and phrases of the text, establishing a strong thesis about the ideas of forgiveness presented in these texts. (R4, W4)
- Students could create an extended definition in which they define forgiveness and give examples of it (W9), from the anchor text studied or other connected texts or from their own experience, that help flesh out that definition. The form this definition takes could be varied: a traditional written piece, a multimedia presentation, a visual collage (W2, W6).

Connected/Supporting Texts	Multimodal Connections
Other Novels: • *Blue Plate Special* by Michelle Kwasney • *The Sin Eater* by Gary Schmidt • *Story of a Girl* by Sara Zarr • *Whirligig* by Paul Fleischman *Poetry:* • *Forgive Me, I Meant to Do it: False Apology Poems* by Gail Carson Levine, illustrated by Matthew Cordell • *Revenge and Forgiveness: An Anthology of Poems* edited by Patrice Vecchione • *This Is Just to Say: Poems of Apology* by Joyce Sidman	*Music:* • "Human" by Brandy • "Please Forgive Me" by Bryan Adams • "Walk" by Foo Fighters • "Working My Way Back" to You" by the Four Seasons • "Prodigal Son" by the Rolling Stones *Film:* • *Forgiveness: A Time to Love and a Time to Hate* (2011), a PBS film directed by Helen Whitney • *The Big Question: A Film about Forgiveness* (2009) made by Vision Video • *The Power of Forgiveness* (2007) directed by Martin Doblmeier • *Amish Grace* (2010) directed by Gregg Champion, starring Kimberly Williams-Paisley

Theme: The Making of a Legend—Robin Hood

Potential Essential Questions	Potential Anchor Texts
• What do we know about legendary figures? How do we know this? • What qualities do legendary figures have that make them seem real? How do authors/ tellers of legends convey these qualities? • Why are these qualities important? • Why are legends often based in historical fact? • How did the telling of legends serve society in the time they were first told? How do they still serve society today? • How and why do legends change over time? How do these changes keep them realistic?	• *In a Dark Wood* by Michael Cadnum • *The Outlaws of Sherwood* by Robin McKinley • *Scarlet* by A. C. Gaughen

Potential Assessments (Unit Projects)

• Have students look only at the cover of the book. From that picture alone have the students make inferences (R1) about what they are going to read. Have them discuss or write about their inferences. Have them brainstorm about what they already know about the legendary figure and answer such questions as, Does what you already know influence your perceptions of the book? How does your previous knowledge of this legendary figure influence your expectations of the book? Have the students collaborate on discussion of these issues (SL1).

• Use one or more works either read together, individually, or in literature circles; also include a film version or other artistic medium. Have the students use graphic organizers or other method to record the important qualities of the legendary figure (or some other character) in the work. Also record how the character changes over time (R3, R6). Either individually or in groups, have the students create power-points, movies, or some other media that conveys the qualities they identified for that legendary figure (or character) and why they are important both to the story and to the reader (W2). Publish these on a website for the unit (W6). Have the whole class compare and contrast how different versions of the story may emphasize different qualities. Answer questions with essays or other form that indicate why they think the stories are different, citing examples from the text (R9, W1, W9).

• Have the students research, using print and electronic sources (both popular and scholarly), the historical facts of the legendary figure's time and persons (for Robin Hood this would be the 12th century and figures like Robin himself and others like Richard the Lionheart). Include research into political, social, and cultural issues of the time by dividing the class into groups and giving them each a different area (W7). Divide the project into manageable sections so students are guided though the steps to gather sources and evaluate them (W8). Have them give group presentations with power-point or other visuals along with supportive evidence from text(s) that show what details of the depiction are historical fact and which are historical fiction (W9). This provides strong text-to-world connections for these novels.

• Using the research done above, have students construct an argumentative essay (W1) about why the stories of the legendary figure would have been important for the time. What situations made the people need to have a figure such as Robin Hood to believe in? Have students combine their historical study with quotes from one or more fictional text to show how the author conveyed time and place and how that time and place connects to the "real" world that they discovered in their research (R4, W9).

(*continued*)

182 From *Integrating Young Adult Literature through the Common Core Standards* by Rachel L. Wadham and Jonathan W. Ostenson. Santa Barbara, CA: Libraries Unlimited. Copyright © 2013.

- Compare and contrast a classic telling of the tale with a modern telling (see above Pyle and Gaughen for example). Have the students create a chart or graphic indicating differences between the two stories (R9). In an evaluative comparative essay have the students, with evidence from the text (W9), contrast the ways the two authors depicted the legend. Have them craft an argument as to why they believe the author created their portrayal that way. Have the students write their own creative narrative (story, poem, drama) (W3) that recrafts the story with a theme that is important to them personally.
- Create a Voki (a speaking avatar, http://www.voki.com/) of the legendary character addressing an issue of modern concern that they might be interested in (W6); for example, Robin Hood addressing the government bailouts of the auto industry. Have the students write the script aimed at a certain audience (W4) of what it would be important to say and defend the style and language they choose. Connect text-to-world issues, and give depth to the study of character creation and how dialogue gives us a sense of character (R3).

Connected/Supporting Texts	Multimodal Connections
Other Novels:	*Movies*:
• *Robbie Forester and the Outlaws of Sherwood Street* by Peter Abrahams	• *Princess of Thieves* (2001) directed by Peter Hewitt, starring Keira Knightley
• Rowan Hood series by Nancy Springer	• *Robin Hood* (1973) directed by Wolfgang Reitherman
Graphic Novel:	• *Robin Hood* (2010) directed by Ridley Scott, staring Russell Crowe
• *Outlaw: The Legend of Robin Hood* by Tony Lee, Sam Hart and Artur Fujita	• *Robin Hood: Prince of Thieves* (1991) directed by Kevin Reynolds, starring Kevin Costner
Classics:	
• *Ivanhoe* by Walter Scott	
• *The Merry Adventures of Robin Hood* by Howard Pyle	
• *The Sword in the Stone* by T. H. White	

From *Integrating Young Adult Literature through the Common Core Standards* by Rachel L. Wadham and Jonathan W. Ostenson. Santa Barbara, CA: Libraries Unlimited. Copyright © 2013.

Theme: Mythological Tales

Potential Essential Questions	Potential Anchor Texts
• What do mythological stories (especially heroic tales) reveal about a culture's values? • What mythological stories do we tell today in our modern culture? • What is the purpose of mythological tales? • How do today's superheroes compare to the heroes of ancient mythology?	• *American Born Chinese* by Gene Luen Yang • *Beowulf* by Gareth Hinds • *The Last Olympian* by Rick Riordan • *The League of Extraordinary Gentlemen, Vol. 1* by Alan Moore • *The Odyssey* by Gareth Hinds • *The Red Pyramid* by Rick Riordan

Potential Assessments (Unit Projects)

• Have students compose a myth of their own—creation myth, heroic tale, etc. (W3). Students will need to make sure that they follow the conventions of the kind of myth they choose (R9): a creation myth should explain how the world came to be, for instance, or a hero myth should follow the outlines of the hero journey archetype. These stories could be published in an online or print form, collecting the "mythos" of a class or grade level. (W6)

• Write an analysis comparing a modern superhero to an ancient mythological hero (W2). This analysis could focus on making connections based on the hero journey, drawing parallels between the ancient and modern tellings of this archetypal journey (R9). Or students could compare and contrast the embedded values in the portrayal of the ancient hero and the modern hero (R5, R9).

• Write a comparison analysis of a handful of modern urban legends, and compare their purposes with purposes of ancient mythological stories (R5, R9). This assignment would allow students to analyze the purposes behind ancient myths and then examine how those purposes are reflected in modern urban legends.

• The teacher can introduce students to the mythic/archetypal theory of literary criticism (see Wikipedia for a comprehensive overview of the theory) (R9), and model and practice with them interpreting modern texts through this theoretical lens. Students could then be tasked to analyze a book they have read (young adult or a classic) through the mythic/archetypal theoretical frame (W2, W4).

Connected/Supporting Texts	Multimodal Connections
Reference Sources: • *Encyclopedia of Urban Legends* by Jan Harold Brunvand • *Mythology for Teens: Classic Myths for Today's World* by Zachary Hamby • *Oh My Gods! A Look-It-Up Guide to the Gods of Mythology* (Mythlopedia) by Megan Bryant • *Star Wars: The Power of Myth* by DK Publishing • *Star Wars: The New Myth* by Michael Hanson and Max Kay *Anthologies and Short Stories:* • *Psyche in a Dress* by Francesca Lia Block • Scary Stories to Tell in the Dark series by Alvin Schwartz	*Films:* • *Clash of the Titans* (1981) Film adaptation of the myth of Perseus directed by Desmond Davis, starring Laurence Olivier • Disney's *Hercules* (1997) Film adaptation of the Greek myth • *Joseph Campbell on the Power of Myth with Bill Moyers* (1988) • Film stories that tell the story of a hero fitting the archetypal hero pattern (e.g., The Lord of the Rings, Star Wars, Harry Potter) • *Urban Legends: The Complete Season One* (2009) The Biography Channel

Theme: The Personal Price of War—The Revolutionary War

Potential Essential Questions	Potential Anchor Texts
• What is the purpose of war? • What is the impact of war on a society? • What is the impact of war on families? • What is the impact of war on an individual? • How are these impacts different during a war compared to when the conflict is over? • When do we consider the costs of war to be too high?	• *Chains* by Laurie Halse Anderson • *Five 4ths of July* by Pat Raccio Hughes • *Soldier's Secret: The Story of Deborah Sampson* by Sheila Solomon Klass • *Woods Runner* by Gary Paulsen

Potential Assessments (Unit Projects)

- Make a bulletin board, placing the word "war" at the center. Have the students brainstorm different words and ideas that relate to the word. As they read the text, have them add additional words and ideas to the board. At the end of the unit have the students write informative essays (W2) on how the words on the board changed over time, emphasizing how the before and after changed their vision of what war is.
- Have the students take on the persona of one of the fictional characters (R3). Have them write a letter (W2) as if they were that person and using the voice and style the author used to convey that person (R4). The letter should be formulated to address a certain audience (W4) that could be anyone from the person's family to a girlfriend to a political leader. In the letter, students could address how the war is or has impacted the individual character.
- Use the BioCube interactive found on the Read, Write Think website (http://www. readwritethink.org/classroom-resources/student-interactives/cube-30057.html) to have students develop an outline based on one of the fictional characters (R3). Have them use this outline to write a complete biography of the character (W5, W2). Have them imagine details (R4, W9) for before and after the events in the novel that are consistent with those events, showing what choices or psychological impact the war would have on the person in their future lives.
- Continue the narrative begun in one of the fictional texts (W3, W9), starting the story 10 years after the last event in the novel. The stories should represent the character in a way consistent with the novel, but they do not necessarily have to duplicate the style of the original text. Have the students add characters and change settings as necessary. Using a peer-review process, revise and edit the stories based on peer feedback (W5).
- Connecting a variety of texts from fiction to nonfiction (R8, R9), have the students create a play in which fictional and real characters interact. Each character in the play should be consistent with the depiction of the character or accurate to the real person (R4, R9). The theme of the play should address the essential question and allow those who view/read the play to understand what a possible answer to that question is (R2).
- Develop an interactive time line (http://www.timetoast.com/). Have students use information from textbooks, websites, and other information resources to do short research (W7) on important events of the war. Plot these points on the time line. Identify important plot moments from the fictional text(s), and place these events on the time line using different visual indicators to show the differences between fiction and nonfiction. Have students analyze the similarities and differences between the two to determine how accurate the author was in portraying history (R9).
- Connect the text(s) to current issues by comparing the experiences of those in the recent wars in Iraq and Afghanistan to the Revolutionary War. Have the student interview or read first-person accounts of veterans who served. Compare these accounts to those given in the text(s) (R9). Have the students write an informative essay (W2) comparing the two experiences. Have them articulate their own answers to the essential questions given the information they gained from this experience.

(continued)

From *Integrating Young Adult Literature through the Common Core Standards* by Rachel L. Wadham and Jonathan W. Ostenson. Santa Barbara, CA: Libraries Unlimited. Copyright © 2013.

Connected/Supporting Texts	Multimodal Connections
Other Novels:	*Documentary Films:*
• *The Astonishing Life of Octavian Nothing: Traitor to the Nation: Pox Party* by M. T. Anderson	• *The History Channel Presents: The Revolution* (2006) directed by Peter Schnall, distributed by A&E Home Video
• *Forge* (sequel to *Chains*) by Laurie Halse Anderson	• *Liberty: The American Revolution* (2007) produced by TPT in association with MiddleMarch Films (http://www.pbs.org/ktca/liberty/)
• *Give Me Liberty* by Laura Elliott	
• *Johnny Tremain* by Esther Forbes	*Fictionalized Movies:*
• *My Brother Sam Is Dead* by James Lincoln Collier	• *1776* (1972) directed by Peter H. Hunt, starring William Daniels and Howard DaSilva
• *Time Enough for Drums* by Ann Rinaldi	• *Johnny Tremain* (1957) directed by Robert Stevenson, starring Hal Stalmaster and Luana Patten
Graphic Novels:	
• Graphic Heroes of the American Revolution series by Gary Jeffrey	• *Revolution* (1985) directed by Hugh Hudson, starring Al Pacino
• *The Sons of Liberty* by Alexander Lagos, illustrated by Steve Walker	*Primary Sources:*
Nonfiction:	The Federalist Papers (http://thomas.loc.gov/home/histdox/fedpapers.html)
• *Alexander Hamilton: The Outsider* by Jean Fritz	Documents from the Continental Congress and the Constitutional Convention (http://memory.loc.gov/ammem/collections/continental/)
• *The Crossing: How George Washington Saved the American Revolution* by Jim Murphy	
• *George Washington Spymaster: How America Outspied the British and Won the Revolutionary War* by Thomas B. Allen	
• *Lafayette and the American Revolution* by Russell Freedman	
• *The Real Revolution: The Global Story of American Independence* by Marc Aronson	
• *The Notorious Benedict Arnold: A True Story of Adventure, Heroism and Bravery* by Steve Sheinkin	
• *Write on Mercy! The Secret Life of Mercy Otis Warren* by Gretchen Woelfle	

From *Integrating Young Adult Literature through the Common Core Standards* by Rachel L. Wadham and Jonathan W. Ostenson. Santa Barbara, CA: Libraries Unlimited. Copyright © 2013.

Theme: Secrets

Potential Essential Questions	Potential Anchor Texts
• Why do people keep secrets? • When is a secret good to keep? When can it be harmful? • How do you know when to keep a secret and when to tell it?	• *Dirty Little Secrets* by C. J. Omololu • *Lie* by Caroline Bock • *Speak* by Laurie Halse Anderson

Potential Assessments (Unit Projects)
• Complete anticipation questions based on the students' own experiences (R1) to make text-to-self connections. Specific questions could be: Have you ever kept a secret? Why did you keep that secret? What happened when the secret was revealed? Additionally, opinion questions could be phrased and students could respond using a Likert Scale from strongly disagree to strongly agree. Specific questions could be: People should never keep secrets, It is important to keep all secrets, My friends ask me to keep secrets. This provides text-to-text connections and allows the students to contextualize the essential questions.
• After looking at the cover or reading the first chapter(s) of the text(s), complete anticipation guides based around the essential questions to guide the students to make inferences (R1) about what they will be reading. Specific questions could be: What secret is the character keeping? What clues make you predict this?
• Create graphic organizers of the plot's twists and turns (R3, R5) to interpret the sequencing and time lines the author uses to reveal information about the characters' secrets. From this sequence, have the students create a cause-and-effect flow chart, indicating the textual evidence (W9) that reveals the event, what characters or plot point affected that event, and the consequences of the event. This could lead to deeper discussion, essays, or presentations that use textual evidence to show why the characters do what they do.
• Create a book trailer (search "Making Book Trailers" on the web for more information on how to do this for free; YouTube and Amazon feature many models too) that emphasizes theme when the focus is on the story's secrets and the consequences or revelation of the secret (R2). Have the students do a rereading of the text to identify most of the important plot points. Have them find visuals that explain the important elements and explain why they do. Find music that fits the tone and style of the work and explain why. Have them create and publish their work on a website (W6); they can find a free tool at http://education.weebly.com/.
• Make text-to-world connections by researching events (W7) when celebrities or public figures have had secrets revealed. How does the media report these events? How does the public respond? How do these events change our view of the individual? Why would they want to keep these things a secret? Argumentative essays (W1) either for or against the revelation of the secret could be constructed.

Connected/Supporting Texts	Multimodal Connections
Other Novels: • *Bluefish* by Pat Schmatz • *Compulsion* by Heidi Ayarbe • *Every Little Thing in the World* by Nina De Gramont • *Identical* by Ellen Hopkins • *Just Listen* by Sarah Dessen • *Not That Kind of Girl* by Siobhan Vivian • *Stupid Fast* by Geoff Herbach • *Three Black Swans* by Caroline B. Cooney	*Music (Videos on YouTube):* • "Dirty Little Secret" by the All-American Rejects • "Do You Want to Know a Secret?" by the Beatles • "Secrets" by the Cure • "A Saucerful of Secrets" by Pink Floyd • "Our Secret Garden" by Peter Murphy • "My Secret Garden" by Depeche Mode • "Jessie's Girl" by Rick Springfield • "Secret Love" by Doris Day

(continued)

From *Integrating Young Adult Literature through the Common Core Standards* by Rachel L. Wadham and Jonathan W. Ostenson. Santa Barbara, CA: Libraries Unlimited. Copyright © 2013.

Nonfiction: • *Can I See Your I.D.? True Stories of False Identities* by Chris Barton • *I Don't Keep Secrets* by Sheila Stewart • *PostSecret: Extraordinary Confessions from Ordinary Lives* by Frank Warren • *Secret American People: From Secret Societies to Secret Agents* by Christopher Forest • *Secrets Girls Keep: What Girls Hide (& Why) and How to Break the Stress of Silence* by Carrie Silver-Stock • *Would You Rather—? Super Secrets* edited by Justin Heimberg and David Gomberg *Poetry:* • *If I Were in Charge of the World and Other Worries: Poems for Children and Their Parents* by Judith Viorst • *Things I Have to Tell You: Poems and Writing by Teenage Girls* illustrated by Nina Nickles • *Weird? (Me, too!): Let's Be Friends* by Sara E. Holbrook	

Theme: Triangle Shirtwaist Factory Fire

Potential Essential Questions	Potential Anchor Texts
• What is the cost of human life? How do we know when that cost is too dear to pay? • What rights do employees have? What responsibilities do employers have to their employees? How has this concept changed over time? • How does one event change the course of history? How can one event still have impact hundreds of years after it happened?	• *Ashes of Roses* by Mary Jane Auch • *Threads and Flames* by Esther M. Friesner • *Uprising* by Margaret Peterson Haddix

Potential Assessments (Unit Projects)

- After reading the text(s), have the students identify a critical scene in the book(s). Focus on those that have incidents that propel the action forward (R3). Have the students identify important structures, descriptions, or character development that are not part of the scene that was chosen but that are integral to understanding the story (R5). Students will then rewrite or modify that scene of the story into a reader's theater script using the elements from the scene as well as adding any context that is necessary. The script should be organized (W4) like any dramatic script. Have groups share their drafts and conduct writing workshops for editing and rewriting (W5), focusing on story details and how they are conveyed. Have students perform the scripts. If possible, film the productions and place them on a website (W6).
- Develop an interactive time line (http://www.timetoast.com/). Have students gather and evaluate primary sources (W7, W8) to consolidate the important events leading up to, during, and after the fire. Plot these points on the time line. Identify important plot moments from the fictional text(s) and place these events on the time line using different visual indicators to show the differences between fiction and nonfiction. Have students analyze the similarities and differences between the two to determine how accurate the author was in portraying history (R9).
- Select one of the minor characters from the text(s). Use character map graphic organizers for students to gather and articulate clues from the text that relate to that character (R3). Fill in the holes left by what the author does not say with individual ideas that are consistent with what the author has given the student. Write a narrative (W3) that recounts a scene that is in the text(s) or one that is not in the text but is consistent with the story from that character's point of view (R6).
- During the reading of a variety of texts, gather words and phrases that the author uses to convey the sense of time and place in the story (R4). Try to identify colloquial words, words that have changed meaning over time, or phrases that give the story cultural context such as the use of words adopted from foreign languages. Create a Wordle (http://www.wordle.net/) of the words gathered. Identify which words are used most often and which are used less frequently. Identify words or ideas that were used by all the authors, and have the students discuss how these words helped everyone portray history (R9). Identify words only one or a few of the authors used. Have the students show how these differences convey the author's style and tone. Discuss how these word choices (R4) connect to the point of view (R6) and structure (R5) that the author used to tell the story (R9).
- Using primary sources, select one of the photographs of the event from the primary sources. Write a poem or story (W3) that is based on the photograph. Take the poem or story though several drafts (W5) to a final version published on a website (W6).
- Have the students conduct short research about the fire (W7) to develop arguments (W1) to be used at a mock trial. Conduct a mock trial or debate over an issue relating to the fire such as the staircases, fire escapes, or wood surfaces. Focus the debate on what the laws were at the time and

(continued)

how the company complied with the laws. Discuss the ethics of the situation where the company complied with the law, but this compliance still put their employees at risk. Try to determine what ethical responsibilities the employers had to their employees. Compare the outcomes of the student trial or debate to those of the real trial.
- Do short research (W7) on the impact of the fire on labor reforms and building safety measures. Write an informative essay (W2) on the topic.

Connected/Supporting Texts	Multimodal Connections
Other Novels: - *Dear Emma* by Johanna Hurwitz - *Lost* by Jacqueline Davies - *Triangle* by Katharine Weber *Nonfiction:* - *Flesh and Blood So Cheap: The Triangle Factory Fire and Its Legacy* by Albert Marrin - *Fire at the Triangle Factory* by Holly Littlefield - *The Triangle Factory Fire* by Victoria Sherrow - *Triangle Shirtwaist Factory Fire* by Donna Getzinger - *The Triangle Shirtwaist Factory Fire: Its Legacy of Labor Rights* by Katie Marsico - *Sweat and Blood: A History of U.S. Labor Unions* by Gloria Skurzynski - *The Woman behind the New Deal: The Life of Francis Perkins, FDR's Secretary of Labor and His Moral Conscience* by Kirstin Downey (contains a chapter on the Triangle Fire) - *Trials of the Century: An Encyclopedia of Popular Culture and the Law* by Scott P. Johnson (contains a chapter on the Triangle Fire trial)	*Documentary Films:* - *American Experience: Triangle Fire* (2011) produced by PBS - *Triangle: Remembering the Fire* (2011) HBO documentary film directed by Daphne Pinkerson *Primary Sources:* - Cornell University: Remembering the 1911 Triangle Factory Fire (http://www.ilr.cornell.edu/trianglefire/) - United States Department of Labor Occupational Safety & Health Administration: The Triangle Shirtwaist Factory Fire (http://www.osha.gov/oas/trianglefactoryfire.html) - Triangle Fire Open Archive (http://rememberthetrianglefire.org/open-archive/) - New York Public Radio: Remembering the Triangle Shirtwaist Fire, 100 Years Later (http://www.wnyc.org/articles/wnyc-news/2011/mar/21/100-years-later-remembering-triangle-shirtwaist-factory-fire/) - Famous Trials: The Triangle Shirtwaist Fire Trial 1911 (http://law2.umkc.edu/faculty/projects/ftrials/triangle/trianglefire.html)

Theme: Unpacking the Story—Beauty and the Beast

Potential Essential Questions	Potential Anchor Texts
• How do different authors tell the same story? Why are there differences in the way authors tell stories? • How do stories change across time and/or cultures? Why do they change? • How do different mediums (text vs. visual) affect the way an author tells a story? • What motifs and/or structures are essential to a story? • Why are some of these motifs and/or structures universal to stories? Why are some only evident in some time and/or cultures?	• *Beauties and Beasts* (The Oryx Multicultural Folktale Series) by Betsy Hearne • *Beastly* by Alex Flinn • *Beastly* (2011 film) directed by Daniel Barnz, staring Alex Pettyfer and Vanessa Hudgens

Potential Assessments (Unit Projects)

- Using two different versions of the tale (R9), have students create graphic organizers (i.e., Story Structure, Story Map, or Story Organizer) for each story. Students will write informative essays (W2) about the differences they found.
- Have students do short biographical research (W7) on the author/creator of one of the versions of the tale. Using a biographical criticism framework, ask students to look for things in the individual's life that possibly affected their interpretation of the story. Students will write critical argumentative essays (W1) about how knowing the author's experiences help the reader to understand the text.
- Using two different versions of the tale in different mediums (i.e., text and visual) (R7, R9), have students create graphic organizers (i.e., Character Maps, Character Traits) for two of the characters in each story focusing on the details the author uses to convey the character (R3). As individuals or in groups, have the students write an biography for each of the different characters (W2) drawing on the details they have found (W9) and conveying though their own style why the character is the same as well as different (W4).
- Study the work of Vladimir Propp in his *Morphology of the Folktale* (University of Texas Press, 1968) and the Aarne-Thompson Tale Type Index (available online http://www.ruthenia.ru/folklore/thompson/index.htm). Select one or two versions of the tale and a classification of motifs (i.e., tests, captives and fugitives, etc.), and have the students classify the motifs in their tale.
- Using two different versions from various times or cultures, use the classification of motifs (i.e., tests, captives and fugitives, etc.) to identify differences in the telling. Have students do short research (W7) on the time or culture. In multimedia presentations, have the students analyze why the motifs are different and show how these differences can be connected to the time or culture of the story.
- Using a shorter version (i.e., short story or television episode) compared to a longer version (i.e., novel or movie), have the students keep graphic organizers of the details the author/creator uses to portray character, setting, or plot elements focusing on the figurative language or powerful images (R4). Compare why the authors chose the words and images that they did. Ask whether the length of the form has any impact on how the author/creator conveys ideas.
- Have students select a time period or culture, doing short research as necessary (W7) to get an idea of the time or place. Using that time or culture as a backdrop, have the students write their own short version of the tale (W3). Through editing and rewriting (W5), help the students use words and figurative language that convey the sense of time and place. Also have them use dialogue, themes, and other structures that relate to that particular time and place.

(continued)

Connected/Supporting Texts	Multimodal Connections
Short Stories: • "Beast" in *The Rose and the Beast* by Francesca Lia Block • "The Beast" in *Ruby Slippers, Golden Tears* by Tanith Lee, edited by Ellen Datlow and Terri Windling • "Beast and Beauty" in *Tales From the Brothers Grimm and the Sisters Weird* by Vivian Vande Velde • "A Beauty in the Beast" in *Untold Tales* by William Brooke *Novels:* • *Beast* by Donna Jo Napoli • *Beauty and the Werewolf* by Mercedes Lackey • *Beauty: A Retelling of the Story of Beauty and the Beast* by Robin McKinley • *Belle: A Retelling of "Beauty and the Beast"* by Cameron Dokey • *The Fire Rose* by Mercedes Lackey • *Heart's Blood* by Juliet Marillier • *Rose Daughter* by Robin McKinley	*TV Shows:* • *Beauty and the Beast* (1987–1990) created by Ron Koslow • *Beauty and the Beast* (2012) directed by Gary Fleder *Movies:* • *Beauty and the Beast* (1946) directed by Jean Cocteau, starring Jean Marais, Josette Day and Mila Parely • *Beauty and the Beast* (1987) directed by Eugene Marner, starring John Savage and Rebecca De Mornay • *Shelley Duvall's Faerie Tale Theatre: Beauty and the Beast* (1984) directed by Roger Vadim, starring Susan Sarandon and Klaus Kinski • *Disney's Beauty and the Beast* (1991) directed by Gary Trousdale and Kirk Wise

Theme: Wildlife Conservation

Potential Essential Questions	Potential Anchor Texts
• What are humans doing to prevent extinction and/or to keep our planets ecological systems sound? • How can we balance the needs of humans and society with the needs of our planets and wildlife? • What role does government, science, construction, or business play in keeping our ecological systems in balance? What role do individuals play?	• *Hoot* by Carl Hiaasen • *The Maze* by Will Hobbs • *Wolves, Boys and Other Things That Might Kill Me* by Kristen Chandler

Potential Assessments (Unit Projects)

- Conduct short research (W7) on the issue of wildlife conservation brought up in the book(s) (i.e., wolves in Yellowstone, condors in the wild, etc.) using scientific and popular sources that they gather and evaluate (W8). Have the students write an explanatory essay (W2) describing the data each source cites explaining why it is may be difficult to understand or why it may confuse the issue. Have the students use a bibliography generator (such as those in Microsoft Word, Easy Bib, or BibMe) to cite their sources (W7, W8). This exploration has strong text-to-world connections.
- Create a character map or diagram for the text to show how the characters interact in the text around the conservation issue. Along with the visual created, cite examples from the text that show how characters influence others during the course of the story and how differing points of view on the issue impact the final outcome of the story (R3, R4)
- Using the character map as a guide, trace the development of one character by using dialogue from the text(s) and show how it conveys a character's attitude about the issue at a point in time and how the author then uses the other characters and situations in the plot to develop the character's ideas (R3).
- Craft an argumentative essay on the issue of wildlife conservation brought up in the book(s) where the student takes a stand on the issue and uses data and supportive points from the short research (W7, W8) to back up his or her claims (W1).
- Research a company, business, or agency (W7, W8) that deals with the issue of wildlife conservation brought up in the book(s). Create group wikis (http://www.wikispaces.com/content/teacher) to collect (W8) and publish (W6) the findings of what the group is doing to support or devalue conservation. Write letters to the group presenting an argument (W1) for what they could do to better help conservation efforts.
- Conduct interviews with the community about their feelings on the issue of wildlife conservation brought up in the book(s) or one of local concern. Write-ups about the issues could be added to the wikis created above that reflect the issues but that are aimed at a certain audience (W4).
- Supported by a study of other wildlife conservation campaigns and how these authors effectively communicate information, create student-generated Glogs (interactive posters at http://edu.glogster.com/) that with visuals and text effectively communicate an argument (W1, W6) for or against conservation that is aimed at a certain audience (W4). Post these posters on a website, and have classes, schools, or communities vote for their favorite (W6).

Connected/Supporting Texts	Multimodal Connections
Other Novels: • *The Last Lobo* by Roland Smith • *Scat* by Carl Hiaasen • *The Weirdo* by Theodore Taylor	*Movies:* • *DisneyNature: Chimpanzee* (2012) • *DisneyNature: African Cats* (2011) • *DisneyNature: The Crimson Wing* (2008) • *DisneyNature: Oceans* (2009)

(continued)

From *Integrating Young Adult Literature through the Common Core Standards* by Rachel L. Wadham and Jonathan W. Ostenson. Santa Barbara, CA: Libraries Unlimited. Copyright © 2013.

Nonfiction:	Television:
• *The Frog Scientist* by Pamela S. Turner • *Kakapo Rescue: Saving the Worlds Strangest Parrot* by Sy Montgomery, illustrated by Nic Bishop • *A Life in the Wild: George Schaller's Struggle to Save the Last Great Beasts* by Pamela S. Turner • *When the Wolves Returned: Restoring Nature's Balance in Yellowstone* by Dorothy Hinshaw Patent, illustrated by Dan Hartman • *World without Fish* by Mark Kurlansky, illustrated by Frank Stratton	• *In the Valley of the Wolves*, an episode of *Nature* (http://www.pbs.org/wnet/nature/episodes/in-the-valley-of-the-wolves/introduction/212/) *Websites:* • National Wildlife Federation: http://www.nwf.org/ • World Wildlife Federation (WWF): http://wwf.panda.org/ • Yellowstone Park Wolves: http://www.yellowstonenationalpark.com/wolves.htm

Chapter 10

Raw Materials for Textual Connections

Introduction

As we speak to and advocate for young adult literature to both pre-service and in-service professionals, we find that one of the greatest challenges teachers face is finding what young adult books are out there. We recognize that keeping up with the scope of the genre, especially with so many new books each year, can be a daunting task. The resources we have already shared should have made you aware of some texts, but in this chapter we want to provide you with even more. What follows are a number of booklists that give you outstanding young adult texts that we feel have great application in the classroom. We hope these lists will assist you in finding some texts that you can then take to apply in your classroom with a variety of pedagogies, assessments, or activities. To show how these texts can connect to the common core, we have organized our recommendations around the 10 anchor standards for reading. There is no way we could make a comprehensive list of all the texts in every category, so these lists are just a starting point. We offer our favorites here and hope that you will expand these lists as you encounter new titles.

As we noted in chapter nine, for all texts we have chosen only to indicate the most basic bibliographic information, and we encourage you to select materials most suited to the readers and situations they are working with. So let's dive in and look at the great variety of young adult texts that can connect the dots between your classrooms and the anchor standards.

Making Inferences

The first anchor standard for reading revolves around the reader making inferences from the text. This ability requires the reader to take clues from the text and figure out something that is not explicitly stated. While almost any text can be used to structure learning about how to make inferences, we find that two types of young adult texts are especially suited to the task, graphic novels and mysteries.

Graphic Novels

Graphic novels are valuable teaching tools as they combine both textual and visual literacy skills to the interpretation of the text. They also provide a strong application of the skills needed to make inferences. Since neither the text nor the illustrations gives us the whole picture, we have to "read" both. This is also how we make inferences in real life, as many of the inferences we make in human interactions are taken from visual as well as textual clues. These texts give us a great opportunity to expand on that real-world context. For those less familiar with the genre of graphic novels we suggest the yearly Young Adult Library Services Association Great Graphic Novels for Teens List (http://www.ala.org/yalsa/ggnt) or an introductory podcast hosted by ReadWriteThink (http://www.readwritethink.org/parent-afterschool-resources/podcast-episodes/introduction-graphic-novels-30326.html) as great resources. We find the following to be good choices for addressing making inferences.

The Accidental Genius of Weasel High by Rick Detorie

Americus by M. K. Reed, illustrated by Jonathan David Hill

Foiled by Jane Yolen, illustrated by Michael Cavallaro

Ghostopolis by Doug TenNapel

Paige by Paige by Laura Lee Gulledge

The Plain Janes by Cecil Castellucci, illustrated by Jim Rugg

Rapunzel's Revenge by Shannon and Dean Hale, illustrated by Nathan Hale

Re-Gifters by Mike Carey, illustrated by Marc Hempel and Sonny Liew

Smile by Raina Telgemeier

The Sons of Liberty series by Alexander Lagos, illustrated by Steve Walker

Mysteries

By their very nature mysteries lend themselves to the study of inferences. for if it were not for the ability to take clues and figure out something that is not explicitly stated, no crime would ever be solved. This genre allows us to take that inherent connection and show readers how authors use characters, plot, and setting to give us the clues we need to make inferences. As well-crafted mysteries will leave clues along the way to help us connect the pieces, a creative professional can use these as a strong basis to help students not only discover how to make their own inferences but also understand how the author uses them to craft a narrative.

The Agency series (*A Spy in the House; The Body at the Tower; The Traitor in the Tunnel*) by Y. S. Lee

Closed for the Season by Mary Downing Hahn

Echo Falls Mysteries series (*Down the Rabbit Hole; Behind the Curtin; Into the Dark*) by Peter Abrahams

Heist Society series (*Heist Society; Uncommon Criminals*) by Ally Carter

Homelanders series (*The Last Thing I Remember; The Long Way Home; The Truth of the Matter; The Final Hour*) by Andrew Klavan

Second Sight by Gary Blackwood

So Yesterday by Scott Westerfeld

Virals by Kathy Reichs

You Killed Wesley Payne by Sean Beaudoin

Young Sherlock Holmes series (*Death Cloud; Rebel Fire*) by Andrew Lane

Themes Connected to Developmental Tasks

As we noted in chapter five, teens are drawn to works of young adult literature because they see themselves reflected in the pages. Because it is told from a teen's point of view, all young adult literature in some way addresses the same developmental challenges that real teens are facing. So while it is possible to connect any young adult novel to teens ongoing development, we would like to offer you some of our favorites. For each of six developmental tasks described in chapter 5, we offer a list of novels that connect to that task. While these tasks could be interpreted in any number of ways, we have chosen to focus on one aspect of each. These novels will do much to advance the needs associated with the reader dimensions of text complexity; we also find they are very suited to the second anchor standard for reading. This standard's focus is on themes and topics that generate knowledge. We find that since the developmental themes connect closely with teen readers, they are also likely those themes that will help those same readers to develop knowledge. Using developmental themes as the basis for explorations related to standard two, paired with activities that show how theme develops over a course of a text and how the theme interrelates with other elements, makes a great combination for ideal student learning.

Creating Mature Relationships

For most young adults, developing romantic relationships is of the utmost importance. So in this section we offer titles whose themes focus on the challenges of finding and keeping love from both the male and female perspective.

Anna and the French Kiss by Stephanie Perkins

An Abundance of Katherines by John Green

Amy and Roger's Epic Detour by Morgan Matson

Just Listen by Sarah Dessen

Scrambled Eggs at Midnight by Brad Barkley

Marcelo in the Real World by Francisco X. Stork

North of Beautiful by Justina Chen Headley

The Possibilities of Sainthood by Donna Freitas

The Statistical Probability of Love at First Sight by Jennifer E. Smith

The Unwritten Rule by Elizabeth Scott

Defining One's Gender Role

How society defines one's gender roles is a very challenging issue, especially for teens who are also facing overall identity issues. In this section we offer titles centered around themes that focus on breaking out of established gender identities to break new ground in defining what it means to be male and female.

Boy2Girl by Terence Blacker

The Dairy Queen series (*Dairy Queen*; *The Off Season*; *Front and Center*) by Catherine Gilbert Murdock

The Education of Bet by Lauren Baratz-Logsted

Eon: Dragoneye Reborn and *Eona: Return of the Dragoneye* by Alison Goodman

How Beautiful the Ordinary: Twelve Stories of Identity edited by Michael Cart

Nailed by Patrick Jones

Peaceweaver by Rebecca Barnhouse

The Pirate Captain's Daughter by Eve Bunting

Parrotfish by Ellen Wittlinger

Spirit's Princess by Esther M. Friesner

Accepting One's Body

Many teens, facing challenges that seem overwhelming, engage in self-destructive behavior to try and gain a sense of control over their lives. Some of these behaviors, like cutting, alcoholism, and eating disorders, give teens the perception of control through their own bodies. In this section we offer titles centered around characters who are self-destructive because they are unable accept their body but who ultimately find hope for their lives with the support of those around them.

Blood Wounds by Susan Beth Pfeffer

Jane In Bloom by Deborah A. Lytton

Looks by Madeleine George

Perfect by Natasha Friend

Purge by Sarah Littman

Scars by C. A. Rainfield

Skin by Adrienne Maria Vrettos

The Spectacular Now by Tim Tharp

Willow by Julia Hoban

Wintergirls by Laurie Halse Anderson

Finding Emotional Independence

Striking out on your own into new territories without adults to help is one of the hallmarks of being a teenager. These forays into new territory are important for teens to establish their own emotional independence and for them to learn how to make choices for themselves. In this section we offer titles centered around characters who step outside of their normal experiences to take a journey of self-discovery.

Accidents of Nature by Harriet McBryde Johnson

Along for the Ride by Sarah Dessen

As Easy as Falling off the Face of the Earth by Lynne Rae Perkins

Car Trouble by Jeanne DuPrau

Defining Dulcie by Paul Acampora

How to Build a House by Dana Reinhardt

Jump by Elisa Carbone

Lost It by Kristen Tracy

Rules of the Road by Joan Bauer

So B. It by Sarah Weeks

Preparing for Adult Life

One of the biggest challenges for teens in preparing for adult life is navigating the world of work. In this section we offer titles centered around characters who are dealing with their own challenges on the job.

Dream Factory by Brad Barkley

The Espressologist by Kristina Springer

The Grimm Legacy by Polly Shulman

Killer Pizza by Greg Taylor

Leaving Protection by Will Hobbs

Past Perfect by Leila Sales

Project Sweet Life by Brent Hartinger

Rules of the Road by Joan Bauer

Shelf Life by Robert Corbet

Working Days: Stories about Teenagers at Work edited by Anne Mazer

Developing a Moral Code and Socially Responsible Behavior

Riding the wave of a trend, some of the best books that address the process of teenagers developing a moral code and socially responsible behavior are actually dystopian science fiction. These books that present teenagers rebelling against a controlling society or surviving an apocalypse allow for deep discussion of morality. In this section we offer titles in this genre.

All These Things I've Done by Gabrielle Zevin

Birthmarked and *Prized* by Caragh O'Brien

Blood Red Road by Moira Young

Bumped and *Thumped* by Megan McCafferty

Candor by Pam Bachorz

Delirium and *Pandemonium* by Lauren Oliver

Divergent and *Insurgent* by Veronica Roth

Little Brother by Cory Doctorow

Legend by Marie Lu

Shipbreaker and *The Drowned Cities* by Paolo Bacigalupi

Thematically Connected to the Classics

As we have noted, young adult literature, like all quality literature, addresses expansive themes of universal significance. When we identify these universal themes, there are no limitations to the ways we can connect novels; finding these text-to-text connections can help us expand our students' vision of any one theme by including different perspectives and ideas.

These connections are also a good way to address anchor standard two, which revolves around the exploration of theme. We can also use it to address anchor standard six, which asks us to explore how different authors from different time periods address the same issues.

While we could have identified any number of themes and outlined numerous novels that address those themes, we have chosen to structure our offerings in this section around classic novels traditionally taught in middle and high school. In this section we first identify the major theme of a classic novel. We then offer a selection of young adult novels that connect to that same theme. These offerings can certainly be used in different ways. One of these novels alone could be used to explore the theme. Two or more of them could also be combined to be used as part of a thematic unit. Using young adult novels as a bridge to the classic text is an approach that has been advocated by many, and this application could also apply to these titles. There is also potential to explore how several of the novels could be used as part of literature circles, group study, or individual reading. No matter the approach, these thematically connected works have great potential in the classroom to create authentic and interesting learning experiences.

Class, Wealth, and Social Standing

The Great Gatsby by F. Scott Fitzgerald

Bright Young Things and *Beautiful Days* by Anna Godbersen

Dumb Lock by Lesley Choyce

King of the Lost and Found by John Lekich

The Realm of Possibility by David Levithan (free verse stories)

When the Sea Is Rising Red by Cat Hellisen

Loss of Innocence

Lord of the Flies by William Golding

Nothing by Janne Teller

Petty Crimes by Gary Soto (short stories)

Shooting the Moon by Frances O'Roark Dowell

This Gorgeous Game by Donna Freitas

Witness by Karen Hesse

Loneliness

Of Mice and Men by John Steinbeck

Butterfly by Sonya Hartnett

Hard Love by Ellen Wittlinger

How to Say Goodbye in Robot by Natalie Standiford

Love and Leftovers: A Novel in Verse by Sarah Tregay

Strays by Ron Koertge

The Nature of Evil

The Scarlet Letter by Nathaniel Hawthorne

Black Juice by Margo Lanagan (short stories)

Envy by Gregg Olsen

Raven Summer by David Almond

Rot and Ruin by Jonathan Maberry

Stolen by Vivian Vande Velde

Racial Injustice

To Kill a Mockingbird by Harper Lee

Copper Sun by Sharon M. Draper

The Land by Mildred D. Taylor

Lizzie Bright and the Buckminster Boy by Gary D. Schmidt

Mississippi Trial, 1955 by Chris Crowe

A Summer of Kings by Han Nolan

Dialogue-Rich Texts

Dialogue is one of the fundamental tools authors use to convey their narrative. Almost any story will have some form of dialogue. In the hands of a skilled author, dialogue will be used to propel actions and develop characters. Focusing on how an author uses structures to convey meaning in a text is a fundamental expectation of the CCSS. Anchor standard three focuses specifically on dialogue as a structure for us to explore. While almost any piece of dialogue could be used to explore connections to plot and character, there are many works that use dialogue most effectively. In this section we will focus on dialogue-rich texts that we feel have particular strengths for use in the classroom to explore how authors use this tool to propel their narrative.

Amplified by Tara Kelly

Aristotle and Dante Discover the Secrets of the Universe by Benjamin Alire Saenz

The Fault in Our Stars by John Green

Life Is But a Dream by Brian James

Lock and Key by Sarah Dessen

Peaches by Jodi Lynn Anderson

Spellbound by Cara Lynn Shultz

Stay with Me by Paul Griffin

Suite Scarlet by Maureen Johnson

You Against Me by Jenny Downham

Comparing and Contrasting Structure

As we discussed in chapter four, how an author uses the structural elements of a narrative impacts the qualitative complexity of a novel. Throughout the anchor standards, there is a strong focus on comparing and contrasting structures that authors use to make meaning. This standard is clearly articulated as part of anchor standard five. The grade-level standards note three specifics: flashbacks, parallel plots, and time manipulations where the novel is set in two time periods. In this section we will offer books that use these three structures to create complex narratives.

Flashbacks

As I Wake by Elizabeth Scott

The Boy Who Dared by Susan Campbell Bartoletti

The Final Four by Paul Volponi

The First Part Last by Angela Johnson

Hanging on to Max by Margaret Bechard

If I Stay by Gayle Forman

Inexcusable by Chris Lynch

Just Listen by Sarah Dessen

Story of a Girl by Sara Zarr

The Survival Kit by Donna Freitas

Parallel Plots

Crossing Montana by Laura Torres

The Dragon Tree by Jane Langton

The Field of the Dogs by Katherine Paterson

A Love Story Starring My Dead Best Friend by Emily Horner

On Wings of Evil by Cora Taylor

Rats Saw God by Rob Thomas

The Summer I Got a Life by Mark Fink

When Kambia Elaine Flew in from Neptune by Lori Aurelia Williams

Where Things Come Back by John Corey Whaley

Witch Hill by Marcus Sedgwick

Manipulating Time—Novels Told in Two Time Periods

Anxious Hearts by Tucker Shaw

Blood Magic by Tessa Gratton

Blue Plate Special by Michelle Kwasney

Bog Child by Siobhan Dowd

Mare's War by Tanita S. Davis

Mercury by Hope Larson

Postcards from No Man's Land by Han Nolan

Revolution by Jennifer Donnelly

Stay by Deb Caletti

Wonderstruck by Brian Selznick

Point of View

An author's selection of point of view has one of the greatest impacts on the creation of a narrative. The characters, plot, style, theme, and conflict are directly impacted by which point of view the story comes from. Helping readers to discover this intricate relationship between elements is one of the significant areas addressed by the standards. Anchor standard six specifically addresses point of view by asking for readers to look critically at how views shape the rest of the story. In this section we offer a variety of texts that will assist in the deep analysis of point of view.

Differing Points of View

Telling a story from more than one point of view not only adds to the complexity of a novel, but it also allows for a lot of diversity in the application of anchor standard six. Showing how one author uses point of view in different ways helps readers to see and understand how our vision changes with the changes in character viewpoint. These books are some of our favorites that offer differing points of view.

Breakout by Paul Fleischman

The Brimstone Journals by Ron Koertge

Bronx Masquerade by Nikki Grimes

The First Part Last by Angela Johnson

How to Build a House by Dana Reinhardt

Leviathan by Scott Westerfeld

Perfect Chemistry by Simone Elkeles

The Realm of Possibility by David Levithan

Shiver by Maggie Stiefvater

You Are My Only by Beth Kephart

World Literature

The grade-level standards of anchor standard six specifically ask students to look at world literature, since viewpoints outside our own offer us a wonderful opportunity to study point of view. With the globalization of our society we have greater access today to world literature than in any previous time; this is true also of world literature written for young adults. Here we offer some works by international authors. We offer only the English translations where books were first written in a foreign language. However, the original versions are certainly recommended where the language ability of the reader allows.

A Bottle in the Gaza Sea by Valerie Zenatti (Israeli)

Brave Story by Miyuki Miyabe (Japanese)

Children of Crow Cove series (*The Crow-Girl; Eidi; Tink*) by Bodil Bredsdorff (Danish)

Dani Bennoni: Long May he Live by Bart Moeyaert (Belgian)

Departure Time by Truus Matti (Dutch)

The Princess Plot by Kirsten Boie (German)

The Princetta by Anne-Laure Bondoux (French)

<u>Steiner Sisters</u> quartet (*A Faraway Island*; *The Lily Pond*) by Annika Thor (Swedish)

A Time of Miracles by Anne-Laure Bondoux (French)

War of the Witches by Maite Carranza (Spanish)

Style and Point of View

Point of view shapes many elements, but it most certainly shapes the style and tone of a text. For certain styles, such as those that use satire and sarcasm, grasping point of view requires distinguishing what is directly stated in a text from what is really meant. Works that rely on this style, then, can be used not only to meet anchor standard six, but they can also be used to address the making of inferences called for in standard one. In this section we offer novels that use satire and sarcasm as integral parts of their stylistic choices.

Satire

Beauty Queens by Libba Bray

Cloaked in Red by Vivian Vande Velde

Doom Machine by Mark Teague

The Fourth Stall by Chris Rylander

Geek: Fantasy Novel by E. Archer

King Dork by Frank Portman

Political Timber by Chris Lynch

Spoiled by Heather Cocks

Story Time by Edward Bloor

Rash by Pete Hautman

Sarcasm

An Abundance of Katherines by John Green

Amplified by Tara Kelly

The Center of the Universe (Yep, That Would Be Me) by Anita Liberty

Croak by Gina Damico

Drums, Girls and Dangerous Pie by Jordan Sonnenblick

The Edumacation of Jay Baker by Jay Clark

<u>Ghostgirl</u> series (*Ghostgirl*; *Homecoming*; *Lovesick*) by Tonya Hurley

Going Bovine by Libba Bray

Love, Inc. by Yvonne Collins

My Awesome/Awful Popularity Plan by Seth Rudetsky

Books Made into Movies

The CCSS reading and writing anchor standards acknowledge that in the 21st century, literacy is about far more than just being able to decode texts. It includes being about to decode visual images as well. In that vein, anchor standard seven asks readers to compare multiple versions of stories that are offered in differing artistic mediums. Looking at how a filmed adaptation follows or departs from another version is a fine critical exercise. Today many filmmakers are turning to young adult books for material. For professionals these book that have been made into movies provide us with a strong connection to apply the CCSS. Here are some of our favorite young adult book-to-movie adaptations.

Aquamarine by Alice Hoffman

Angus, Thongs and Full-Frontal Snogging by Louise Rennison

Blood and Chocolate by Annette Curtis Kaluse

Confessions of a Teenage Drama Queen by Dyan Sheldon

Derby Girl by Cross Shauna (Film title: *Whip It*)

Flipped by Wendelin Van Draanen

Hoot by Carl Hiaasen

Howl's Moving Castle by Diana Wynne Jones

I Love You Beth Cooper by Larry Doyle

Inkheart by Cornelia Funke

It's Kind of a Funny Story by Ned Vizzini

Portraying History

This selection offers outstanding young adult novels that offer realistic, accurate, and interesting portrayals of a variety of historical time periods. Historical fiction is strongly connected to anchor standard nine, which asks readers to show how fiction is used to portray history. Historical novels also find strong connections to standard four, which asks us to analyze how authors use language to express a sense of time and place. The scope of historical fiction written for young adults, especially when it comes to important historical events, is very broad. In this text it is impossible to represent this diversity, so in this section we offer only some of our recent favorites in the genre.

Ancient

The Ancient Ocean Blues by Jack Mitchell

Bearing the Saint by Donna Farley

I Am the Great Horse by Katherine Roberts

The Moon Riders by Theresa Tomlinson

Pharaoh's Daughter: A Novel of Ancient Egypt by Julius Lester

Middle Ages (10th–13th centuries)

Daughter of Xanadu by Dori Jones Yang

Feast of Fools by Bridget Crowley

The Golden Rat by Don Wulffson

The Humming of Numbers by Joni Sensel

<u>Pagan Chronicles</u> series (*Pagan's Crusade; Pagan in Exile; Pagan's Vows; Pagan's Scribe; Babylonne*) by Catherine Jinks

Peregrine by Joan E. Goodman

<u>Perfect Fire</u> trilogy (*Blue Flame; White Heat; Paradise Red*) by K. M. Grant

The Queen's Daughter by Susan Coventry

Troubadour by Mary Hoffman

The Wager by Donna Jo Napoli

Renaissance (14th–16th centuries)

Belle's Song by K. M. Grant

Cate of the Lost Colony by Lisa M. Klein

Dante's Daughter by Kimberley Heuston

The Falconer's Knot: A Story of Friars, Flirtation and Foul Play by Mary Hoffman

A Golden Web by Barbara Quick

Hurricane Dancers: The First Caribbean Pirate Shipwreck by Margarita Engle

Primavera by Mary Jane Beaufrand

The Red Queen's Daughter by Jacqueline A. Kolosov

Redemption by Julie Chibbaro

The Sorcerer of Sainte Felice by Ann Finnin

Enlightenment (17th–18th centuries)

The Academie by Susanne Dunlap

Beyond the Burning Time by Kathryn Lasky

Fever, 1793 by Laurie Halse Anderson

Five 4ths of July by Pat Hughes

The Fool's Girl by Celia Rees

No Shame, No Fear and *Forged in the Fire* by Ann Turnbull

Sovay by Celia Rees

A True and Faithful Narrative by Katherine Sturtevant

Wicked Girls: A Novel of the Salem Witch Trials by Stephanie Hemphill

Woods Runner by Gary Paulsen

Modern Era (19th–20th centuries)

Anya's War by Andrea Alban

Between Shades of Gray by Ruta Sepetys

The Braid by Helen Frost

Child of Dandelions by Shenaaz Nanji

Desperate Journey by Jim Murphy

Flygirl by Sherri L. Smith

<u>Luxe</u> Series (*Luxe*; *Rumors*; *Envy*; *Splendor*) by Anna Godbersen

Phantoms in the Snow by Kathleen Benner Duble

Strings Attached by Judy Blundell

Three Rivers Rising: A Novel of the Johnstown Flood by Jame Richards

Drawing on Tradition

We now offer a selection of texts that use the traditional forms of myth, fairy tale, folklore, and legend to create new stories. Some of these texts will be more literal retellings of a traditional story, others will be modern visions of the same story. Still others will offer a different take on the story by telling it from a different point of view or changing the setting to bring new life to the story. These texts will be particularly useful in achieving anchor standard six, which calls for students to determine how different points of view affect a story. In addition, these texts are strongly connected to anchor standard nine, which asks for students to show how modern works draw on themes and types of traditional literature, including myth and legend.

Mythology

Greek

Cupid

   Cupid: A Tale of Love and Desire by Julius Lester

   "Cupidity" by Caroline Goode in *Love, Love, Love* by Deborah Reber and Caroline Goode

   The Cupid War by Timothy Carter

   Destined by Jessie Harrell

   Mad Love by Suzanne Selfors

   Psyche in a Dress by Francesca Lia Block

   Stupid Cupid by Rhonda Stapleton

   Thwonk by Joan Bauer

Medusa

   Dread Locks by Neal Shusterman

   Dussie by Nancy Springer

   Singer to the Sea God by Vivien Alcock

   Snakehead by Ann Halam

   <u>Medusa Girls</u> series (*Sweet Venom*; *Sweet Shadows*) by Tera Lynn Childs

Persephone

Abandon by Meg Cabot

Everneath by Brodi Ashton

The Goddess Text and *Goddess Interrupted* by Aimee Carter

Psyche in a Dress by Francesca Lia Block (Novel in Verse)

Radiant Darkness by Emily Whitman

Nordic

Icefall by Matthew Kirby

Need series (*Need; Captivate; Entice*) by Carrie Jones

Odd and the Frost Giants by Neil Gaiman

Runemarks by Joanne Harris

Sea of Trolls trilogy (*The Sea of Trolls; The Land of the Silver Apples; The Islands of the Blessed*) by Nancy Farmer

Stork Trilogy (*Stork; Frost; Flock*) by Wendy Delsol

Celtic

The Coming of the Dragon by Rebecca Barnhouse

Darkhenge by Catherine Fisher

The Fire Opal by Regina McBride

Goblin Wars series (*Tyger Tyger; In the Forests of the Night*) by K. R. Hamilton

The Scorpio Races by Maggie Stiefvater

SnowWalker by Catherine Fisher

The Stones Are Hatching by Geraldine McCaughrean

Warriors of Camlann by N. M. Browne

Selkie

The Folk Keeper by Franny Billingsley

Sea Change by Aimee Friedman

Selkie Girl by Laurie Brooks

Tempest Rising by Tracy Deebs

Egyptian

Another Pan by Daniel Nayeri

Sphinx's Princess and *Sphinx's Queen* by Esther M. Friesner

The Ugly Goddess by Elsa Marston

Other

Dingo by Charles De Lint (Aboriginal)

Guardian of the Dead by Karen Healey (Maori)

The Qalupalik by Elisha Kilabuk (Inuit)

<u>Tiger's Apprentice</u> series (*The Tiger's Apprentice; Tiger Blood; Tiger Magic*) by Laurence Yep (Chinese)

Vodnik by Bryce Moore (Slavic)

Fairy Tales and Folklore

Beauty and the Beast

Beast by Donna Jo Napoli

Beastly by Alex Flinn

Beauty by Robin McKinley

Belle by Cameron Dokey

Rose Daughter by Robin McKinley

Cinderella

Ash and *Legend* by Malinda Lo

Cinder by Marissa Meyer

Just Ella by Margaret Peterson Haddix

Princess of Glass by Jessica Day George

Shadows on the Moon by Zoe Marriott

The Frog Prince

Enchanted by Alethea Kontis

The Frog Princess by E. D. Baker

Geek Charming by Robin Palmer

Water Song by Suzanne Weyn

Little Red Riding Hood

Cloaked in Red by Vivian Vande Velde

Little Miss Red by Robin Palmer

Red Rider's Hood by Neal Shusterman

Scarlet Moon by Debbie Viguie

Sisters Red by Jackson Pearce

Rapunzel

Golden by Cameron Dokey

Letters from Rapunzel by Sara Holmes

Rapunzel's Revenge by Shannon and Dean Hale, illustrated by Nathan Hale

The Tower Room by Adele Geras

Zel by Donna Jo Napoli

Rumpelstiltskin

The Crimson Thread by Suzanne Weyn

A Curse Dark as Gold by Elizabeth C. Bunce

The Rumpelstiltskin Problem by Vivian Vande Velde

Spinners by Donna Jo Napoli

Straw into Gold by Gary Schmidt

Sleeping Beauty

Beauty Sleep by Cameron Dokey

A Kiss in Time by Alex Flinn

A Long, Long Sleep by Anna Sheehan

Thornspell by Helen Lowe

The Wide-Awake Princess by E. D. Baker

Snow White

Fairest by Gail Carson Levine

Mira, Mirror by Mette Ivie Harrison

The Poison Apples by Lily Archer

Snow by Tracy Lynn

Snow in Summer: Fairest of Them All by Jane Yolen

The Twelve Dancing Princesses

Entwined by Heather Dixon

The Night Dance by Suzanne Weyn

The Phoenix Dance by Dia Calhoun

Princess of the Midnight Ball by Jessica Day George

Wildwood Dancing by Juliet Marillier

Legend

Robin Hood

Forbidden Forest: The Story of Little John and Robin Hood by Michael Cadnum

In a Dark Wood by Michael Cadnum

Outlaws of Sherwood by Robin McKinley

<u>Rowan Hood</u> series (*Rowan Hood: Outlaw Girl of Sherwood Forest; Lionclaw: A Tale of Rowan Hood; Outlaw Princess of Sherwood; Wild Boy; Rowan Hood Returns*) by Nancy Springer

Scarlet by A.C. Gaughen

King Arthur

<u>Arthur</u> trilogy (*The Seeing Stone; At the Crossing Place; King of the Middle March*) by Kevin Crossley-Holland

Black Horses for the King by Anne McCaffrey

The Book of Mordred by Vivian Vande Velde

Here Lies Arthur by Philip Reeve

Song of the Sparrow by Lisa Ann Sandell

Retelling the Classics

Just as myth, fairy tale, and legend provide inspiration for modern authors, so do works of classic literature. In this selection we offer young adult novels that take a classic work and reenvision it in a new way. These are very directly connected to the original work in that they often use the same character names and plot elements as the original. Some continue the story or change the story into something new by reinventing the plot. Others tell the story from a different point of view or change the setting. While the modern works make changes, they are still clearly connected to the original work. These texts will be particularly useful in achieving anchor standard nine, which calls for students to show how an author uses source material such as Shakespeare to build a new work.

Pride and Prejudice by Jane Austen

  Enthusiasm by Polly Shulman

  Epic Fail by Claire LaZebnik

  Pride and Popularity by Jenni James

  Prom and Prejudice by Elizabeth Eulberg

Sense and Sensibility by Jane Austen

  The Dashwood Sisters' Secrets of Love by Rosie Rushton

  Sass and Serendipity by Jennifer Ziegler

Jane Eyre by Charlotte Bronte

  A Breath of Eyre by Eve Marie Mont

  Jane by April Lindner

Wuthering Heights by Emily Bronte

  Catherine by April Lindner

  The Heights by Brian James

  The House of Dead Maids by Clare B. Dunkle

The Great Gatsby by F. Scott Fitzgerald

   Jake, Reinvented by Gordon Korman

Faust by Johann Wolfgang von Goethe

   Devilish by Maureen Johnson
   Another Faust by Daniel and Dina Nayeri
   On the Devil's Court by Carl Deuker

The Iliad by Homer

   Goddess of Yesterday by Caroline B. Cooney
   Inside the Walls of Troy: A Novel of the Women Who Lived the Trojan War by Clemence McLaren
   Troy High by Shana Norris
   Nobody's Princess and *Nobody's Prize* by Esther M. Friesner
   Starcrossed by Josephine Angelini
   Troy by Adele Geras

The Odyssey by Homer

   Ithaka by Adele Geras
   King of Ithaka by Tracy Barrett
   The Odyssey by Gareth Hinds
   Waiting for Odysseus by Clemence McLaren

Cyrano de Bergerac by Edmond Rostand

   At Face Value by Emily Franklin
   Cyrano by Geraldine McCaughrean

Frankenstein by Mary Shelley

   Department 19 by Will Hill
   Mister Creecher by Chris Priestley
   Monster High by Lisi Harrison
   This Dark Endeavor: The Apprenticeship of Victor Frankenstein and *Such Wicked Intent: The Apprenticeship of Victor Frankenstein Book Two* by Kenneth Oppel

Shakespeare

Hamlet

Dating Hamlet: Ophelia's Story by Lisa Fiedler

Falling for Hamlet by Michelle Ray

Hamlet by James Marsden

Ophelia by Lisa Klein

Ophelia's Revenge by Rebecca Reisert

Macbeth

Enter Three Witches by Caroline Cooney

Lady Macbeth's Daughter by Lisa M. Klein

Something Wicked: A Horatio Wilkes Mystery by Alan Gratz

The Third Witch: A Novel by Rebecca Reisert

A Midsummer's Night Dream

Come Fall by A.C.E. Bauer

This Must Be Love by Tui Sutherland

Othello

Othello Julius Lester

Exposure by Mal Peet

Romeo and Juliet

Juliet Immortal and *Romeo Redeemed* by Stacey Jay

The Juliet Spell by Douglas Rees

Romeo's Ex: Rosaline's Story by Lisa Fiedler

Romiette and Julio by Sharon M. Draper

Saving Juliet by Suzanne Selfors

Real People in Fiction

The characters that populate fiction are not always entirely fictional; from time to time real people make appearances. In this selection of works we give you texts that feature real people. These works offer a range of text-to-world connections and will be particularly useful in achieving anchor standard nine, which calls for students to compare a fictional portrayal of a character to a historical account to show how fiction changes history. Unless the person who appears is obvious from the title of the work, we name them in parentheses at the end or for those featured in multiple titles as a heading at the beginning of the citations.

Artists

David by Mary Hoffman (Michelangelo)

I Am Rembrandt's Daughter by Lynn Cullen

The Master's Apprentice by Rick Jacobson (Michelangelo)

Marie, Dancing by Carolyn Meyer (Edgar Degas)

Primavera by Mary Jane Beaufrand (Botticelli)

Leonardo Da Vinci

Lady with an Alien: An Encounter with Leonardo da Vinci by Michael D. Resnick

Leonardo's Shadow: Or, My Astonishing Life as Leonardo da Vinci's Servant by Christopher Grey

The Smile by Donna Jo Napoli

Authors

Belle's Song by K. M. Grant (Geoffrey Chaucer)

Cassandra's Sister by Veronica Bennett (Jane Austen)

Dante's Daughter by Kimberley Heuston (Dante Alighieri)

The Haunting of Charles Dickens by Lewis Buzbee

I Was Jane Austen's Best Friend by Cora Harrison

The Man Who Was Poe by Avi (Edgar Allen Poe)

A Voice of Her Own: Becoming Emily Dickinson by Barbara Dana

William Shakespeare

Fool's Girl by Celia Rees

King of Shadows by Susan Cooper

Kissing Shakespeare by Pamela Mingle

Loving Will Shakespeare by Carolyn Meyer

The Playmaker by J. B. Cheaney

The Shakespeare Stealer and *Shakespeare's Scribe* and *Shakespeare's Spy* by Gary Blackwood

Shakespeare's Daughter by Peter Hassinger

Swan Town: The Secret Journal of Susanna Shakespeare by Michael J. Ortiz

The True Prince by J. B. Cheaney

The Two Loves of Will Shakespeare by Laurie Lawlor

Musicians

Beethoven Lives Upstairs by Barbara Nichol

Hidden Voices: The Orphan Musicians of Venice by Patricia Lowery Collins (Vivaldi)

In Mozart's Shadow: His Sister's Story by Carolyn Meyer

The Musician's Daughter by Susanne Emily Dunlap (Franz Joseph Haydn)

Royals

Doomed Queen Anne by Carolyn Meyer (Anne Boleyn)

Duchessina: A Novel of Catherine de Medici by Carolyn Meyer

Isabel: Jewel of Castilla by Carolyn Meyer (Isabel I, Queen of Spain)

The King's Arrow by Michael Cadnum (King William II)

The King's Rose by Alisa M. Libby (King Henry VIII)

Mary, Bloody Mary by Carolyn Meyer (Mary Tudor)

Nine Days a Queen: The Short Life and Reign of Lady Jane Gray by Ann Rinaldi

Patience, Princess Catherine by Carolyn Meyer (Catherine of Aragon)

Prisoners in the Palace: How Victoria Became Queen With the Help of her Maid, A Reporter and a Scoundrel by Michaela MacColl

A Proud Taste for Scarlet and *Miniver* by E. L. Konigsburg (Eleanor of Aquitaine)

The Queen's Daughter by Susan Coventry (King Henry II and Eleanor of Aquitaine)

The Queen's Own Fool: A Novel of Mary Queen of Scots by Jane Yolen

Sphinx's Princess and *Sphinx's Queen* by Esther M. Friesner (Nefertiti)

Treason by Berlie Doherty (Prince Edward, Son of King Henry VIII)

Cleopatra, Queen of Egypt

Cleopatra Confesses by Carolyn Meyer

Cleopatra's Moon by Vicky Shecter

Elizabeth I, Queen of England

Beware Princess Elizabeth by Carolyn Meyer

The Counterfeit Princess by Jane Thomas

The Redheaded Princess by Ann Rinaldi

The Red Queen's Daughter by Jacqueline A. Kolosov

The Stolen One by Suzanne Crowley

A Sweet Disorder by Jacqueline A. Kolosov

Grand Duchess Anastasia

Anastasia's Secret by Susanne Emily Dunlap

The Diamond Secret by Suzanne Weyn

<u>Dreaming Anastasia</u> trilogy (*Dreaming Anastasia; Haunted; Anastasia Forever*) by Joy Preble

The Fetch by Laura Whitcomb

The Lost Crown by Sarah Elizabeth Miller

Marie Antoinette

The Bad Queen: Rules and Instructions for Marie-Antoinette by Carolyn Meyer

The Lacemaker and the Princess by Kimberly Brubaker Bradley

Revolution by Jennifer Donnelly

Napoleon Bonaparte

The Academie by Susanne Dunlap

Betsy and the Emperor by Staton Rabin

Napoleon and Josephine: The Sword and the Hummingbird by Gerald Hausman

Scientists and Inventors

Ashes by Kathryn Lasky (Albert Einstein)

The Girl in the Clockwork Collar by Kady Cross (Nikola Tesla)

The Inquisitor's Apprentice by Chris Moriarty (Thomas Edison)

Invisible Things by Jenny Davidson (Alfred Nobel)

The True Adventures of Charley Darwin by Carolyn Meyer (Charles Darwin)

A Variety of Others

Al Capone Does My Shirts and *Al Capone Shines My Shoes* by Gennifer Choldenko

Booth's Daughter by Raymond Wemmlinger (John Wilkes Booth)

Distant Waves by Suzanne Weyn (Nikola Tesla, Sir Arthur Conan Doyle, and Harry Houdini)

The Five Fists of Science by Matt Fraction (Mark Twain and Nikola Tesla)

The Houdini Box by Brian Selznick

In the Shadow of the Lamp by Susanne Emily Dunlap (Florence Nightingale)

Miss Spitfire: Reaching Helen Keller by Sarah Miller

Ripper by Stefan Petrucha (Theodore Roosevelt)

Novels and Picture Books

A variety of texts have usefulness in the classroom. When it comes to middle and high school classrooms, one of the more overlooked formats is that of picture books. Picture books are very accessible to teens and offer a great variety of interesting connections for the classroom. We find that pairing novels and picture books is a good way to achieve anchor standard nine, which ask students to analyze how two or more authors write about the same subject. In this selection we offer a novel and picture book pairing that have potential in discovering how authors address cultures and themes in both long and short formats.

Black Boy White School by Brian F. Walker

These Hands by Margaret H. Mason, illustrated by Floyd Cooper

These stories both encompass feelings of trying to be accepted and yet not fitting in because of the perceived differences that come with the color of your skin.

Seedfolks by Paul Fleischman

A Bus Called Heaven by Bob Graham

These books display how communities can come together to make something extraordinary happen.

No Such Thing as Dragons by Philip Reeve

The Paper Dragon by Marguerite W. Davol, illustrated by Robert Sabuda

These books share the plot elements of two unlikely heroes facing down dragons. They both have strong thematic discussion points relating to courage and doing something even if you think it is impossible.

The Smile by Donna Jo Napoli

Who Stole Mona Lisa? By Ruthie Knapp, illustrated by Jill McElmurry

Both revealing secrets and back stories behind Leonardo da Vinci's *Mona Lisa*.

The Devil's Paintbox by Victoria McKernan

The Buffalo Storm by Katherine Applegate

Both recount the experiences of two pioneers as they travel across the plains to the Pacific Northwest.

The Pirates of Turtle Rock by Richard W. Jennings

The Pirates Next Door by Jonny Duddle

Brings pirates and their treasures into a modern suburban setting with relationships with characters who are bored with life and enjoy seeing a wider perspective.

Novels and Nonfiction

The CCSS places significant emphasis on nonfiction. While a great deal of our work with nonfiction will be contained in other content areas, the potential for using nonfiction in ELA classrooms is great. A significant way to bring nonfiction into ELA classrooms is using it in conjunction with fiction. In this section we offer a novel and then give one or more works of nonfiction that matches it. Including these nonfiction texts as part of the study of a novel will provide depth to our study of fiction as well as provide needed support for the knowledge demands of a text.

Annexed by Sharon Dogar

> *The Anne Frank Case: Simon Wiesenthal's Search for the Truth* by Susan Rubin
> *Anne Frank: Her Life in Words and Pictures from the Archives of the Anne Frank House* by Menno Metselaar and Ruud Van der Rol

Anya's War by Andrea Alban

> *Amelia Lost: The Life and Disappearance of Amelia Earhart* by Candace Fleming
> *Around the World in 100 Days* by Gary L. Blackwood
> *Around the World* by Matt Phelan

The Berlin Boxing Club by Robert Sharenow

> *Hitler Youth: Growing Up in Hitler's Shadow* by Susan Campbell Bartoletti
> *Jazz Age Josephine* by Jonah Winter, illustrated by Marjorie Priceman
> *A Nation's Hope: The Story of Boxing Legend Joe Louis* by Matt de la Pena, illustrated by Kadir Nelson
> *Superman versus the Ku Klux Klan: The True Story of how the Iconic Superhero Battled the Men of Hate* by Rick Bowers

Bicycle Madness by Jane Kurtz, illustrated by Beth Peck

> *Wheels of Change: How Women Rode the Bicycle to Freedom (With a Few Flat Tires along the Way)* by Sue Macy

The Breaker Boys by Pat Hughes

> *Growing Up in Coal Country* by Susan Campbell Bartoletti
>
> *Trapped: How the World Rescued 33 Miners from 2,000 Feet below the Chilean Desert* by Marc Aronson

Chasing Vermeer by Blue Balliett, illustrated by Brett Helquist

> *The Vermeer Interviews: Conversations with Seven Works of Art* by Bob Raczka

Dairy Queen by Catherine Gilbert Murdock

> *Let Me Play: The Story of Title IX: The Law That Changed the Future of Girls in America* by Karen Blumenthal

Evolution, Me and Other Freaks of Nature by Robin Brande

> *Billions of Years, Amazing Changes: The Story of Evolution* by Laurence Pringle, illustrated by Steve Jenkins
>
> *Evolution: The Story of Life on Earth* by Jay Hosler, art by Kevin and Zander Cannon

Fever, 1793 by Laurie Halse Anderson

> *The Secret of the Yellow Death: A True Story of Medical Sleuthing* by Suzanne Jurmain

Five 4ths of July by Pat Raccio Hughes

> *The Notorious Benedict Arnold: A True Story of Adventure, Heroism, & Treachery* by Steve Sheinkin

Flappers series (*Vixen; Ingénue*) by Jillian Larkin

> *Bootleg: Murder, Moonshine and the Lawless Years of Prohibition* by Karen Blumenthal

Flygirl by Sherri L. Smith

> *Flying Higher: the Women Airforce Service Pilots of World War II* by Wanda Langley
>
> *The Tuskegee Airmen: Black Heroes of World War II* by Jacqueline L. Harris
>
> *Yankee Doodle Gals: Women Pilots of World War II* by Amy Nathan

The Girl Who Became a Beatle by Greg Taylor

> *John Lennon: All I Want Is the Truth* by Elizabeth Partridge

Hurricane Dancers: The First Caribbean Pirate Shipwreck by Margarita Engle

> *Piracy and Plunder: A Murderous Business* by Milton Meltzer

I Was Jane Austen's Best Friend by Cora Harrison

> *Jane Austen: A Life Revealed* by Catherine Reef

The Miner's Daughter by Gretchen Moran Laskas

> *Brother, Can You Spare a Dime? The Great Depression 1929–1933* by Milton Meltzer
>
> *Children of the Great Depression* by Russell Freedman
>
> *Our Eleanor: A Scrapbook Look at Eleanor Roosevelt's Remarkable Life* by Candace Fleming

Mississippi Trial, 1955 by Chris Crowe

> *Simeon's Story: An Eyewitness Account of the Kidnapping of Emmett Till* by Simeon Wright and Herb Boyd
>
> *A Wreath for Emmett Till* by Marilyn Nelson

Miss Peregrine's Home for Peculiar Children by Ransom Riggs

> *Picture Yourself Writing Poetry: Using Photos to Inspire Writing* by Laura Purdie Salas

Rebel Fire (Sherlock Holmes: The Legend Begins #2) by Andrew Lane

> *Chasing Lincoln's Killer* by James L. Swanson
>
> *Good Brother, Bad Brother: The Story of Edwin Booth and John Wilkes Booth* by James Cross Giblin
>
> *Mr. Lincoln's High-Tech War* by Thomas B. Allen and Roger MacBride Allen

Ripper by Stefan Petrucha

> *Bully for You, Teddy Roosevelt!* by Jean Fritz
>
> *Jack the Ripper* by Jennifer Joline Anderson
>
> *What to Do about Alice? How Alice Roosevelt Broke the Rules, Charmed the World, and Drove Her Father Teddy Crazy* by Barbara Kerley

Three Rivers Rising: A Novel of the Johnstown Flood by Jame Richards

> *The Johnstown Flood* by David McCullough

Troy by Adele Geras

> *Digging for Troy: From Homer to Hisarlik* by Jill Rubalcaba

Soldier's Secret: The Story of Deborah Sampson by Sheila Solomon Klass

> *I'll Pass for Your Comrade: Women Soldiers in the Civil War* by Anita Silvey

The White Darkness by Geraldine McCaughrean

> *Antarctica: Journeys to the South Pole* by Walter Dean Myers
>
> *Frozen Secrets: Antarctica Revealed* by Sally Walker

Wicked Girls by Stephanie Hemphill

> *The Devil on Trial: Witches, Anarchists, Atheists, Communists, and Terrorists in America's Courtrooms* by Phillip Margulies and Maxine Rosaler
>
> *Witches! The Absolutely True Tale of Disaster in Salem* by Rosalyn Schanzer

Appendix A

Blank Analysis Form

Title: **Author:**

Quantitative Dimensions of Text Complexity

Lexile	
ATOS	
Other:_____	
Other:_____	

Qualitative Dimensions of Text Complexity

Format

	Comments	Rating
Size		
Font		

(continued)

	Comments	**Rating**
Layout		
Construction		
Organization		
Illustrations		

Audience

Comments	Rating

Levels of Meaning

	Comments	Rating
Theme		
Conflict		
Connections		

Structure

	Comments	Rating
Setting		
Plot		

(*continued*)

	Comments	Rating
Character		
Point of View		

Language Conventions

	Comments	Rating
Style and Tone		
Literary Devices		

Knowledge Demands

Comments	Rating

Reader Dimensions of Text Complexity

Envisioning Independent Readers

Comments	Rating

The Adolescent Reader

	Comments	**Rating**
Adolescent Development		
Individual Makeup and Experience		

The Reader's Aptitude

	Comments	**Rating**
Interest		

(continued)

	Comments	Rating
Experience		
Motivation		

Task Dimensions of Text Complexity

Comments	Rating

Overall Assessment

Comments

Appendix B

Blank Raw Materials Planning Sheet

Theme

Potential Essential Questions	Potential Anchor Texts

Potential Assessments (Unit Projects)

Connected/Supporting Texts	Multimodal Connections

Appendix C

Model Unit Materials

Full Analysis of *Out of the Dust* **by Karen Hesse**

Quantitative Dimensions of Text Complexity

Lexile	NP: NonProse (Lexile will only score prose texts, not poetry, so this novel does not have a Lexile score.)
ATOS	5.3 (5th/6th Grade): Middle-grade interest level
Flesch-Kincaid Grade Level	3.8 (4th Grade)
Coleman-Liau	4 (4th Grade)
SMOG	2.8 (3rd Grade)
Gunning Fog	5.9 (fairly easy to read)
Dale-Chall	7.62 (9–10th Grade)

Qualitative Dimensions of Text Complexity

Format

	Comments	Rating
Size	The paperback edition of this book (likely the most common version) measures 7.5″ × 5.3″. It is 227 pages long, which is in the middle range for young adult books, but we have to keep in mind that since these are poems, there is more blank space on these pages than we would normally encounter in a novel.	2
Font	A serif font is used throughout the book, and the size of the font is larger than typically used in novels, which makes for easier reading.	2
Layout	Given that the book is actually a collection of poems, the layout of text in the book is standard for poetic verse—line breaks occur in unusual places, stanzas are separated by a blank line, etc. Some poems feature unusual layouts as a device purposefully used to reflect something	3

(continued)

From *Integrating Young Adult Literature through the Common Core Standards* by Rachel L. Wadham and Jonathan W. Ostenson. Santa Barbara, CA: Libraries Unlimited. Copyright © 2013.

	Comments	Rating
	concrete (e.g., the keys on a piano). This layout is unusual for students expecting a prose book and may take some getting used to given students' prior experience with poetry.	
Construction	The paperback copy is of typical construction—glue binding, lower-quality paper, soft cover.	2
Organization	The book is divided into individual poems, each of them titled in bold text at the beginning of the poem, with each poem beginning on a new page; these poems are grouped by seasons. The Scholastic paperback version includes a section of additional information about the author and the book in an "After Words" section.	2
Illustrations	There are no illustrations in the book itself.	×

Audience

Comments	Rating
The publisher denotes a reading level of 6th grade, or ages 10 and above. While this is certainly true given the syntactic demands of the text, older readers (grades 7 and above) are likely to benefit more from reading this book given their stronger comprehension skills and greater experience with poetry. The thematic content and characterizations of the book would be appropriate for grades 6+. In terms of interest level, the book is likely to interest readers who are 12 and older, with middle-grade readers being likely the most interested in the book. Younger readers may be turned off by the poetic form (that doesn't fit with poetry by Silverstein or other poets for younger children), while upper high school readers may not find the 14-year-old narrator as compelling.	3

Levels of Meaning

	Comments	Rating
Theme	The book treats a variety of themes, and these themes are integrated in sophisticated ways. Billie Jo must learn to forgive herself and her father for the terrible accident that takes her mother; she must also learn to accept the place where she lives, the land that sustains and threatens her existence at the same time. Billie Jo, her mother, and her father also find hope and strength when circumstances seem likely to tear them down—the source of that hope that gives them strength is treated throughout the book. The book also treats the theme of loss and grief, not only in how Billie Jo and her father deal with the loss of Ma, but also in how they respond to repeated failures and setbacks in farming or in playing the piano.	4
Conflict	A major conflict throughout the book is against the forces of nature that seemed at this time to conspire against human beings in the dust bowl: the lack of rain, the howling dust storms, even the ravenous	4

From *Integrating Young Adult Literature through the Common Core Standards* by Rachel L. Wadham and Jonathan W. Ostenson. Santa Barbara, CA: Libraries Unlimited. Copyright © 2013.

	Comments	Rating
	grasshoppers. Much is made throughout the book of the repeated times that people are overwhelmed by nature's devastation but pick themselves up again and start anew or clean up the mess (as represented so often by the omnipresent dust). While this conflict dominates the background of the book, there are other significant problems, too: Billie Jo must struggle with internal questions about her and her father's role in her mother's (and unborn baby brother's) death; she must reconcile with her father and build a new relationship with him; and she must overcome the internal doubts that where she comes from (both in terms of the place and her biological connections to her father) has value. These are multilayered conflicts that are tightly integrated with the setting, the plot, and the themes of the story.	
Connections	The text expects some familiarity with the dust bowl and conditions during the Great Depression. Migrants leaving for California are mentioned frequently in the book, and dust storms and poor crops are repeated challenges. These elements play such an important role in understanding the conflicts and the themes of the story that their importance should not be underestimated.	3

Structure

	Comments	Rating
Setting	The story is set in Oklahoma, in the dust bowl during the Great Depression. The ecological disasters and the financial problems of the time form a significant part of the background against which the story is set. The events of the story take place in less than a year—from the winter of 1934 to the fall of 1935. The setting plays a crucial role in the conflicts in the book and, consequently, in the character development and thematic elements as well.	3
Plot	The events of the story are told in chronological order, and there is actually a limited set of events portrayed in the book. Although these events are significant and end up being formative for Billie Jo and her father, they are relatively simple in structure.	2
Character	Billie Jo, the protagonist, is the most explored and complex character in the story; her father is similarly dynamic, but the mother does not appear in the story long enough to be portrayed in a complex way. The other characters are minor, playing roles that provide some texture (as in the storekeeper who makes an error in giving change to Billie Jo) or some background against which elements of Billie Jo's character can stand in relief (as in Mad Dog, who gets a job singing for the local radio station—performing for money in a way that Billie Jo, before the fire, once might have done). Billie Jo resists being defined by the place she lives or the features she shares with her father. Always on her mind early in the book is the	4

(continued)

	Comments	Rating
	thought of leaving—either through her piano playing or through education. She implies a confusion or judgment even about her father's unfailing optimism and his—in her mind—vain efforts to combat the overwhelming power of nature. She even wonders about the apples that symbolize her mother's hope. The loss of her mother drives Billie Jo into a time of despair, where she implicitly blames herself for the loss and questions her relationship with her father; the loss of her ability to play the piano haunts her, suggesting that she may never escape the reality of her situation. When she hops on a train to actually leave, she soon comes to realize just what her family and her home mean to her, and she returns, willing to take steps toward healing and rebuilding (as evidenced in going to the doctor for help with her burned hands so she can play the piano again). Early in the book Pa is portrayed as unfailingly optimistic, sure that the rains will come and the wheat will grow, regardless of signs of the opposite. He reacts in authentic and complex ways to the loss of his wife, at first spending precious money on getting drunk and distancing himself from Billie Jo as if she were to blame for the events. In his grief, he casts about for purpose and starts digging the hole for the pond that Ma wanted—an effort that seems vain to Billie Jo and makes her question what others will think of him. He eventually takes steps toward healing by visiting the doctor to investigate possible skin cancer and going to school to learn skills that might help if the farm isn't enough. While the small number of characters would suggest a less complex book, Hesse's treatment of primarily Billie Jo but also Pa provides something much more sophisticated. The tight integration among characters, conflict, and themes in this book adds to its complexity.	
Point of View	The story is told through Billie Jo's perspective, in first-person voice. It wouldn't be fair to classify her as an unreliable narrator, but she is naïve about many things. The demands of farming at the time seem to escape her at first, and her reaction to her mother's loss, while understandable, reflects Billie Jo's young age. This is presented in the way Billie Jo interprets events and especially in the way she views her father. Readers will need to understand these naïve aspects of her point of view to have an accurate picture of events and characters in the book.	3

Language Conventions

	Comments	Rating
Style and Tone	The poetic style of the writing makes this text much more complex. While it allows Hesse to communicate vivid images and give powerful insights to readers, it also packs a lot of meaning into short passages. While the syntax may seem simple, this text is dense with meaning.	5

	Comments	Rating
Literary Devices	Understandably, the book is filled with poetic devices and figurative language. Rich descriptions abound that give life to the dust storms and the resulting destruction; daily life in the dust bowl is starkly and vividly illustrated in Hesse's writing. She makes use of abundant symbols—the dust that permeates life and serves as a reminder of the forces aligned against the family, the apples that represent Ma's hope for the future and her unwillingness to surrender to despair, the half-finished pond that symbolizes a lost wife and a desire to find purpose in a changed world. These devices, while they add immeasurably to the power of the text, make it more challenging to read and understand.	5

Knowledge Demands

Comments	Rating
Readers must use different skills to unpack the meaning here than they might with prose texts, and an understanding of poetic devices and figurative language becomes important. Where with prose texts, students naturally read to punctuation marks, they tend to forget about this with poetry and will need to be reminded to continue to pay attention to punctuation in spite of the more frequent line breaks in poetry. In addition to the structural complexities, the text demands some understanding of the Great Depression and especially the dust bowl; students will have some familiarity with these topics, but building additional knowledge will enhance their understanding of the text.	4

Reader Dimensions of Text Complexity

Envisioning Independent Readers

Comments	Rating
Readers read a wide variety of texts, and while many students may not initially pick up a book of free verse like this one, by reading this book they can come to understand that powerful texts can take a variety of shapes and forms. Readers also make choices about reading based on their own interests, and some students may find the dust bowl era of interest; all students can find connections to Billie Jo and the challenges she faces in the poems of this book. Additionally, independent readers can make strong connections between their own lived experiences and those of characters in books, even if the settings of those books are different from the readers'. This book, with its historical setting but familiar conflicts and problems, can help readers develop those skills.	3

The Adolescent Reader

	Comments	Rating
Adolescent Development	Adolescents are moving from a more naïve worldview to one that more authentically embraces adult perspectives. Billie Jo experiences changes along these lines as she progresses in this book, and her growth will mirror that of many teen readers. Child-parent	2

(continued)

	Comments	Rating
	relationships play a significant role in teens' lives and development, and those roles are highlighted and explored in some depth in this book, another piece that is likely to reflect readers' own worlds. Billie Jo's increased responsibilities after her mother's death also parallel the growing responsibilities that teens see as they mature.	
Individual Makeup and Experience	While most students have not experienced exactly the same kinds of struggles that Billie Jo and her family face, many teens can identify with financial challenges and the threats to hope and optimism that she and her parents encounter in Great Depression America. Readers who have lost a parent (to death or divorce) can empathize with Billie Jo's loss; readers whose parent has lost a job can identify with the worries about money and the future. Most teens have found themselves in situations they wanted to escape, just as Billie Jo longs for something better away from home. These personal experiences will help color the way that readers interpret Billie, her parents, and their choices in the book. These connections provide a meaningful pathway into the book for teen readers.	3

The Reader's Aptitude

	Comments	Rating
Interest	There are some factors in the book that might put off some readers initially: the poetic verse form, the historical setting, and the female protagonist. These do complicate the matching of this text to a wide variety of readers, but these demands can be easily addressed so a wide variety of readers can be drawn into the text. Given the connections to teens and their experiences and development illuminated above, this is a book that can grab and maintain the interest of many readers.	4
Experience	While they're cast in a historical setting, the challenges and experiences that Billie Jo faces will be recognizable to many students. Some readers will need some help seeing those connections, but once they can see them, these connections should be rewarding for teen readers.	3
Motivation	The characters and conflicts of the book are likely to motivate readers to continue reading. Besides their connection to teens' lives, these are compelling things in and of themselves. The shortness of texts (there is far less text per page in this book than in the traditional novel) will also be a positive motivating factor for many readers.	3

Task Dimensions of Text Complexity

Comments	Rating
There are many instructional opportunities with this book. The one that stands out the most, perhaps, is the poetic nature of the book and what we could explore with	4

Comments	Rating
students in this vein. Poetry analysis, especially for middle-grade readers, will be more complicated than what they've done with prose texts, but it is within their reach. When it's contextualized within the study of a book like this, it can be more powerful for students; a gripping and accessible story like the one in *Out of the Dust* can minimize some of the traditional challenges with poetry instruction. The study of language—from figurative language to more technical issues of syntax—is also suitable for a text like this. The book also provides meaningful opportunities to explore characterization, as the major themes and conflicts of the text are intricately revealed mostly through the characters. In all, the number and connectedness of the different instructional possibilities make this a more complex text, well suited to classroom study.	

Overall Assessment

Comments

Out of the Dust tells the compelling story of a young girl's coming of age in the midst of the hardships of the dust bowl; to do so in poetic verse makes the emotions, questions, and challenges she faces all the more vivid and evocative. While its poetic form may make this book more complex, the complexity allows for a more sophisticated exploration of significant themes. While the historical setting may seem to make things disconnected from today's readers, there is much in this book that they can relate to. We're sure that teenagers can find inspiration and sympathy in the character of Billie Jo.

Anticipation Guide

Directions: Read each of the following statements carefully and decide whether you agree or disagree with each. Use the numbered scale below each statement to indicate how you feel about it (4=strongly agree, 1=strongly disagree). Be prepared to discuss your reasons for your response.

1. If you've tried something a few times and can't succeed, it's probably better to give up than waste more effort on something you're not good at.

    4   3   2   1

2. It can be good for us to work at things we're not good at.

    4   3   2   1

3. If you know you're not going to succeed at something from the beginning, don't waste time and effort even trying.

    4   3   2   1

4. Music is just for entertainment; it doesn't really do much besides give people a good time.

    4   3   2   1

5. We always hear to "never give up," but that doesn't apply to everything—it's okay to give up on things that don't really matter.

    4   3   2   1

6. If you really care about something, it won't matter if you're good at it or if you succeed at it; you should keep doing it just because you care about it.

    4   3   2   1

7. There's not really a difference between persevering (not giving up no matter what) and an obsession; you can go too far with obsessions, and they can become unhealthy.

    4   3   2   1

Scenarios

1. Lydia has played soccer for years, starting since she was in first grade. She really enjoys playing soccer, and she's pretty good at it. She doesn't play in the most competitive league in the area, but she's played on some pretty good teams and has done well. Next year, she enters high school, and tryouts for the high school soccer team are coming up at the end of the summer. Lydia knows that, in the past, about 100 girls have usually tried out for 15–20 open positions on the team; she knows many of the girls who are trying out, and they've been playing in the best leagues for many years. She doesn't think she has much of a chance of making the team, but she could do some summer camps and work really hard for the next two months to prepare herself. There are other fun things she could do this summer, though, and she wonders if it's worth the sacrifice.
   a. Should Lydia spend her summer getting ready for the high school tryouts?
   b. What other things could she spend her summer doing? Would they be more worthwhile than preparing for tryouts?
   c. Would spending the summer getting ready for tryouts be beneficial even if she doesn't make the team? Why or why not?

2. Tony knows he has the next best fantasy novel for teenagers in his head, but he's had a hard time convincing anyone else of that. He's sent his novel off to three different publishers, but each one has rejected it; he's used the feedback they sent, though, and each time he feels like the book is getting better. However, it takes a long time to make those changes and keeps him away from time with his friends and family and even from some training he's doing for his job. He's just received his third rejection letter, but it has some good suggestions, and Tony feels like he's getting closer to having a novel someone will want to publish. But the recommendations in this letter will take him four or five months to complete before he could send the book off again. He's wondering if he should just stop and spend his time differently.
   a. Should Tony keep working on his book and resubmit it? If he gets rejected again, should he keep trying?
   b. What other things could Tony be doing with his time? Are these things more valuable than working on his book?

3. Andrew loves the game World of Warcraft, and he's spent a lot of time the past three years playing; right now, he has a couple of really powerful max-level characters. He belongs to a guild (a group of players that play together frequently) that's trying to beat the hardest dungeon in the game, something that only a handful of guilds on his server have done. His guild is pretty close to completing the dungeon, but there's one final boss that's very difficult to beat. Andrew and his in-game friends know they need better equipment if they hope to beat the boss. But getting that equipment would be a matter of many, many more hours in other dungeons; it would be a big commitment to do this.
   a. Should Andrew continue to commit the kind of time and energy to play the game and get the equipment he will need to beat the game's boss? Why or why not?
   b. How is Andrew's challenge different from the challenges that Tony or Lydia are facing?

4. Maria adopted Jeffrey 12 years ago when he was five years old; he came from an orphanage in Eastern Europe where he wasn't cared for very well. Maria has given him lots of love, helped him for hours with school homework, paid for him to play

sports, and driven him to practices and games. She's tried to devote her time and energy to him because she loves him as if he were her biological son. Instead of working as a lawyer, a career she loves, she has stayed home to be Jeffrey's mother. But Jeffrey has struggled in school and has not fit in well in the United States; since he's become a teenager, he's started acting out in violent and unhealthy ways. He fights Maria on everything from homework to the friends he hangs out with—when he's home, he sulks in his room and doesn't want to talk; when he's away from home, Maria worries about who he's spending time with and what he's doing. At school, he's been suspended a couple of times for fighting with other students. He'll graduate next year, and Maria wonders sometimes if he'll flee home and never come back, and whether or not all her effort is worth it.

   a. Is all Maria's sacrifice for Jeffrey worth it? Why or why not?

   b. Does it matter how Jeffrey reacts to her? If he hates her forever, does it still make all Maria's sacrifice worth it?

   c. How is Maria's situation different from or similar to the other situations here?

5. Shawn always wanted to be a farmer; he dreamed of owning his own land and farming it ever since he was a young child. But he let other people convince him that farming was too hard to make a good living at, and so he pursued computer programming in college; now he has a good job as a programmer and a family he loves and is able to support well. However, he keeps thinking about that farm and the dream he used to have; he wonders if he's given up something really valuable in leaving that dream behind. He's talked with his wife, and she's actually supportive of his dream and would be fine with his leaving his job and trying to make a go at farming. But it would be a real upheaval for his children, and it might not make much money for a long time.

   a. Should Shawn change careers and embrace his dream to be a farmer? Why or why not?

   b. How would his life be different? What risks would he take? Would those risks be worth pursuing the dream?

   c. How are Shawn's dream and the decision facing him (and his family) different from and similar to the others in this group of scenarios?

Character Tracking Chart

Character	Challenges/ Failures/Setbacks	Response	Explanation	Lines
Pa				
Ma				
Billie Jo				

From *Integrating Young Adult Literature through the Common Core Standards* by Rachel L. Wadham and Jonathan W. Ostenson. Santa Barbara, CA: Libraries Unlimited. Copyright © 2013.

"Keepin' the Faith"

As we read *Out of the Dust* and other texts, we'll talk a lot about the trials and setbacks, even failures, that people (real and fictional) face. We'll also see how they manage to hold on to hope or stay optimistic in the face of these potentially devastating events. On this graphic organizer, you'll keep track of the conclusions you draw while we read about different people and different events. At the end of our unit, this sheet will provide you with details you'll need to complete assignments.

Name of the Person/ Character and the Text	Describe the Challenge/ Failure/Setback	Describe how the character(s) held on to hope, what inspired optimism, etc. (use quotes and page numbers!)
Phil, Lou, and Mack from *Unbroken*	Their plane crashes and they're adrift in the ocean without food or water or shelter. Sharks even attack them.	One guy gives up and doesn't do anything to help out; the other two work hard to catch some birds to eat, to gather water, even beating off the sharks. They were "inspired to work toward their survival" while the other guy's hopelessness was "becoming self-fulfilling."

Positive-Negative Chart for Pa

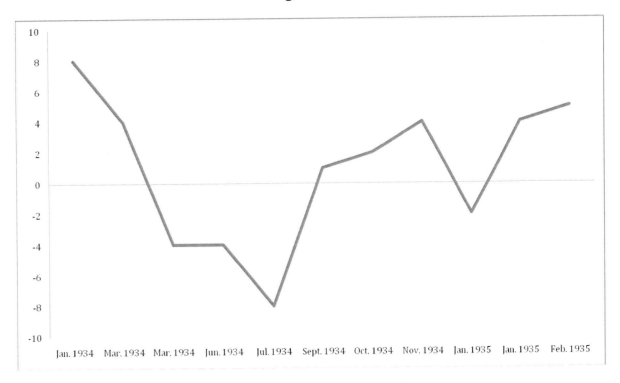

(Jan 1934) Ma announces she's pregnant; Pa might get a boy.	Dust storm covers the fields in dirt; Pa is beaten but won't cry.	Ma and the unborn son are killed in the accident with the bucket of kerosene.	Hires on with Wireless Power digging holes for towers; brings in some money.	Christmas dinner without Ma; Billie Jo tries but it isn't the same.
(Mar 1934) Pa thinks about borrowing money for wheat seeds.	Pa will be lucky to get five bushels to his acre, in spite of all his hard work.	Starts digging a hole for a pond, repairing the windmill.	Real snow falls and brings moisture to the land.	More rain, farmers are optimistic, and the plants start to revive.

Hope Photo-Essay Storyboard

In the boxes below, make a simple sketch of the image you want to use and the accompanying text (from *Out of the Dust*). While you may place the text elsewhere on the screen in your photo-essay, for now we'll just put it to the side. Once you've filled in all your images and text, cut these boxes out so you can manipulate and play with the order of the pieces.

From *Integrating Young Adult Literature through the Common Core Standards* by Rachel L. Wadham and Jonathan W. Ostenson. Santa Barbara, CA: Libraries Unlimited. Copyright © 2013.

Instructional Handout Example

(for working with Microsoft Movie Maker)

Saving Your Movie

In order to submit this assignment, you need to turn your project into a movie file. To do so, select the **Save Movie File** option from the **File** menu. Follow the steps of the wizard that appears (as shown below).

Leave the default option selected here (My Computer). Click "Next."

Enter a file name here for your movie (make sure that your first and last names are part of the file name so that I know this is your movie). Leave the default location here alone – DO NOT change this to your network (H:) drive! Click the "Next" button. This will save the movie to the "My Videos" folder inside the "My Documents" folder on the computer hard drive. You can then transfer it to your thumb drive or upload it directly.

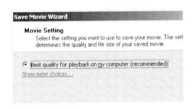

Again, leave this setting ("Best quality for playback . . .") as it is. Click the "Next" button one last time. Movie Maker will now make a movie from your project. When it's finished, click the "Finish" button and your movie will automatically load into Media Player and you can see your finished product!

REMEMBER: Your final movie file will need to be uploaded to the designated site. Please make sure that you upload this movie file and not the project file you've been saving and opening in Movie Maker.

From *Integrating Young Adult Literature through the Common Core Standards* by Rachel L. Wadham and Jonathan W. Ostenson. Santa Barbara, CA: Libraries Unlimited. Copyright © 2013.

Index

About the Authors

RACHEL L. WADHAM, MEd, is librarian and professor of adolescent literature at Brigham Young University, Provo, UT. Her published works include Libraries Unlimited's *This Is My Life: A Guide to Realistic Fiction for Teens* and Linworth's *Bringing Fantasy Alive for Children and Young Adults*. Wadham holds a master's degree in library science from the University of North Texas and a second master's degree in curriculum and instruction from Pennsylvania State University.

JONATHAN W. OSTENSON, PhD, is professor in the English Education program at Brigham Young University, Provo, UT, where he teaches courses in English teaching methods and young adult literature. Previously, he taught junior high and high school English for 11 years.